In a postmodern era of simulation, mass communication and disenchantment, how are we to distinguish sincerity from irony?

Irony is both a figure of speech – saying one thing and meaning another – and an attitude to existence, in which the ironic subject adopts a position of scepticism and mistrust in relation to everyday language. In this clear, user-friendly guide, Claire Colebrook provides an historical and theoretical overview of irony, tracing its development from Socrates to the present day, and explores the challenge that irony presents to communication and representation in literature today.

This is the essential guide for any student of literary theory looking to unravel the many theories of this complex subject.

Claire Colebrook teaches English at the University of Edinburgh. Her publications include *Gilles Deleuze* (2002), in the Routledge Critical Thinkers series, and *Irony in the Work of Philosophy* (2003).

THE NEW CRITICAL IDIOM

SERIES EDITOR: JOHN DRAKAKIS, UNIVERSITY OF STIRLING

The New Critical Idiom is an invaluable series of introductory guides to today's critical terminology. Each book

- provides a handy, explanatory guide to the use (and abuse) of the term
- offers an original and distinctive overview by a leading literary and cultural critic
- relates the term to the larger field of cultural representation.

With a strong emphasis on clarity, lively debate and the widest possible breadth of examples, *The New Critical Idiom* is an indispensable approach to key topics in literary studies.

Also available in this series:

IRONY

Claire Colebrook

Routledge
Taylor & Francis Group
LONDON AND NEW YORK

First published 2004 by Routledge
2 Park Square, Milton Park, Abingdon, Oxon OX 14 4RN

Simultaneously published in the USA and Canada
by Routledge
270 Madison Ave, New York, NY 10016

Reprinted 2005

Routledge is an imprint of the Taylor & Francis Group

Typeset in Adobe Garamond and Scala Sans by
Keystroke, Jacaranda Lodge, Wolverhampton
Printed and bound in Great Britain by
TJ International Ltd, Padstow, Cornwall

British Library Cataloguing in Publication Data
A catalogue record for this book is available from the British Library

Library of Congress Cataloging in Publication Data
Colebrook, Claire.
   Irony / Claire Colebrook.
     p. cm. — (New critical idiom)
Includes bibliographical references and index.
1. Irony in literature. I. Title. II. Series.
   PN56.I65C65 2003
   809'.918—dc21

                        2003009700

ISBN 0–415–25133–8 (hbk)
ISBN 0–415–25134–6 (pbk)

Contents

SERIES EDITOR'S PREFACE

The New Critical Idiom is a series of introductory books which seeks to extend the lexicon of literary terms, in order to address the radical changes which have taken place in the study of literature during the last decades of the twentieth century. The aim is to provide clear, well-illustrated accounts of the full range of terminology currently in use, and to evolve histories of its changing usage.

The current state of the discipline of literary studies is one where there is considerable debate concerning basic questions of terminology. This involves, among other things, the boundaries which distinguish the literary from the non-literary; the position of literature within the larger sphere of culture; the relationship between literatures of different cultures; and questions concerning the relation of literary to other cultural forms within the context of interdisciplinary structures.

It is clear that the field of literary criticism and theory is a dynamic and heterogeneous one. The present need is for individual volumes on terms which combine clarity of exposition with an adventurousness of perspective and a breadth of application. Each volume will contain as part of its apparatus some indication of the direction in which the definition of particular terms is likely to move, as well as expanding the disciplinary boundaries within which some of these terms have been traditionally contained. This will involve some re-situation of terms within the larger field of cultural representation, and will introduce examples from the area of film and the modern media in addition to examples from a variety of literary texts.

ACKNOWLEDGEMENTS

I would like to acknowledge the careful criticism and encouragement offered by Liz Thompson and John Drakakis. I am also, as ever, extremely grateful for the detailed and intelligent advice of my good friend David Neil.

1

THE CONCEPT OF IRONY

Despite its unwieldy complexity, irony has a frequent and common definition: saying what is contrary to what is meant (Quintilian 1995–98 [9.2.44], 401), a definition that is usually attributed to the first-century Roman orator Quintilian who was already looking back to Socrates and Ancient Greek literature. But this definition is so simple that it covers everything from simple figures of speech to entire historical epochs. Irony can mean as little as saying, 'Another day in paradise', when the weather is appalling. It can also refer to the huge problems of postmodernity; our very historical context is ironic because today nothing really means what it says. We live in a world of quotation, pastiche, simulation and cynicism: a general and all-encompassing irony. Irony, then, by the very simplicity of its definition becomes curiously indefinable.

THE HISTORY OF IRONY: FROM *EIRONEIA* TO *IRONIA*

In the comic plays of Aristophanes (257–180 BC) *eironeia* referred to lying rather than complex dissimulation. When *eironeia*, not much later than Aristophanes, came to refer to a dissimulation that was not deceitful but clearly recognisable, and intended to be recognised, irony intersected with the political problem of human meaning. The problem of irony is at one with the problem of politics: how do we know what others really mean, and on what basis can we secure the sincerity and authenticity of speech? The word *eironeia* was first used to refer to artful double meaning in the Socratic dialogues of Plato, where the word is used both as pejorative – in the sense of lying – and affirmatively, to refer to Socrates' capacity to conceal what he really means. It was this practice of concealment that opened the Western political/philosophical tradition, for it is through the art of playing with meaning that the interlocutors of a dialogue are compelled to question the fundamental concepts of our language.

Plato's Socrates has, from Quintilian to the present, been identified with the practice of irony. Socrates often spoke as though he were ignorant or respectful, precisely when he wished to expose his interlocutor's ignorance. He would ask someone for the definition of friendship or justice and then allow the confident and ready definitions of everyday speech to be exposed in all their contradictory incompleteness. By demanding a definition from those who presented themselves as masters of wisdom, Socrates showed how some terms were less self-evident and definitive than everyday meaning would seem to suggest. It is no accident that Socrates used irony to challenge received knowledge and wisdom at a historical moment when the comfort and security of small communities were being threatened by political expansion and the inclusion of other cultures. The tribal cultures of Ancient Greece were opening out to imperial expansion and the inclusion of others. It is at this moment of cultural insecurity – in the transition from the closed community to a polis of competing viewpoints – that the concept of irony is formed. *Eironeia* is no longer lying or deceit but a complex rhetorical practice whereby one can say one thing – such as Socrates' claim to be ignorant – but mean quite another, as when Socrates' exposes the supposedly wise as lacking in all insight. Socrates tried to show that it is always possible that what we take to be the self-evident sense of a context or culture is far from obvious; it may be that what is being said is *not meant*.

Today, despite its major differences, 'postmodern' irony also has this distancing function: we wear 1980s disco clothing or listen to 1970s country and western music, not because we are committed to particular styles or senses but because we have started to question sincerity and commitment in general; everything is as kitsch and dated as everything else, so all we can do is quote and dissimulate. But even in a world of postmodern irony, the very sense that everything is somehow quoted or simulated relies on a lost sense of the truly valuable or original. Both Socrates' questions and the contemporary use of parody and quotation rely on distinguishing between those statements and actions that we genuinely intend and those that we repeat or mime only to expose their emptiness. How do we acquire the sort of insider knowledge that allows us to interpret a text or context and distinguish the ironic from the non-ironic? How do we know when a speaker is *not* sincere? This chapter provides a history and overview of competing approaches to irony but in doing so it is already within the problem of irony. For the very practice of charting and explaining a series of epochs and cultures relies on being able to identify and understand each writer's specific culture or context. In many ways, then, we have to be ironic: capable of maintaining a distance from any single definition or context, quoting and repeating various voices from the past. But we also have to be wary of irony; we have to be sure that the past we grasp means what it seems to mean.

It is a peculiarly modern gesture to think of differing epochs, each with their own standard of truth. In order to think of the relative truth and difference of historical contexts or epochs we have to imagine that certain contexts may be meaningful and coherent and yet no longer be held as true. We read the sense of past texts and contexts without belief or commitment, seeing and recognising the 'truths' of the past but not holding to those truths. Only with some concept of irony is it possible to range across literary history. The idea of past contexts that are meaningful in themselves but which are no longer 'ours' requires the ironic viewpoint of detachment. Through irony we can discern the meaning or sense of a context without participating in, or being committed to, that context.

Hayden White (1973, 375) argues that the very notion of modern history is essentially ironic: for the historian must *read* the past as if there were some meaning of the past not apparent to the past itself. The past always means more than it explicitly 'says'. The historian must not take the past at its word but always be other than the worlds she surveys. Furthermore, once we become aware of, and sensitive to, the notion of irony and specific historical contexts it becomes possible to read irony back into earlier texts. Irony destroys the immediacy and sincerity of life; through irony we do not just live the meanings of our world, we can ask what these meanings are *really* saying. Not only, then, does irony share the fluidity and context-dependency of all general concepts; it is the very notion of irony that allows us to think of competing and discontinuous contexts. Reading ironically means, in complex ways, not taking things at their word; it means looking beyond standard use and exchange to what this or that might *really mean*. This can be simple. If I say, 'This is paradise!' and our context – the weather outside – is clearly not blissful, then you know I am being ironic. But what happens in literature where, precisely because texts circulate from other contexts, we have no obvious context to refer to? Irony therefore raises the question of literary interpretation: if we know what a word means according to its context, how do we know or secure a proper context?

Shakespearean drama, for example, was once read and received as a sincere defence and representation of the well-ordered, pre-modern cosmos (Bradley 1905). Such a reading was possible only because of a (then) widely shared notion about historical context: the Elizabethan world-view was one of unquestioning belief and obedience to ordained law (Lovejoy 1936). Today, however, Shakespeare is often read ironically: not as a writer who represented the standard world-view, but as a dramatist who displayed and invented that world-view as a position to be questioned (Dollimore and Sinfield 1985; Drakakis 1995). Such new readings are possible because critics have recreated the supposedly original context. According to the new historicist criticism that was dominant in the 1980s, contexts are not passive backgrounds to the texts we read; contexts are created by texts, with each text also presenting the instabilities and insecurities of context. A text is never just what it says; it also displays the production and force of different ways of speaking. According to Stephen Greenblatt, the Renaissance was an era of competing and contested representations (Greenblatt 1988). Texts were anything but sincere; they presented standard Elizabethan myths of power *as* myths. The very practice of re-reading the past and of suspecting that all those texts that were once read as sincere might actually be critical of the power they describe depends upon the structure of irony. It is always possible, particularly if we question or re-invent a context, that a text can be read as having a meaning *other than* what it says. The twentieth-century writer Jorge Luis Borges gives a stunning example of how even the most sacred texts can be exposed to irony. In 'Pierre

Menard, Author of Don Quixote', Borges describes the project of a twentieth-century author who sets himself the task of rewriting Miguel de Cervantes' *Don Quixote*. Simply transcribing the novel would be too facile a task, so Pierre Menard decides to project himself into the position of the original Cervantes. Eventually, he produces one identical paragraph of the 'original' text. Of course this completely identical paragraph is stunningly ironic, for the very circumstance of its new context gives it an entirely transformed sense. Borges then suggests that all the texts of Western culture could benefit from this imaginative device. What if we were to imagine *The Imitation of Christ* as authored by James Joyce (Borges 1965, 51)?

This process of ironic re-reading, where we dare to imagine a text as somehow meaning something other than what it explicitly says, characterises much of what counts as literary criticism. Indeed, one could argue – as many twentieth-century critics were to do – that literature is characterised by its potential for irony, its capacity to mean something other than a common-sense or everyday use of language. To see Shakespeare as ironic is not just to see him, as a playwright, as distanced from the world he presents. It is also a recognition of our capacity as readers to question whether a literary text is at one with what it 'says'; for a text can always be read as if it were presenting or 'mentioning' a world-view, rather than intending that world-view. This is one mode of irony: a writer uses all the figures and conventions of a context while refraining from belief or commitment. We can imagine an author behind the work who presents certain positions but does not really intend or mean what is said. It is possible to read Shakespeare ironically, not because we are secure about context, but because the very idea of what counted as *the* Elizabethan context is, and was, up for question. Shakespeare would be read as sincere and non-ironic if we simply believed in the Renaissance past as a time of unquestioned duty and belief; he would be ironic, however, if we felt that his drama, as art, displayed that belief in order to show its limits and fragility.

Nowadays there are countless books and articles referring to the irony of medieval, Renaissance and even biblical texts. Such forays into the past are justified by the continual use of the word *ironia* throughout the Middle Ages. Authors as early as Bede (672/3–735) and Erasmus found *ironia* in the bible (Knox 1989, 29). Their cited examples were those of explicit mockery, such as the taunt made by the chief priests and elders to Christ: 'Prophesy to us, O Christ, who he is that smote you' (Matthew xxvi 68). Today, though, the analysis of irony in biblical and ancient texts extends beyond such isolated and explicit examples to an irony that pervades the text as a whole (Camery-Hoggatt 1992; Duke 1985; Good 1965; Plank 1987). What needs to be understood in any history of irony is the complex and ironic process of 'reading back'. Once we have the concept and theory of irony it is possible to discern ironic strands in literature that did not, itself, use or theorise the concept of irony.

Before the explicit and extended theorisation of irony in the nineteenth century, irony was a recognised but minor and subordinate figure of speech. The first significant instances of the Greek word *eironeia* occur in the dialogues of Plato (428–347 BC), with reference to Socrates. It is here that *eironeia* no longer meant straightforward lying, as it did for Aristophanes, but an intended simulation which the audience or hearer was meant to recognise. As we will see in the next chapter, Socratic irony was defined not just as the use of irony in conversation but also as an entire personality. Aristotle (384–322 BC) also referred to irony, most notably in his *Ethics* and *Rhetoric*, but it was the Platonic and Socratic use that became definitive for later thought. Aristotle's ironist was, like Plato's Socrates, one who played down or concealed his virtues and intelligence (Aristotle 1934 [*Nicomachean Ethics* 4.7.3–5], 241). Aristotle regarded such an ironic personality as neither pernicious nor ideal. Irony was not a vice but it was far from being a virtue. The truly virtuous citizen would be neither boastful, nor ironic, but sincere in his self-presentation.

It would seem to make sense, then, to look at Socrates as the very beginning of irony. For it was in Plato's Socratic dialogues that irony referred to both a complex figure of speech and the creation of an enigmatic personality. Many nineteenth- and twentieth-century writers have done just this, and placed Socrates at the centre of the concept of irony (Kierkegaard [1841] 1989; Nehamas 1988 and 1999).* Some go so far as to say that Socrates' ironic personality inaugurated a peculiarly

---

*Dates in square brackets are those of first publication. Dates in curved brackets are those of modern editions listed in the references, and page numbers refer to these.

Western sensibility (Lefebvre 1995, 12; Vlastos 1991, 29, 44). His irony, or his capacity *not* to accept everyday values and concepts but live in a state of perpetual question, is the birth of philosophy, ethics and consciousness. The problem with seeing Socrates as the origin of irony, and irony as the essence of Western consciousness, is that the awareness of Socrates and Socratic irony was virtually absent from medieval and Renaissance works on irony and rhetoric. Although Quintilian referred to Socrates, it was his distinction between verbal irony, as a figure of speech, and irony as an extended figure of thought that led to a strictly rhetorical tradition of defining irony. Irony was explained by isolated literary examples, such as those Quintilian himself drew from Homer and Virgil, and not by the complexity of the Socratic personality. The Latin manuals on rhetoric written up until the Renaissance knew the Greek sources primarily through what was available of Cicero and Quintilian. Even in the Renaissance, when the Socratic dialogues and the fuller works of Cicero became available, *ironia* was not considered to be the full-scale mode of Socratic existence that it was for nineteenth-century writers. *Ironia* was a trope or figure of speech, an artful way of using language.

Until the Renaissance, irony was theorised within rhetoric and was often listed as a type of allegory: as one way among others for saying one thing and meaning another. When the Greek and Latin descriptions of Socrates became available to Renaissance writers, irony was still not what it was to become for the Romantics (an attitude to existence). Irony was a rhetorical method. The Latin rhetorical manuals known in the Middle Ages had their origin in juridical and manifestly political situations; they instructed how best to construct speeches for the purposes of defence, praise or public persuasion. There was very little that was 'literary' or creative in such uses of rhetoric. *Ironia*, as defined by those who followed Cicero and Quintilian, had little to do with creating an artful mode of self and consciousness. *Ironia* was a way of making what one said and meant more effective; it was not a way of abstaining from belief or commitment. Later, in the Middle Ages, the prime purpose of rhetorical treatises was instruction for religious sermons and writing, although the models used were still the original Latin contexts of juridical defence and persuasion (Kennedy 1980, 24). Again, *ironia* was a limited technique, part of the method of effective speaking. It was ultimately in the service of getting one's point across. It did not constitute an entire style or mode of delivery, but could be used within speeches and writings to serve the overall effect. One could not have said that a text or person was 'ironic' any more than it would have made sense to refer to someone as 'metaphorical'; irony was a specific device, not a sensibility or attitude.

When the Renaissance became aware of the original Greek and extended Latin references to Socrates as an ironist the concept of irony was expanded from being one figure of speech among others to being a figure that could characterise an entire personality. Socrates' irony was habitual or extended: he tended to use irony frequently and as a mode of argument. But even here Socrates was certainly not celebrated as the epitome of Western consciousness, nor was irony granted a fundamental role in the definition of literature or literary awareness. If Socrates, today, is the beginning of irony and Western consciousness, he is so in a quite modern sense. Aristotle, Cicero and Quintilian all defined irony in reference to Socrates, but they did not see irony as a radically transformative political position; Socrates' irony was one technique among others for political discussion. Since the nineteenth century, however, Socratic irony has come to mean more than just a figure of speech and refers to a capacity to remain distant and different from what is said in general. If there has always been irony, both in practice and in name, it has not always taken the same form. This historical problem places us in an ironic predicament: how justified are we in reading past texts as ironic; do they mean what they seem to be saying?

So, in thinking about irony historically we have to try to separate the sources for the definition of irony (which range from Ancient Greece to the present) from the past texts to which we can now apply the idea of irony. On the one hand, there are uses of the word 'irony' throughout literary history to name varying levels of linguistic complexity. On the other, there are instances of language that we can now identify as ironic, even if they were not explicitly labelled as such. In addition to specific references to irony and uses of irony throughout history there is also a historical shift in the status of irony. At a certain point in history, particularly with the self-conscious recognition of being modern in the eighteenth and nineteenth centuries, irony was seen to characterise life as a whole. Once irony was expanded to this degree it was then possible to look back, not just at Socrates but at Shakespeare or Chaucer, and see their writing as subtly ironic.

MEDIEVAL AND RENAISSANCE IRONY

As noted above, the most recognised definitions of irony came from Cicero and Quintilian. Medieval and Renaissance authors who did not have access to these texts directly were nevertheless aware of the tradition of Ciceronian rhetoric through later sources. The most important of these later sources were the widely used grammars by Aelius Donatus (AD 4), and Isidore of Seville (*c.*570–636), whose *Origines* or *Etymologiae* served as rhetorical encyclopedia throughout the Middle Ages. Both these sources continue the idea of irony as saying the opposite or contrary of what is meant and make no reference to a broader irony that would characterise an entire personality or even an entire text. Donatus, in his monumental *Ars Grammatica*, defined irony as a trope where the real meaning is the opposite of the apparent meaning: *tropus per contrarium quod conatur ostendens* (Donatus 1864, 401). Irony was employed within texts and speeches for clearly intended and recognisable reasons. Like Quintilian, Isidore of Seville defined irony as a figure of speech and as a figure of thought – with the figure of speech, or clearly substituted word, being the primary example. The figure of thought occurs when irony extends across a whole idea, and does not just involve the substitution of one word for its opposite. So, 'Tony Blair is a saint' is a figure of speech or verbal irony if we really think that Blair is a devil; the word 'saint' substitutes for its opposite. 'I must remember to invite you here more often' would be a figure of thought, if I really meant to express my displeasure at your company. Here, the figure does not lie in the substitution of a word, but in the expression of an opposite sentiment or idea. When medieval and Renaissance writers were ironic, it was this local and rhetorical mode of irony that was employed: an irony that could be explained either through the substitution of a word for its opposite or as adopting, say, an expression of praise when derision is really implied.

When later writers have looked back at pre-modern examples of irony they have argued that writers from Bede to Chaucer were aware of the concept of irony (Knox 1989, 8–9), and they have also been able to identify cases of irony. They have done so by appealing either to the context of the literary work as a whole, or to the social context in which such works were written. D.H. Green (1979) has not only argued that cases of simple and complex irony can be found in medieval literature and that medieval writers were aware of the rhetoric of irony; he has also described specific reasons for irony in the medieval romance tradition. We can discern irony in medieval literature, Green argues, because works are no longer circulated anonymously and orally but are attributed to specific authors (Green 1979, 6). So, we can ask, 'Is this meant ironically?' and refer not just to the odd word, but to entire speeches within a work. We can question an overall intent. Also, Green argues, the writer of romances would have occupied a distanced and critical position in relation to the courts and would have used irony to say implicitly what it might not have been politic to say outright. This is, of course, a crucial feature and possibility of irony in any age, but as Green notes, the conditions of court and patronage would have been particularly constraining on expression and would have been conducive to using indirect modes of expression such as irony (Green 1979, 359). Furthermore, at the time of the writing of romances there were remnants of the social ideal of the ironic citizen – going back to Socrates – as an elevated and urbane individual; such an ideal is perfectly in keeping with the values of courtly life (ibid. 341). Most of the examples cited by Green, however, are cases of simple irony, clearly identified by being incongruous with their context. When Gawain, prior to having his head chopped off, is greeted with, 'Now, Sir swete', the politeness is clearly *not* intended (ibid. 206).

Green, arguing for irony in medieval romances, gives a wealth of extended examples of irony. His analyses are typical of many arguments in literary criticism that identify irony across the range of literature in English, from Chaucer and Shakespeare to Austen and Eliot. Here the irony can either lie in the situation, where what the character says is undermined by what they do or say elsewhere; or, the irony can lie in the speech itself where the rhetoric is so excessive or clichéd that we suspect the author of ironising the character's own limited imagination. The opening of Chaucer's *Merchant's Tale* offers two modes of extended irony. To begin with, the irony is a typical example of excessive praise signalling irony. We read the celebration of marriage ironically because the merchant has already expressed his dissatisfaction with his wife ('I have a wyf, the worste that may be' [1218]), so the context signals that the character cannot mean what he says. However, as in all literature, we are challenged as to where the irony lies: does the character intend the irony, by wanting to be understood as not praising marriage, or does

Chaucer intend the irony, by suggesting that all such praises and eulogies will be undermined by real love and marriages? It is not just the context that gives away irony in this case. The speech is so excessive that even if there were no contextual clue we might suspect irony. Our context could be human life and marriage in general: could anyone really love his wife and marriage *this much*? If one did want to offer such an exceeding praise of love and do so sincerely, then we would need a more elaborate context: say, the plot of *Romeo and Juliet* where the circumstances and characters would seem to be able to mean and intend such words sincerely. And, as anyone who tries to write on love knows, in order for the words to appear as sincere, we cannot just use everyday language excessively. So, when we do hear characters using praise in a clichéd but intense manner, we expect that the author wants us to hear more than, or something other than, praise. The ironic meaning is, perhaps, 'how ungrounded, insincere and empty all this excessive praise must be!' The irony here does not lie in a single word but requires the whole passage to alert us that what is being said is not what is meant.

Many commentators on pre-modern irony give examples where praise is so excessive that it *must* be ironic. But if excessive rhetoric triggers this suspicion we would still require some confirmation or assumption about context to conclude that irony were present. What distinguishes an ironic use of excessive and contradictory rhetoric from a text that simply is excessive? Green's examples of medieval irony are all explained from the context of the narrative as a whole, what characters have said, or what the author (we assume) must have meant. Dilwyn Knox (1989), who also argues for the frequent use of irony in medieval literature, does, however, cite an example where such contextual clues were not read, and the obviously ironic text was read as sincere. The excessive and inappropriate praise did not arouse suspicion and, as a consequence, the text did not have its intended force and effect. The late medieval poem, *Liber de Statu Curie*, probably written between 1261 and 1265 by Magister Henricus Würzburg, is a dialogue that appears to praise the clergy and the holy city. The character Ganfridus assures his interlocutor of the honesty, safeness and integrity of Rome. He insists that the doctors charge moderately for their services, that the cardinals eat frugally and refuse all wine, and are generous to the poor and destitute. Now, two things need to be noted. The first is the excessiveness of the praise. Ganfridus is not offering a moderate defence; indeed, he assumes the clergy and Rome to be beyond all reproach. To any astute reader who knows about the supposed corruption of the clergy at this time, such unquestioning praise will be obviously ironic. Second, the irony is signalled in the text, with the speaker lamenting that 'hic fuit antiphrasis' – there has been antiphrasis, or saying what is contrary. Knox notes, however, that this conclusion was not in all texts, and was not in the copy lodged in the papal library of Eusebius IV. From this he concludes that the obvious irony was not always recognised. The text was read as a sincere praise of the clergy, and would need to be so if included in the papal library.

This raises two issues. First, even the most 'obvious' ironies bear the possibility of not being read, and they do so precisely *because* of the contextual nature of irony. How could the papacy itself conclude that a eulogy of Rome was *obviously* ironic? Irony, even at its most obvious, is always diagnostic and political: to read the irony you do not just have to know the context; you also have to be committed to specific beliefs and positions *within* that context. Irony must be partial and selective. If the context were unanimous – if we *all* believed without question in the corruption of the clergy – then how could we present a character as ironically praising the clergy? His words would not make sense if praise were not a possible position within our context. In order for the irony to work there must be some possible speakers who would believe or intend what is being said. Second, this example is taken from dialogue. The author presents possible voices and positions, allowing those positions to disclose their own incoherence. In these cases of extended irony, then, what is actually intended is not what the *speaker* wants to say. In fact, just where the intention or irony lies becomes difficult to discern. In the case cited from Knox, we would say that the author of the dialogue really meant to say that the clergy are corrupt and did so by having a character utter praise that was obviously incongruous. The irony of *Liber de Statu Curie* works towards another intended meaning, and it does so by appealing to another context: those of us who recognise the clergy as corrupt. But irony cannot always be determined in this way; in any collection of competing voices it is always possible that the underlying or unifying intention is undecidable.

The idea that 'behind' the voices of Shakespeare, Chaucer or even Plato *there is* a univocal intent, and that such an intent is secured by context, is highly problematic. For part of what we do when we read *literature* is to look at what a text can do in contexts beyond its original intent and conventions (Miller 1998, 172). Something like this is given in the example already cited by Knox: how much greater the force and irony of an anti-clerical text when it is lodged in the papal library and read as sincere! The irony here is not intended; it occurs or 'happens' when texts diverge from their original contexts. Such an irony is only later discerned, and so perhaps is not even present. Similarly, once we have the concept of complex irony, an irony that extends beyond a word or figure substituted within the text, we are capable of questioning the sincerity or authenticity of any text. To what extent can a text be controlled or governed by its original context? When the Romantic poets argued that Milton's devil was the hero of *Paradise Lost* (1667), and was so in spite of Milton's intention (Wittreich 1991), they relied on the notion that a text has a force that is not reducible to what the author wanted to say. Milton may have wanted to present Satan as evil, but the force of the words that the character of Satan used had an appeal and implication well beyond Milton's piety. By the same token, when we isolate irony in Homer, Chaucer or Shakespeare – even when those authors did not refer to their texts *as ironic* – we acknowledge that there must be clues for reading irony that go beyond authorial intent.

Irony is just this capacity to consider a work as a text: as a production that is not reducible to conscious intent or the manifest work. But if we are to give irony any specificity we need to ask just how it is that we take some texts to mean what they say, and other texts to be other than, or distanced from, what they say.

COSMIC, TRAGIC OR DRAMATIC IRONY AND EVERYDAY IRONY

Before going on to look at the complexities of literary irony in the following chapters, we can consider the ways in which we use the concept of irony in everyday and non-literary contexts. There are two broad uses in everyday parlance. The first relates to cosmic irony and has little to do with the play of language or figural speech. A Wimbledon commentator may say, 'Ironically, it was the year that he was given a wild-card entry, and not as a seeded player, that the Croatian won the title.' The irony here refers, like linguistic irony, to a doubleness of sense or meaning. It is as though there is the course of human events and intentions, involving our awarding of rankings and expectations, that exists alongside another order of fate beyond our predictions. This is an irony of situation, or an irony of existence; it is as though human life and its understanding of the world is undercut by some other meaning or design beyond our powers. It is this form of irony that covers everything from statements such as, 'Ironically, Australians are spending more than ever on weight-loss formulas while becoming increasingly obese', to observations like, 'The film ends ironically, with the music of the young and hopeful cellist played as we see her crippled and wasted body.' In such cases, the word irony refers to the limits of human meaning; we do not see the effects of what we do, the outcomes of our actions, or the forces that exceed our choices. Such irony is cosmic irony, or the irony of fate.

Related to cosmic irony, or the way the word 'irony' covers twists of fate in everyday life, is the more literary concept of dramatic or tragic irony. This is most intense when the audience knows what will happen, so that a character can be viewed from an almost God-like position where we see her at the mercy of the plot or destiny (Sedgwick 1935). If irony is taken in its broadest sense as a doubleness of meaning, where what is said is limited or undercut by what is implied, then we can start to include ironies that are not rhetorical, that have little to do with speech or language. Such ironies were not labelled as ironies until the nineteenth century (Thirlwall 1833, 490), but it is frequently argued that even ancient texts display this mode of irony. Tragic irony is exemplified in ancient drama and is intensified by the fact that most of the plots were mythic. The audience watched a drama unfold, already knowing its destined outcome. There was already a sense of irony or mourning in the predetermined plot, as though the drama could only unfold an already given destiny, as though the time when human action could be open and determining was already lost. In Sophocles' *Oedipus the King*, for example, 'we' (the audience) can see what Oedipus is blind to. The man he murders is his father, but he does not know it. In so doing he not only does more than he intends, he also fulfils a destiny that he and the audience have heard at the opening of the play from the prophet Teirisias, but whose meaning only 'we' fully hear:

You have your eyes but see not where you are
in sin, nor where you live, nor whom you live with.
Do you know who your parents are? Unknowing
you are an enemy to kith and kin
in death, beneath the earth, and in this life.
A deadly footed, double striking curse,
from father and mother both, shall drive you forth
out of this land, with darkness on your eyes,
that now have such straight vision.

(Sophocles 1942, 128, 413–19)

We might say that we can get a sense of this tragic or dramatic irony
today, either by the fact that we know the plot of *Macbeth* and can see
Macbeth hurtling towards his end, despite his ambitions, or by the fact
that we are aware of the forces of plot and genre (Blissett 1959). In the
case of *Macbeth* we may know the meaning of the witches' prediction and
see Macbeth misinterpret what they say, precisely because he believes too
readily in his power to act and determine his own end. But even if we do
not know or see the actual plot we can experience a tragic or dramatic
irony through the experience of plot as such. We can watch a film, and
once we get a sense that its genre is one of tragedy or horror, we can
'know' that the central character will meet his end; we can see all his hopes
and efforts as ironic. We see that he is blind to what *must* befall him.

Dramatic, cosmic and tragic irony are ways of thinking about the relation between human intent and contrary outcomes. This sense of irony is
related to verbal irony in that both share a notion of a meaning or intent
beyond what we manifestly say or intend. In dramatic and cosmic irony
this other meaning is plot or destiny. In verbal irony the other meaning is
either what the speaker intends or what the hearer understands; but how
do we know just what this other meaning is?

On the one hand, we might say that cosmic irony is something we
can discern across history, from Sophocles to Shakespeare to modern
film, and we might also say the same about verbal irony: that it is always
possible for texts to play with contexts and assumptions. On the other
hand, we might want to ask why the problem of these modes of irony was
made explicit in the nineteenth century.

THE PROBLEM OF IRONY

Why is irony a problem? And why, from its emergence in Ancient Greece to the present, has irony been perceived as a political problem? If we take the simplest definitions of irony that date back to Cicero and Quintilian, where irony is saying something contrary to what is understood, then we begin to get a sense of irony's problematic and contested nature. The simplest and most stable forms of irony rely on the audience or hearer recognising that what the speaker says can *not* be what she means (Booth 1974; Muecke 1980; Searle 1994). And this is because in order to speak at all we have to share conventions and assumptions. A word does not have *a* meaning independent of its social exchange. We know a word is being used ironically when it seems out of place or unconventional. Recognising irony, therefore, foregrounds the social, conventional and political aspects of language: that language is not just a logical system but relies on assumed norms and values.

If I say of a recently shamed, and long suspected, cabinet minister, 'True to the tradition of integrity and honesty that characterised his career, he defended his name until the end', then this statement will be read ironically if 'we' all know that the minister was anything but honest. Understanding something *other than what is said* does not rely on perceiving some private or hidden meaning behind my words; we understand if a word is being used ironically because of context. To use the word 'honest' in this case would be a bad move in a language game, or would not make sense, *unless* I were using the word 'honest' to show just how *dis*honest the minister is, how incongruous the word 'honest' is to describe such a *clearly recognised* fraud. Stable or simple cases of verbal irony tend to prove how shared and clearly recognisable our social norms and assumptions are. If we think of irony as primarily stable, or as exemplified by clear and simple cases, then we will also think of social and political life as primarily reciprocal, common, and operating from a basis of agreement. Complex, undecidable or insecure ironies, where we are not sure about sense, or where what is meant is not *clearly* recognisable, would then be regarded as special and marginal cases that deviate from the common ground of human understanding. Stable irony, with its process of obviously contradicting the conventions of a context and thereby signalling an opposite meaning, would be the ground from which less obvious or distinct cases might be explained. The norm would be a language of shared recognition and conventional exchange, a norm reinforced by the fact that for the most part we all know when someone is being ironic. The very fact that you can know that I mean something other than what I am saying shows that we have fixed conventions and that we seek reasons, such as irony, when those conventions are flouted.

By extension, in literary irony, it is because we assume that a recognised great writer *is great* that clumsy, unpalatable or inhuman expressions are assumed to be ironic. According to Wayne Booth irony does not just rely on shared social values; it also relies on literary value (Booth 1974, 193). Jonathan Swift (1667–1745) would not be a great author if we took his argument for cannibalism in *A Modest Proposal* (1729) as sincere (Swift 1984, 492–9). The speaker in the proposal suggests a perfectly rational method to deal with the hungry and overly populous poor of Ireland; their babies could be consumed and 'thus' the problem solved. Swift's text is 'clearly' ironic not just because its bigotry is excessive but also because it is bigoted; the very fact that its position is so objectionable forces us to read it as *not* saying what it appears to say. What makes the text great, according to Booth, is that it draws both on shared human values, insofar as we all abhor injustice, *and* shared literary values: a great text does not present blind, confused and incoherent dogma. *A Modest Proposal* is more satisfying if we assume that it is ironic: that it is critical of, or distanced from, the prejudiced incoherence it seems to mouth. We can assume a speaker is being ironic only if we share the same norms: Swift cannot *really mean* that it would be economically efficient to consume the poor. We also, according to Booth's account of irony, have to assume the value of textual coherence: it is because Swift expresses the argument in *A Modest Proposal* so clumsily – the proposal is anything but modest – that we assume he intended the text to be read ironically. Irony, for Booth, assumes a set of shared assumptions *and* the assumption of all communication: that we speak in order to be understood:

> It is always good, I have assumed, for two minds to meet in symbolic exchange; it is always good for an irony to be grasped when intended, always good for readers and authors to achieve understanding (though the understanding need not lead to mutual approval – that is another question entirely).
>
> (Booth 1974, 204–5)

If what I say seems not to make sense, then you might start to ask whether I were being ironic. Simple cases of irony therefore reveal something about the nature of communication: that we know what our words mean because we share contexts and conventions, along with the general expectation of sincerity and coherence.

DETERMINING IRONY THROUGH VALUE

From the earliest definitions of irony a distinction was made between a verbal and local irony, which was clearly contrary and delimited, and an extended figure of irony which pervades an entire speech, text or personality, such as the figure of Socrates. It is the first form of simple, stable and clearly recognisable irony that formed the basis of definitions and theories of irony from classical times to the eighteenth century, when irony was still defined in Samuel Johnson's (1709–84) dictionary of 1755 as a mode of speech in which the meaning is clearly contrary to the words. Johnson's example, 'Bolingbroke is a holy man', is not essentially ironic or ambiguous. To be read ironically we must know something about Bolingbroke. The fact that, for Johnson, he was obviously *not* holy allows the irony to confirm what we already know, and what we can safely assume as already known.

Recently, however, greater stress has been placed on irony that is undecidable and on modes of irony that challenge just how shared, common and stable our conventions and assumptions are. Many have argued that our entire epoch, as postmodern, is ironic (Eco 1992; Hassan 1987, 91–2; Hutcheon 1994; Mileur 1998; Sim 2002; Wilde 1980). We no longer share common values and assumptions, nor do we believe there is a truth or reason behind our values; we always speak and write provisionally, for we cannot be fully committed to what we say. Usually, this form of postmodern irony is argued to be inherently politically liberating; because no common ground is assumed, a life marked by irony remains open and undetermined (Handwerk 1985; Lang 1988). But the extension of irony from being a local 'trope' within an otherwise literal language to characterise life and language in general has also served clearly conservative political tendencies, tendencies that have closed literature off from its political and cultural forces. At the very least, irony is elitist: to say one thing and mean another, or to say something contrary to what is understood, relies on the possibility that those who are not enlightened or privy to the context will be excluded. We might be able to argue that irony is inherently ethical precisely because it prompts us to look at the communal nature of language (Handwerk 1985); but we can also say that it is conservative to assume that there simply is *a* community. How many readers, today, would find Johnson's example of irony, 'Bolingbroke is a holy man', so clearly ironic as to be exemplary? If we define irony as a *clearly recognised* figure of speech, then we need to question just how such communities of clear recognition are formed or assumed.

When the American New Critics of the 1940s used irony and paradox as the hallmark of literary and poetic discourse they did so by regarding the text as a self-contained organism. Poems are ironic because they take the words we use in everyday language and give them a richness of meaning. It is not by referring to the world and its conflicts that texts are ironic; the irony lies in the tensions of language. Wordsworth, for example, in the sonnet 'Composed upon Westminster Bridge, September 3, 1802', takes the worn-out metaphor of the city as a natural organism and re-injects it with life (Brooks 1947, 4). Everyday language thinks of life in terms of human bodies and daily action. By contrast, Wordsworth takes the present image of life, the city, and describes it in natural rather than urban terms. He does this by showing the city *not* when it is teeming with life – during the day when it is filled with faceless crowds – but in the solitude of morning: 'the very houses seem asleep/And all the mighty heart is lying still.' Here is the irony: the city is at its most *human* and alive when it can be described as deserted and asleep. For the New Critics, literary sensibility and irony rejuvenate an everyday language that has become worn out *because it is everyday* (unquestioning, lifeless and mechanical). Irony is essentially, avowedly and positively elitist: it works against common sense, the unrefined intellect and the social *use* of language (rather than its reflection, complexity and tension). Cleanth Brooks quotes both T.S. Eliot and I.A. Richards to insist on the superior sensibility of the poet:

> the poet, the imaginative man, has his particular value in his superior power to reconcile the irrelevant or apparently warring elements of experience. As Eliot has put it, 'When a poet's mind is perfectly equipped for its work, it is constantly amalgamating disparate

experience, the ordinary man's experience is chaotic, irregular, fragmentary' . . . [Brooks goes on to quote Richards:] '. . . the ordinary man
suppresses nine-tenths of his impulses, because he is incapable of
managing them without confusion'

(Brooks 1947, 42)

The history of irony's elitism goes back to its emergence in Greek
thought. Not only was irony defined as an art in keeping with an urbane
and elevated personality, it was also recognised as practised primarily in
sites of political power. Irony, as a trope, is a means of effective persuasion
in speeches and therefore already relies on the established speaking
position and force of the orator. As a figure or extended mode of thought
irony allows the speaker to remain 'above' what he says, allowing those
members of his audience who share his urbanity to perceive the true sense
of what is really meant. This sense of irony's necessary exclusiveness was
reinforced in the twentieth century in *Fowler's Modern English Usage*:
'Irony is a form of utterance that postulates a double audience, consisting
of one party that hearing shall hear and shall not understand, and another
party that, when more is meant than meets the ear, is aware both of that
more and of the outsiders' incomprehension' (Fowler 1968, 305).

Because of its ambivalent political history, perceived both as a force of
liberation and as a mode of elitism, there have been recent attempts
to move beyond or redefine irony. If irony *means* something other than
what it says, then this will (according to its supporters) allow language to
be liberated from a fixed and stable context. On the other hand, the idea
of an *other meaning* refers irony back to some speaker or original intent, to
ideas or a sense that lies outside language. Irony may well be tied up with
the long history of Western subjectivism: the idea that behind language,
actions, difference and communication there is a ground or subject *to be
expressed*.

For Douglas Muecke, who wrote a book on irony just as 'deconstruction' was gaining a foothold as a discernible movement, the acceptance of
texts as pure play without grounding sense would lead to the death
of irony. He concluded his own book ironically by suggesting that the
inability to deal with irony would prove just how empty deconstruction
was:

The establishment in recent years in both France and America of Deconstructionist criticism based on a view of writing as, in the words of Jacques Derrida, 'a structure cut off from any absolute responsibility or from consciousness as ultimate authority' . . . will probably lead to a recognition of the decreased usefulness to literary criticism of the term 'irony.' It seems likely that the usefulness of the term will delay the establishment of Deconstructionism or some related movement.

(Muecke 1982, 101)

Given that neither irony nor deconstruction have withered away we need to recognise the *problem* of irony. How can there be an *other* or ironical meaning if all we have are texts? For does not the very notion of 'meaning' demand that there is a sense or depth to a text, that there is more to a text than its surface? And if there *is* this other meaning, and we only know this meaning through what is said explicitly, just what is the nature and location of this meaning? If language is nothing more than a set of conventions and recognised uses, how do we recognise the difference between an ironic and a sincere use? Does the very thought of irony commit us to some linguistic stability and meaning, or does irony problematise and disrupt meaning? It is this problem of discerning the difference between stable meaning with a secure sense, and merely quoted or mentioned words with no clear depth, that will be charted in the following chapters that examine the various theories and values of irony.

2

THE PHILOSOPHY OF IRONY

Plato and Socrates

Irony in its broadest definition, as a sense of life's capacity to thwart language and understanding, emerges in the early nineteenth century with Romanticism. What came to be known as dramatic, cosmic and tragic forms of irony – where irony is just a recognition of the futility or inhumanity of destiny – are species of the Romantic tendency to define irony in terms of life's contradictions (Muecke 1980, 159). Prior to the nineteenth century, as we have already noted, irony took two dominant forms: rhetorical irony as a figure of speech and extended irony. Today, explanations of both forms usually begin by referring to Plato's dialogues and the figure of Socrates, who is the first figure to be described using an *eironeia* that is ethical and complex. Socrates was both an actual historical figure, Plato's philosophical mentor, and a literary character; Socrates did not produce written philosophical theories but practised his philosophies through dialogue. He is known only as Plato presents him, only as a questioning and inscrutable personality, never as a theorising voice in his own right.

Socrates, it is most often argued, used irony to bring about truth and recognition, even if that truth was mysterious or enigmatic. Socrates asks for a definition of friendship, justice or love from those who speak as though words possessed an unproblematic and secure sense. When those he questions give quick definitions, Socrates questions them further in order to show that such definitions cannot hold: if justice is paying back what one owes, would it be just to return an axe to a deranged man? So if love is *not* possessing what one desires can we say that we know what love is? Either Socrates uses irony to bring his interlocutors to ethical knowledge or, he uses irony to show that the knowledge they thought they had was not so certain. Perhaps the words we use in order to say what we mean are not fully meaningful; perhaps there is more to the word 'love' or 'justice' than we think. The everyday irony that, today, we identify in simple cases of verbal 'irony' has its origin in this Socratic technique of *eironeia*. We use a word but expect others to recognise that there is more to what we are saying than the uses of everyday language. The dialogues and the personality of Socrates create the possibility of a meaning that is latent, hidden or implied.

According to Gregory Vlastos even the simple cases of irony presented by Plato are evidence of an entirely new and specifically Western philosophical moral consciousness. This is because irony as used by Socrates, although clearly ironic and with no sense of deceit, was part of a new mode of dialogue and education. The achievement of Socrates, for both his early defenders (including Plato in *The Laws*) and his detractors (including Cicero), is his defeat of sophistry, or the idea that speaking effectively is an art in itself, with no reference to a transcendent or extra-linguistic truth (Vlastos 1991, 23). Against the Sophists who offered artful definitions and turns of phrase, Socrates insists that truth cannot be reduced to figures of speech alone; it must be possible to decide between a skilful and a true argument. What is true, furthermore, is not just what we conventionally agree upon or say is true; truth transcends language. For Plato's Socrates, however effective our skill as speakers may be, the art of speaking is not the same as the art of living: there is a difference between what we conventionally *say* is good and the *good itself.* There is a truth or law that cannot be reduced to convention, artful rhetoric or everyday discourse.

Socrates achieves this moral victory over sophistry through irony. Take a simple case. In Book 1 of the *Republic* the sophist, Thrasymachus, defines justice as the advantage of the powerful (Plato 1963, 588 [338c]).

Justice is nothing more than what those in power present as justice; justice is defined in order to benefit the stronger; and justice according to Thrasymachus is reducible to this simple and effective definition. In this dialogue Socrates' irony works on two levels, the verbal and the ethical. He uses stable verbal irony to tackle the sophist. He refers to his interlocutors as 'wise' and knowledgeable and continually defers to, and accepts, their definitions in order that they might spell out what they mean. Thrasymachus has just been offered money for his definition of justice. Socrates recounts the following exchange between himself and Thrasymachus, with Thrasymachus accusing him of irony:

> Oh yes, of course, said [Thrasymachus], so that Socrates may contrive, as he always does, to evade answering himself but may cross-examine the other man and refute his replies.
>
> Why, how, I said, my dear fellow, could anybody answer if in the first place he did not know and did not even profess to know, and secondly, even if he had some notion of the matter, he had been told by a man of weight that he mustn't give any of his suppositions as an answer? Nay, it is more reasonable that you should be the speaker. For you do affirm that you know and are able to tell. Don't be obstinate, but do me the favor to reply and don't be chary of your wisdom, and instruct Glaucon here and the rest of us.
>
> (Plato 1963, 587–8 [337e–338a]).

Here, as elsewhere, Socrates attributes 'wisdom' to the sophists, and we might see this as a standard verbal irony: one that is meant to be, and is, recognised. Socrates calls the sophists clever, and asks them to pity his ignorance: 'It is pity then that we should far more reasonably receive from clever fellows like you than severity' (Plato 336e–337a, 587). But such an attribution of cleverness is quickly recognised by Thrasymachus as meaning its opposite; it is by deferring to the sophist's cleverness, by asking the sophist to display and prove how clever he is, that Socrates leads the sophist into difficulty. Already, Thrasymachus has accused Socrates of irony. He suggests that Socrates is calling him clever, when Socrates clearly does *not* mean that. But even this clear case is complex. It is not just that Socrates substitutes one word for another, 'clever' for 'ignorant'. He might not mean the opposite; he might not be saying that

Thrasymachus is stupid or ignorant. He might be hinting that there is something altogether different from wisdom, knowledge or *cleverness* when it comes to knowing how to live well, or consider justice. All we have is the negative: that Socrates does not mean what he says. What Socrates *really* thinks or means is not given. Socrates' verbal ironies are therefore more than rhetorical ornaments. They have an ethical purpose, and possibly an ethical form. They place the reader and interlocutor in a position of not knowing, of having to decide just what value to place on words like 'clever'.

The difference between irony, say, and metaphor is that other figures of speech make a comparison, contrast or likeness while irony invokes an absent or hidden sense. Even in a complex metaphor such as 'the mind is a mirror' we may be unclear as to just what comparison is being made, but we are nevertheless given some term other than the literal. If we say 'the mind is a computer', we may be referring to its speed, materiality, complexity, structure, simplicity or memory. But in irony we are given one term that is negated, so that when Socrates refers to Thrasymachus as clever, and we assume this is ironic, we have no other term to replace 'clever' with. If being just or good is *not* about being clever, what is it? Perhaps moral wisdom or a sense of justice is something that cannot be said, defined or spelled out in explicit axioms. Socrates' irony regarding wisdom is tied in with the very nature of wisdom. He uses words like 'clever' and 'wise' ironically, and this has the effect of creating uncertainty about everyday language. Socrates tackles a certain use or convention regarding 'wisdom'. For the sophists, wisdom and cleverness lie in the art of speaking, in skilful phrases, apposite quotations and remembered truisms. But, through irony, Socrates exposes and undermines this conventional understanding of wisdom: if you are wise you will know about justice. But once the sophists attempt to define and speak artfully about justice Socrates leads them into contradiction. Socrates' 'deferential' argument, which accepts – ironically – the sophist's wisdom, takes the following form. Before he has encountered Thrasymachus's definition of justice as power he has already been offered a definition that the sophist Polemarchus has received from Simonides:

> [Socrates:] Tell me, then, you the inheritor of the argument, what it is that you affirm that Simonides says and rightly about justice.

[Polemarchus:] That it is just, he replied, to render to each his due. In saying this I think he speaks well.

[Socrates:] I must admit, said I, that it is not easy to disbelieve Simonides. For he is a wise and inspired man. But just what he may mean by this you, Polemarchus, doubtless know, but I do not. Obviously he does not mean what we were just speaking of, this return of a deposit to anyone whatsoever even if he asks it back when he is not in his right mind. And yet what the man deposited is due to him in a sense, is it not?

[Polemarchus:]Yes.

[Socrates:] But rendered to him it ought not to be by any manner of means when he demands it not being in his right mind.

True, said [Polemarchus].

[Socrates:] It is then something other than this that Simonides must, as it seems, mean by the saying that it is just to render back what is due.

Something else in very deed, [Polemarchus] replied.

(Plato 1963, 580–81 [331e–332b])

It is not the case that Socrates is playing the sophists at their own game, saying whatever will win the argument. On the contrary, Socrates' irony commits itself to the very sense of what wisdom or justice *must mean*. If the sophists are really wise, then they ought to be able to define justice; and if they really know what justice is, then they ought to be able to explain exactly what they have said and all that it entails. But when Socrates and the dialogue follow the sophists' 'wisdom', when the word wisdom is really used with all its force, then the sophist no longer appears wise.

[Socrates:] So justice, according to you and Homer and Simonides, seems to be a kind of stealing, with the qualification that it is for the benefit of friends and the harm of enemies. Isn't that what you meant?

No, by Zeus, he replied. I no longer know what I did mean.

(Plato 1963, 584 [334b–c])

Socratic irony is, therefore, not just saying one thing and meaning another. It is an insistence that what we say must have *some* meaning; that we cannot just offer wisdoms and definitions as rhetorical strategies without commitment to what they mean.

Already, then, there is a difference between Socratic irony in the Platonic dialogues and a merely rhetorical irony. We can imagine a banal everyday irony where we said to a driver who turned out in front of us: 'Well, that was *clever!*' where clever clearly means stupid or unthinking. We are substituting one word for another, its opposite or contrary. But Socrates' irony is not just a substitute of one word for another. Even at its clearest, he uses irony, not to say something else or opposite, but to question the use of a concept. He does not necessarily offer another or clearly recognisable opposed meaning. His ironic strategy, even for those like Vlastos who believe that Socratic irony is a vehicle for displaying truth, is to show that we cannot mean that the sophist is wise, or that justice is power. But we are then led to question for ourselves just what wisdom or justice would genuinely be (Vlastos 1991, 44). Socratic irony, therefore, suggests or implies what a concept ought to mean: we use a concept as though it had moral coherence and force, but we then go on to act and speak in ways that undermine that claimed coherence. The sophists in the *Republic* offer all sorts of seemingly clever definitions of justice, but when Socrates presses the sophists to spell out what these definitions entail or *must mean* the sophists are led into contradiction. This ironic strategy has several levels and implications.

First, when Socrates means something other than what he says this meaning is not just the opposite. His irony is not just a local ornament; it is there to expose the sophist as *not* clever, and so what we recognise as cleverness, knowledge and wisdom may not be so clear and apparent after all. Maybe cleverness and wisdom are not simple arts or *techne* that can be learned and passed around like so much know-how. Perhaps wisdom requires irony: *not* speaking literally and explicitly, recognising that there is always more to what we say. Vlastos emphasises this dimension of Socratic irony. When Socrates stresses that he is not a teacher, is not wise and has no knowledge, he is saying that he does not have these things in the form of the empty, unquestioning and ready-made definitions of the sophists. He has no wisdom or knowledge if by wisdom we mean the clear and sellable catch phrases of sophistry. But he is in possession of wisdom if being wise refers to a truer and higher knowledge of virtue and self-education. We can see that Socrates is being ironic only if we recognise the emptiness and incoherence of the sophists' rhetoric and only if we acknowledge that there must be a higher moral truth and knowledge that is more than just transmitted skill or oratory.

Second, it is because Socrates stresses irony in this way, by not just saying the opposite but suggesting another *moral* meaning, that Socratic irony is linked to ethical pedagogy and Eros. Pedagogy, because Socrates does not offer another meaning; rather he prompts his inter-locutors to ask for themselves what Socrates means, thereby leading to reasoned rather than received definitions (Vlastos 1991, 44). Eros, because Socrates' game, unlike the sophists, is not one of power over others through rhetoric, but dialogue. His interlocutors must be engaged and attracted by Socrates' irony in order to follow his questions. Socrates' appeal lies in what is not presented. One is drawn, not to what Socrates *is*, but to his desire for the truth or what is not given. But Socrates must also be motivated by the desire to achieve the good for his interlocutors, and not just to win the argument for his own sake. This is true Eros, not the attempt to grasp this or that object, prize or person, but the love of wisdom, a wisdom that lies above and beyond any single speaker or rhetorical position. In *not* meaning what he says Socrates' irony has two consequences, the pedagogical and the erotic. First, it challenges the way words are conventionally used: is this really what we mean by 'clever'? Irony speaks a word in such a way that its meaning is open to question. Second, Socrates allows his own standpoint, intention or position to remain open to question: Socrates is not a presented object that we might possess but an implied desire, a movement towards truth or a love of truth, rather than a given definition.

The first effect of irony, or the challenge to the conventional and merely rhetorical use of concepts, is ethical and political, for it allows our conventions and assumptions to be questioned and valued, without imposing or offering another value. Socratic irony was therefore tied up with a politics of discussion and contestation, where law was examined and freely chosen, rather than simply opposed or obeyed. Socratic dialogue shifts the concept of irony from simple rhetorical use to complex rhetorical engagement, such that the boundary between an accepted literal meaning and an ironical meaning is shown to be political and ethical.

Consider a more contemporary use of this style of irony from the twentieth century by W.H. Auden (1907–73) in his poem 'September 1, 1939':

I sit in one of the dives
On Fifty-Second Street
Uncertain and afraid
As the clever hopes expire
Of a low dishonest decade
(Auden 1979, 86)

Auden's use of the word 'clever' is ironic. The irony is Socratic insofar as
it works against common usage and value. By calling a low, dishonest
decade 'clever' he does not just mean the opposite; rather, Auden is using
the word clever in all its emptiness and poverty. It is precisely because
of 'cleverness', a confidence, unquestioning superiority and glib self-
assurance, that the times were shown to be lacking in wisdom. The word
'clever' is divided: on the one hand it refers to what passes as clever (blind
self-assurance), and on the other it points to its own contradiction and
negation: how clever is a decade that culminates in war and violence?
What we thought of as clever, what we said was clever, *cannot* really be
clever. The concept means more than it says. The Socratic mode of irony
does not simply negate a concept; it must bring out *both* how the concept
is misused or corrupted *and* what the concept seems required to mean.

In addition to showing that what we say, or how our concepts are used,
can often *not* be rendered fully meaningful, Socratic irony also created a
unique position within the Platonic dialogues. In being ironic, Socrates'
own position remains undisclosed. This is why Thrasymachus *accuses*
Socrates of irony, of attacking everyone else by calling them clever and
demanding wisdom, but never offering his *own* viewpoint. Those who
stress the ultimate truth function of the dialogues explain this by saying
that the Socrates we do not see is clearly the Socrates of autonomous
moral wisdom and virtue (Vlastos 1991, 44). But many have regarded
this absence of Socrates' real self as a far more disturbing and disruptive
effect of irony: for in *not* saying what he means Socrates is able to remain
above and beyond any context or dialogue, creating an absence or
negativity, and not just *something* that is hidden (Kierkegaard [1841]
1989). Perhaps Socrates is *nothing* other than his distance from received
rhetoric. Perhaps there is no Socratic soul or self. If this were so, the
Socratic ironic legacy would not lead to truth, recognition and moral
education, but would leave us with a character, mask or persona that is

ultimately enigmatic. Socrates would be more like a literary and created character, formed to question life, rather than one more person within life (Nehamas 1998). According to many writers, from Sören Kierkegaard ([1841] 1989) and Friedrich Nietzsche ([1889] 1968, 34) to Pierre Hadot (1995, 147–78), Sarah Kofman (1998) and Jacques Derrida (1995), Western thought has been haunted by this absent and ironic Socrates. Plato creates a character who lives well and who is virtuous, but who offers no definition or logic by which we might fix and explain just what living well *is* (Nehamas 1998, 86). Socratic irony is an art or process of self-formation in opposition to fixed meanings, definitions and conventions. In many ways, then, Socrates typifies the impossibility of philosophy. He is a superior sophist. Through dialogue and ongoing praxis he shows that all our simple definitions are not fully adequate – that we *must mean* more by 'justice' than mere advantage. At the same time, his irony offers no other definition; we are left with the negation of *mere* rhetoric but no *other* skill or art, no set of better rules. What needs to be noted at this stage is that the celebration of the negativity, absence and indeterminacy of Socratic irony was only emphasised from the nineteenth century on, and then with a zeal that continues today.

PLATO'S *SYMPOSIUM*

All these levels and possibilities of Socratic irony are brought out in Plato's *Symposium*, a text that is rich in ironies and which has also been influential in the re-reading of irony in modernity. Writers as diverse as Sören Kierkegaard ([1841] 1989), Sigmund Freud ([1920] 1984), Pierre Hadot (1995), Luce Irigaray ([1974] 1985), Gregory Vlastos (1991), Alexander Nehamas (1998) and Thomas Mann ([1912] 1971) have all worked with the voices of the *Symposium*. This is a dialogue from Plato's middle period, by which time, supposedly, he had recognised the need to do more than negate the sophists' 'wisdom'; he would need to offer a logic or art of his own. This would be a logic of Ideas (from *eidos*, or the essence which remains there, in potential, to be seen and viewed by all). All our uses of the words 'justice', 'beauty', 'wisdom' and so on would be guided by an Idea or pure form of justice or wisdom, a form that only philo-sophical contemplation could discern. There would be an *eidos* above and beyond rhetoric and the practice of dialogue. Such an *eidos* or essence might be revealed or hinted at through dialogue but it would ultimately transcend any single speaker. In the later dialogues, Socrates' irony, framed by Plato's commitment to Ideas, becomes subordinate to truth. Speech and dialogue become vehicles to arrive at a wisdom above and beyond any specific context.

The *Symposium* is a great ironic text precisely because it expresses this anti-ironic idea ironically. Apollodorus recalls the description of a symposium that he has heard about from Aristodemus, so the dialogue is already removed from its original context by being recounted and quoted. The dialogue opens with Aristodemus describing a gathering to Apollodorus where various voices attempt to define love. The concluding voice of the dialogue that appeals to a truth above and beyond any specific voice or desire is also a quoted voice. Socrates' definitive speech repeats a definition of beauty that he has received from a woman outside the Athenian political context. Socrates says that he has learned about the truth of beauty and love from Diotima, a woman from Manitea (Plato 1963, 553 [201d]). In this recounted scene, Socrates repeats Diotima's speech, where Diotima argues that one loves specific things and bodies for their beauty, and in so doing one comes to love and discern the beautiful as such. Eventually, she tells Socrates, one loves this or that thing not just for *its* beauty, but as a way of revealing the essence, Idea, or truth of beauty. And, as truth, this idea would be eternal: unaffected by the changes, errors and corruptions of this world (Plato 1963, 562 [210e–211a]). There is a difference between beautiful things and the essence of beauty. Love or desire moves from this or that instance of beauty to the beautiful as such. Socrates, in recalling Diotima's speech, says that he once thought differently about love but after hearing Diotima realises that love is not itself beautiful or loveable but only a desire *for* what is beautiful. And all 'desiring *for*' strives to achieve, end or consummate its desire; it must reach an end in the beautiful itself. Love, therefore, necessarily moves beyond the things of this world, including human products of love such as children, to a true love of what is eternal, for only this love achieves its fulfilment. Eternal love is love of what remains the same, regardless of time or space: love of truth (Plato 1963, 563 [211e]).

The *Symposium* has already presented other voices and their definitions of Eros, but it is only with Diotima's speech, via Socrates, that we are no longer given this or that benefit, instance or definition of love, but the very essence and end of love: that which must *necessarily* be sought and desired is truth. Through realising the limit and fragility of any worldly thing of beauty we are led to the essence of beauty, which is also the eternal *truth* of beauty: that which must be loved for its own sake.

To a certain extent, then, this position described by Socrates is remarkably anti-ironic: there simply *is* a truth that we can arrive at, and discern, beyond all particular points of view. Such a truth is what all love, speech and dialogue is directed towards, and is independent of any specific lovers or speakers. I say that this is anti-ironic because, unlike the enigma, suggestiveness and allusion of Socratic irony, this positing of essence and truth is literal. There simply are Ideas and forms towards which our words and actions ought to strive. Even so, the *Symposium* remains ironic at several levels. To begin with, despite the stress on truth and beauty *itself*, the dialogue takes the form of repeated and recollected speech. On several occasions Aristodemus says that he cannot remember this or that detail, that the gathering *may* have taken the form he remembers. Second, despite Socrates' reported *definition* of Eros as love of the true and eternal, there is another model of ironic Eros *performed*, rather than stated, in the dialogue.

Socrates is enamoured of the youth Alcibiades. He arrives at the symposium where the various participants decide to deliver eulogies to love. Alcibiades is not yet present but the other guests offer various conflicting praises and definitions until Socrates begins with his characteristic irony. He demands that Agathon repeat and clarify what he has *said*, spelling out what he really *means*, what his words and rhetoric must entail if he is really committed to his speech: 'But now that we've had the pleasure of hearing your magnificent description of Love, there's just one little point that I'm not quite clear about. Tell me. Do you think it is the nature of Love to be of somebody, or of nobody?' (Plato 1963, 551 [199c]). From there, Socrates leads Agathon further and further into his ideas:

> Then isn't it probable, said Socrates, or rather isn't it certain that everything longs for what it lacks, and that nothing longs for what it doesn't lack? I can't help thinking, Agathon, that that's about as certain as anything could be. Don't you think so?
>   Yes, I suppose it is.
>
> (Plato 1963, 552 [200a–b])

Eventually, and characteristically, Socrates leads Agathon to an inherent contradiction:

> Then, if Love is lacking in what is beautiful, and if the good and the beautiful are the same, he must also be lacking in what is good.
>
> Just as you say, Socrates, he replied. I'm afraid you're quite unanswerable.
>
> No, no, dear Agathon. It's the truth you find unanswerable, not Socrates.
>
> (Plato 1963, 553 [201 c–d])

When Socrates finally reports Diotima's speech on the form or Idea of love, this is not the last word of the dialogue. Alcibiades arrives and we are given a performance of a quite different mode of Eros: Eros as an ironic engagement between master and pupil, rather than Eros as a fixed essence or what love ultimately grasps. Both modes of Socratic irony, the verbal and the extended, are at work here. Socrates playfully refers to Alcibiades' cleverness. Alcibiades, Socrates says, is trying to seduce Socrates through beauty, but this attempt at seduction is motivated by Alcibiades' recognition of the *real* beauty of Socratic wisdom. Alcibiades is offering a bodily beauty for Socrates' inner beauty. In so doing he is guilty of trickery. But, Socrates warns, how can Alcibiades be so sure that this beautiful wisdom he is vying for is really worth it? After all, his young eyes, which see the world so clearly, are perhaps not yet able to see the beauty that is not physically visible. This mode of irony sees Socrates playing with language in order to suggest what lies beyond language: a beauty *other than* the bodily beauty of Alcibiades and an Eros *other than* the meeting of bodies. Alcibiades has offered his body to Socrates only to be refused, suggesting that Socrates' love is directed not to what Alcibiades at present *is* (his body), but perhaps to what he may *become* through the master–pupil relation (his potential for wisdom).

Perhaps the Eros lies in the encounter itself, and not some end (either physical or eternal) that the encounter might achieve. There is an irony in this Eros, for in refusing Alcibiades but desiring him nevertheless Socrates remains enigmatic, and the erotic encounter remains in suspense. An entirely different mode of Eros is at work here than that recounted by Diotima. This is not an Eros that meets with its object and achieves its end. It is an ironic Eros that enjoys sustained dialogue, encounter and being *other than* any fixed end. What Alcibiades loves in Socrates is not what Socrates *is* or *presents*, but the ongoing creativity, questioning and openness of Socrates: 'Yes, I've heard Pericles and all the other great orators, and very eloquent I thought they were, but they never affected me like that; they never turned my whole soul upside down'. Alcibiades then continues his homage to Socrates:

> there's not one of you that really knows him. But now I've started on him, I'll show him up. Notice, for instance, how Socrates is attracted by good-looking people, and how he hangs around them, positively gaping with admiration. Then again, he loves to appear utterly uninformed and ignorant – isn't that just like Silenus? Of course it is. Don't you see that it's just his outer casing, like those little figures I was telling you about? But believe me, friends and fellow drunks, you've only got to open him up and you'll find him so full of temperance and sobriety that you'll hardly believe your eyes. Because, you know, he doesn't really care a row of pins about good looks – on the contrary, you can't think how much he looks down on them – or money, or any of the honors that most people care about. He doesn't care a curse for anything of that kind, or for any of us either – yes, I'm telling you – and he spends his whole life playing his little game of irony, and laughing up his sleeve at the whole world.
>
> I don't know whether anyone else has ever opened him up when he's been being serious, and seen the little images inside, but I saw them once, and they looked so godlike, so golden, so beautiful, and so utterly amazing that there was nothing for it but to do exactly what he told me.
> (Plato 1963, 567–68 [215e–217b])

Socrates achieves this enigmatic persona through irony, in being playfully distant from what he says.

But the *Symposium* also brings out more than Socrates' *use* of irony. Socrates' entire personality or existence can be, and has been, read as ironic. This is given, not in what Socrates says, but in Alcibiades' description of him. Here, Socratic irony is not an art of speech or dialogue, a way of playing with language in order to lead the discourse beyond fixed definitions; it is a mode of self or way of life. Socrates is enigmatic. He lives and acts, not as a person or subject with an essence and identity revealed through speech, but as a character in constant creation and formation. To love Socrates is, then, not to love a fixed form but to be enamoured with a process of creativity.

We might say, then, that Plato's dialogues open the problem and politics of irony. There is no doubt that they offer examples of rhetorical irony, where Socrates' refers to ignorance, wisdom, cleverness or beauty, suggesting that the sophists are anything but wise, and that Socratic 'ignorance' is of greater value. There are cases where irony is used as a device to deflate and defeat the sophists or those who believe that all life and value can be managed through rhetoric and forceful oratory. But these ironies are neither simple opposites nor contraries. By ironically presenting himself as committed to what the sophists say, Socrates exposes the lack of sense at the heart of sophistry. Through this defeat of *mere* rhetoric and contingent definitions Socratic irony has been identified with the birth of Western reason, or the commitment to *a* truth and logic that is valid and present for any possible speaker or subject. Irony opens the possibility of moral autonomy, where we do not just receive definitions of what moral concepts mean but must intend these for ourselves. In this sense, according to Vlastos, Socratic irony merely makes explicit the ethical norms of all discourse: 'Socratic irony is not unique in accepting the burden of freedom which is inherent in all significant communication' (Vlastos 1991, 44). By exposing how empty and unstable rhetoric is, Socratic irony demands a more rational understanding freed from opinion, received ideas and ad hoc justifications.

Plato's dialogues fulfilled a political and ideological imperative (Lycos 1987), which the concept of irony sustains today. Plato's dialogues present various voices, usually of Socrates and a gathering of sophists or friends, where the argument is ordered logically: not just by force or skilful persuasion but by *right reason*. Irony is crucial here for two reasons. In its limited sense, as a simple rhetorical device, irony must appeal to common sense or right reason. In order to say what is other than understood, or say one thing and mean another, we require a shared context in which hearers would be able to recognise what is really being meant. This includes Socrates' interlocutors who are the first to describe him as being ironic when he leads them into absurdities, contradictions and reversals in their argument. Irony relies on a crucial feature of language as shared recognition. In ironic speech acts we become aware of a feature that marks all language: we do not just exchange signs; we recognise a *meaning* that is other than the sign, or what the sign intends. This dimension of meaning and sense requires shared conventions and presupposed values. Examples of stable or simple irony, where there is a clear meaning achieved because of a common recognised context, are already present in the Platonic dialogues. As we have already noted, the Platonic dialogues are the first instances where the word irony (or *eironeia*) is used to describe such feats of language, although later commentators have found instances of irony as early as Homer. The important point is that the dialogues are the first recorded occasion of this shared recognition of implied meaning being made explicit, labelled as irony, and given an important political function. For the Socratic 'method' is not one of stating values in the form of commands or propositions, or even of alluring rhetoric, but appealing to assumptions 'we' all obviously share. In the dialogues rhetorical irony, as a simple figure of speech, explicitly relies on, and develops, a shared context of understanding.

The dialogues therefore institute a new mode of politics. Politics is not just the site of competing opinions; it is a reasoned discussion leading to a 'higher', universal and necessary value. Politics is achieved through philosophy: reflection on the idea of the good *behind* what we say, and not through rhetoric or literature, as mere style. Politics is not just *praxis*: the ongoing activity of participants. It is *theoria*: the contemplation of an end above and beyond any single life or action. We reach this philosophical mode of politics through irony. Politics is not just the exertion of authority, but authority based on legitimate values that transcend any specific opinion: values that 'we' share and recognise behind different uses of a word. Such transcendent or universal values can only be recognised, not by being imposed and asserted arbitrarily (as what is effective now and on this occasion), but by being discovered (as what *would* be recognised in any discussion of justice, wisdom or honesty).

Interpretations of the dialogues differ as to whether Socrates or Plato inaugurates the politics of irony. Socrates' irony may be enigmatic and problematic, showing the incoherence of everyday definitions but offering no secure and fixed *techne* or repeatable set of axioms for securing the good. Socrates may be an exemplary literary character, created by a Plato who then goes on to define the good (Nehamas 1998). Alternatively,

Socrates' irony may well be the essence of transcendent goodness: in being other than opinion, conversation and rhetoric the art of irony creates a value above and beyond any speech act. Socrates' irony – his refusal to say exactly what he means – prompts his participants to think for themselves. They are not told what to think but are awakened from their dogmatism (Vlastos 1991). To this day, many writers stress the mobilising, dynamic, diagnostic and politically libratory force of Socratic irony:

> The sophistic, undialectizable Socrates, devoid of positive content, who played upon his interlocutors' discourse in order to draw it out, to develop its possibilities in a dialogue destined to end in aporia, both incarnates the postmodern text and exemplifies that stance of the poststructuralist literary critic.
>
> (Lang 1988, 38)

Everyday speaking merely exchanges accepted and expected phrases; by implying something *other* than what we say Socratic irony at least prompts us to question our conventions and expectations. Rather than deciding between the late Platonic Socrates, who uses irony to arrive at truth, and the early or pre-Platonic Socrates, who implies that there is no single truth or discernible moral *techne*, we might say that Socrates is ironic because he is a figure of both stability and instability. He disrupts conventions and opinions by suggesting a higher moral truth, but in refusing to state just what this truth is he leaves us in a position of perpetual reading: for Socrates is a figure to be interpreted, an enigma presenting contradictory possibilities.

THE POLITICS OF IRONY AFTER SOCRATES

From Socrates' own time until today Socratic irony has been regarded with ambivalence, nostalgia, mourning, blame and celebration. Indeed, the two tendencies in reading Socratic irony are mirrored in the political ambivalence and divergence that surrounds Socrates today. The politics of Socratic irony also concerns the relation between philosophy and literature. There are those who regard the *repression* of Socratic irony as both the birth of philosophy and the death of style and rhetoric: 'the attribution of a hidden truth to Socratic irony constituted the denial of a conception of language as wordplay or production of meaning in favor of the reassuring belief that meaning preexists language' (Lang 1988, 33). By subordinating active, practical and lived Socratic irony to detached knowledge and true ideas, the dynamic and creative power of literature was supplanted by a fixed, necessary and transcendent body of law. Language was no longer a force that *created* order and differences; language was subordinate to an eternal truth – the representation or mirror, rather than production of, truth.

The first person to notice this repression of the force of rhetoric by Socrates was the Roman orator Cicero (106–43 BC), whose *De Oratore* and *De Inventione* were important sources for later works on rhetoric. On the one hand, according to Cicero, Socrates was a master of irony and rhetoric, an active performer and participant in political life. On the other hand, Cicero argued, Socrates believed that rhetoric was ultimately unimportant and ought to be subordinated to the truth of ideas. In so doing Socrates disengaged pure thought from action and public life, subordinated politics to philosophy and creative language to the intuition of truth. It is with Socrates that the man of reason, with certain uses of language such as philosophy, appears as the law and ground of all language. There can only be irony of the Socratic form because there is a commitment to a truth beyond mere act, force and speech. Like Friedrich Nietzsche many centuries later, Cicero accuses Socrates of turning life against itself, of inventing a distinction between pure truth as contemplation and the engaged speech of persuasion and self-formation. Socrates achieved this distinction between truth and rhetoric or performance *through rhetoric*. Socrates himself was both a contemplative philosopher and a political performer, but those who have slavishly followed him are nothing more than men of 'ideas'. After Socrates 'philosophy' is divorced from rhetoric and politics and becomes a narrow 'theory':

> persons have been found who being themselves copiously furnished with learning and with talent, but yet shrinking on deliberate principle from politics and affairs, scouted and scorned this practice of oratory. The chief of these was Socrates, the person who on the evidence of all men of learning and the verdict of the whole of Greece, owing not only to his wisdom and penetration and charm and subtlety but also to his

eloquence and variety and fertility easily came out top whatever side in a debate he took up; and whereas the persons engaged in handling and pursuing and teaching the subjects that we are now investigating were designated by a single title, the whole study and practice of the liberal sciences being entitled philosophy, Socrates robbed them of this general designation, and in his discussions separated the science of the wise thinking from that of elegant thinking, though in reality they are closely linked together; and the genius and varied discourses of Socrates have been immortally enshrined in the compositions of Plato, Socrates himself not having left a scrap of writing. This is the source from which has sprung the undoubtedly absurd and unprofitable and reprehensible severance between the tongue and the brain, leading to our having one set of professions to teach us to think and another to teach us to speak.

(Cicero 1942, 60)

This subordination of rhetoric was implied in the very nature of a specifically Socratic irony: the idea that there is a meaning or 'said' behind the particular utterance. Plato's Socrates inaugurated an ideal of pure knowledge independent of human praxis. The philosopher as contemplator of eternal ideas was created, through Plato's Socrates, as the true representative of political speech, while the orator, as effective speaker and personality, was marginalised. When the German Romantics elevated irony to an ultimate principle of life they, not surprisingly perhaps, turned back both to the active and conversational Socrates *and* to the Latin or Ciceronian model of philosophy as rhetoric – active and plural conversation – rather than detached and pure idealism. Socrates was both a great literary character, aware of the absence, difficulty and impossibility of truth, but he was also the beginning of a tendency to depart from everyday life in order to theorise. His irony could lead to the elevation of a truth in itself, above and beyond any particular political context.

Today, this argument that life 'falls' from active and creative speech into a submission to an external meaning and truth above life is typified in celebrations of irony. And such celebrations frequently refer back to Socrates, with camps divided as to whether Socrates is the beginning or end of radical irony. There is an active and ironic Socrates, whose irony is pure play and creation. This Socrates is then unfortunately represented in the later Platonic dialogues, and later Western thought, as one who uses irony, rhetoric and play only to reveal some ultimate truth (Lang 1988; Nehamas 1998). The repression and destruction of Socratic irony, the repression of a language that *creates* rather than represents is, it is argued, the inauguration of a model of politics where active participation is ultimately subjected to some higher and predetermined truth or end that is simply there to be known. According to Michel Foucault (1926–84), it is with the routing of the sophists, or those who saw rhetoric as the ultimate political art, that human life becomes subordinated to some putative objective truth (Foucault 1972, 218). Foucault draws on a tradition going back at least as far as Nietzsche, a tradition that sees the elevation of philosophy (or pure truth) over literature (or active and creative speech) as symptomatic of Western politics and its model of ethics as *knowledge* rather than as active self-formation. Socrates is poised at the brink of this repression. On the one hand, his irony is a mode of practical and affirmative self-creation, always different and distant from what is said and presented. On the other hand, Socratic irony is subsequently interpreted, from as early as Plato and Aristotle, as a play with language that moves from the instability of irony to the fixity of ultimate moral truths. It is precisely the Socratic occupation of an ambivalent place that is neither within nor outside Platonism that, according to Jacques Derrida, precludes us from closing the truth claims of philosophy and its supposed purity:

> In this theatre of irony, where the scenes interlock in a series of receptacles without end and without bottom, how can one isolate a thesis or a theme that could be attributed calmly to the 'philosophy-of-Plato', indeed to *philosophy* as the Platonic thing? This would be to misrecognize or violently deny the structure of the textual scene, to regard as resolved all the questions of topology in general, including that of the places of rhetoric, and to think one understood what it means to receive, that is, to understand.
>
> (Derrida 1995, 119)

STABLE IRONY AND RECOGNITION

There is, however, a second tradition that celebrates the stability of irony precisely because, far from being disruptive and actively questioning, irony allows us to discern fixed and enduring, and ultimately human, truths. Cicero, as we have seen, was already aware of this tendency in Socratic irony: that it played with language but only in an appeal to some ultimate and pre-rhetorical truth. Many argue that this emphasis on the stability of Socratic irony goes back to Plato and Aristotle (Lang 1988). Socrates can ask questions, dissimulate and create uncertainty in the early dialogues, but the later Platonic texts find him offering ultimate definitions (Nehamas 1998). His personality is neither entirely ironic nor essentially absent and enigmatic; his irony is employed as a method to lead to truth. On this picture, irony would be a figure of speech within language, and language would be ultimately stable, shared and conducive to political recognition rather than disruption.

In the twentieth century most of the material on irony in philosophy and literary theory argued that irony reveals and reinforces shared human assumptions. We recognise irony, it is argued, because we have fixed conventions. Irony is possible when language is used in ways that run *against* our norms; it thereby brings our norms into focus. We recognise it as irony precisely because what *is* meant or what is *really* being said is so obviously *not* what is manifestly spoken. John Searle, for example, argues that an ironic speech-act does not harbour any hidden or mysterious 'meaning', some ineffable truth or enigma above human speech. Meaning is not something that lies behind our words; nor is there a sense or truth that precedes human dialogue. On the contrary, language only works with shared conventions, and when language is *not* used conventionally or in ways that 'we' recognise, we can all clearly see what is *really* being meant (Searle 1994).

This type of explanation that looks at irony *within* a stable and shared community of understanding is expressed most explicitly in Wayne Booth's *A Rhetoric of Irony* (1974). The title is significant. We can have a rhetoric of irony – a theory about its recognition, creation and effects – precisely because irony is a specific type of speech act. Booth, in ways similar to Douglas Muecke's work on irony, tends to regard any irony that goes further than a literary event, any irony that creates wholesale uncertainty, misrecognition or instability as *secondary* and, also, as destructive of the inherent decisiveness of irony. The problem reaches its zenith, for Muecke, when poststructuralism argues for a general 'writing' freed of all intentions, meanings and contexts:

> This separating out of writing as something independent of communication is now becoming widespread. In so far as it amounts to a denial of both mimesis and the relevance of intentionality it may well have been, as I have heard it explained, a translation, on the part of the French intellectual left, of the *refus de pouvoir* and the distrust of authority and propensity of the French marxists into the terms of literary theory. Be that as it may, any such distinction between writing and communication *ipso facto* rules out irony as I have defined it. I have taken being ironical to mean transmitting a literal message in such a way or in such a context as to challenge a response in the form of a correct interpretation of one's intent, the transliteral meaning.
>
> (Muecke 1982, 100)

What is primary is speech that 'we' all know and understand. Irony is *rhetorical* because it is used as a figure or technique to *say* or *convey* some other meaning, albeit with greater force, economy or effect. If irony were to become absolute then we would lose the rich value of shared understanding.

Searle, relatively recently, attacked literary critics for treating all texts ironically. Literary critics, he argued, tend to treat all texts as though they were not grounded in stable and recognisable contexts; they tend to see all texts as distanced or divorced from their original intention. This predicament can be solved, Searle argues, through philosophy: if we are made aware of language as a shared and conventional system, then we will not be led into the naive belief that texts are ultimately unstable or undecidable (Searle 1994). Wayne Booth, much earlier, also insisted that far from leading to nihilism or the insecurity of all sense and value, irony tended to show just how reliable most literary meaning is. It is because what the author says is so obviously false that 'we' know something else must have been meant. If a text is manifestly racist, bigoted, confused and narrow then we either assume that this is not a work of literature, in that it lacks all sense and value, *or* the author is being ironic. As an example

Booth turns to one of Robert Browning's (1812–89) dramatic mono-
logues, where Browning typically presents the voice of a speaker who
unintentionally reveals more than they mean to say.

'Soliloquy of the Spanish Cloister' (1842) is spoken in the voice of
a hypocritical and malicious monk who, in condemning the lewdness
and immorality of one of his fellows, shows himself to be all too aware
of the 'flesh' and its perils. As Booth notes, it is the *speaker* who notices
and describes at length the girl who is supposedly the object of desire; and
it is the speaker who assumes the presence of lust, acknowledging that it
is so well hidden as to remain unseen. It is the speaker who perceives
corruption and then projects it onto his rival who supposedly hides it so
well:

> . . . While brown Dolores
>   Squats outside the Convent bank
> With Sanchicha, telling stories,
>   Steeping tresses in the tank,
> Blue-black, lustrous, thick like horsehairs,
>   – Can't I see his dead eye glow,
> Bright as 'twere a Barbary corsair's?
>   (That is, if he'd let it show!)
>
> (Browning [1842] 1988, 200–1 [4.25–32])

This humorous contradiction is, Booth argues, clearly ironic. If the poem
were not ironic then it would be a mere rant. It is because we assume a
readership and authorship that is insightful, rather than malevolent and
hypocritical, that we can also assume that the poem is ironic, and this
irony presents us with no special problems of interpretation:

> The task of deciding precisely what emotional load Browning gave
> to his ironic portraiture, or what response a reader does or should
> give him, is not necessarily less difficult, once that portrait has been
> constructed, than in works that make no ironic demands.
>
> (Booth 1974, 148)

The author could not himself be endorsing religious hypocrisy; and no
enlightened reader would miss this point:

> To me, the very nature of the speaker's sins undercuts any effort to read
> the poem with solemnity or even gravity. But to say that 'solemnity is
> ironically undercut' by many details in the poem I must, once again,
> make certain inferences about the author . . . I . . . must either assume
> in advance or derive from the poem some picture of his artistic skill,
> including his concern for artistic coherence.
>
> (Booth 1974, 149)

Irony, for Booth, is most often a rhetorical figure or trope within an
otherwise stable context of human sense and understanding. Given the
choice, we opt for charity: we assume that the author's meaning is what
we would agree with. We assume that the author is human, benevolent
and enlightened, ironically distanced from the text, and *not* the incoherent and self-incriminating voice of the ironised speaker. For Booth,
irony assumes, rather than disrupts, a common ground.

For philosophers like Searle and literary critics like Booth and Muecke,
all of whom were wary of the tendency for modern 'theory' to over-
emphasise linguistic instability, irony is evidence of the fundamental
coherence of language and literature. By contrast, for philosophers more
interested in literature and negativity like Sören Kierkegaard (1813–55)
and Nehamas and twentieth century literary critics with an interest in
the postmodern like Candace Lang and Linda Hutcheon, irony tends
towards the multiplication of viewpoints and incoherence. This dispute
over irony is also a dispute over the status of politics – whether politics
begins with agreement and recognition or difference and incommen-
surability. On the one hand, there are those who see irony as a rhetorical
figure that is ultimately recognised because there is something like shared
human understanding. Socrates' irony would, or should, be a rhetorical
move in order to reinforce truth and consensus. Literary effect or rhetoric
could then be judged from some external point of knowledge, theory or
truth. On this model, politics would not just be *praxis* or effective speech;
it would be speech directed to some end or ideal, such as the human or
shared good that we must all presuppose. On the other hand there are
those who see irony as a way of life, embodied in the figure of Socrates
who refused to present virtue and the good life as a fixed ideal that could
be known. Irony – the continual questioning or distance from fixed
norms – is the possibility of politics as *praxis*: as engaged activity achieved

through dynamic speech and collective participation. Those who emphasise the stability of irony value, or assume the value of, a politics directed towards community and unity. Those who celebrate the destabilising force of irony, by contrast, insist that politics is the rejection, contestation or disruption of shared norms.

According to Candice Lang (1988), who argues that the tradition of irony's repression is only now being liberated through postmodern humour, the restriction of irony to a 'merely' literary effect goes back to Quintilian. Following Cicero, Quintilian introduces a distinction between irony as a trope and irony that is habitual or an extended figure. With this distinction it becomes possible to decide against the wholesale personality of Socratic irony and focus, as most would do, on the rhetorical *uses* of irony. Socrates' irony and dismissal of rhetoric suggested a truth available to private philosophical contemplation. Socrates instituted a model of truth above and beyond political discussion. Rhetoric henceforth would be subordinated to a *techne* or skill which ultimately served some end outside rhetorical ploys.

In Quintilian this tendency, recognised by Cicero, for irony to be subjected to some non-rhetorical truth is extended and intensified. What is significant is that, from Quintilian to the Renaissance, mention of Socratic or extended and habitual irony falls away. Further, the entire political context of rhetoric also shifts. In Cicero's time rhetoric was not an isolated literary or technical skill. Rhetoric was a political practice, to do with advocating causes, deciding questions of law and public good. The main tradition of rhetoric to which Cicero was already appealing went back to Aristotle's *Rhetoric*, where rhetoric was also defined as an art subordinate to some ultimate purpose or argument, to logic or dialectic. Aristotle had also defined irony as a trope or rhetorical strategy within argument, and when he referred to Socratic irony he insisted that Socrates' pretended ignorance or downplaying of his knowledge ought to give way to an honest model of good citizenship. The truly virtuous soul accurately and honestly presents himself as he is, and does not dissimulate. From Aristotle, through Quintilian and onwards, the Socratic or extended irony which makes all speech questionable becomes less important. The rhetorical or Ciceronian model of politics as explicit rhetoric and active persuasion gave way to a theoretical politics concerned with a contemplative intuition of the good. As Cicero warned, the

Platonic subordination of rhetoric to truth led to the downplaying of active speech and engagement and an emphasis on truth as private contemplation, with rhetoric as mere ornament. Rhetoric itself shifts from being what it was in Cicero's day – active politics and public engagement – and becomes an art of skilled speech and presentation.

Today, when writers defend the stability of irony they do so because they assume that politics is primarily directed towards consensus, communication and the minimisation of ambiguity and conflict. They also assume that there are norms or truths outside political performance or rhetoric. The idea that one might aim, as Socrates appears to have done, to disrupt consensus and be *other than* shared norms would be unacceptable for any politics based on modern notions of transparency and justification. Both the philosopher, John Searle, and the literary critic, Wayne Booth, insist on stable irony as the proper example for an understanding of irony precisely because they understand rhetoric as a device and practice within human understanding; rhetoric can only work because there is some presupposed context. Neither Booth nor Searle consider a sense or truth beyond context to which irony might refer; nor do they see irony as disruptive of contexts. It is the unremarkable, uncontested and trans-historical form of irony, in which the contrary meaning is clearly intended, that gives us the possibility of irony in general. Irony is part of a more general process of understanding and recognition, where we discern intentions and meanings through the assumption of common conventions and projects and an overall ideal of coherence. The ironies within a literary text are signalled either by plot or by disjunctions of character and context. We should not take a modern or postmodern concept of irony, such as the Romantic or post-structuralist suspicion of fixed definitions, and apply that concept to pre-modern or stable contexts.

In the next chapter we will look at the tradition of theorising irony that emphasises instability and negativity, the Socrates who was an enigmatic character rather than a philosopher in pursuit of truth. It was the German Romantics who both retrieved the ambiguous Socrates in order to react against a tradition of enlightenment reason and who also influenced the radical theorisation of irony in the twentieth century.

3

ROMANTIC IRONY

Romantic irony is most commonly associated with the Jena Romantics: the Schlegel brothers – August Wilhelm (1767–1845) and Friedrich (1772–1829) – Ludwig Tieck (1773–1853), Karl Wilhelm Ferdinand Solger (1780–1819) and Novalis (1772–1801). The main source of the writings with regard to irony was the journal, *Athenaeum*, which in its brief history from 1798 to 1800 published a series of texts that crossed the genres of philosophy, literature, criticism and review and included a highly influential collection of fragments (Behler 1993). As the name *Athenaeum* indicates, the German Romantic movement valorised the ancient past, but like the English Romantics they were also entranced by Shakespeare, medievalism and certain key moderns, such as the French encyclopaedist Denis Diderot (1713–84) and the German proto-Romanticist J.W. Goethe (1749–1832). What they were against, predominantly, was reason and the enlightenment restriction of reason to a universal human norm.

At the same time, they were aware of the paradoxes of a critique of reason. In order to argue against or challenge reason one needed to speak, but such speech would seem to demand understanding and would therefore rely on the very norms of reason it set out to delimit. The only possible response to this predicament would be irony: a speech which at once made a claim to be heard, but which also signalled or gestured to its own limits and incomprehension. While the Jena romantics were the group that came closest to offering a theory of irony, 'Romantic irony' has since been identified with Romanticism in general, with Friedrich Schlegel's fragments often providing the theory through which English Romantic irony can be read (Alford 1984; Mellor 1980; Simpson 1979).

THE IRONIC FALL

Romantic irony, broadly defined, regards irony as something like a human condition or predicament. Romantic irony is also one of the earliest and most intense modes of anti-humanism. It is precisely because we are human and capable of speaking, creating and engaging with others that human life has no fixed nature; any definition it gives of itself will only be one more creation, which can never exhaust the infinite possibilities for future creation: 'If every infinite individual is God, then there are as many gods as there are ideals' (Schlegel 1991, 92). The German Romantics emphasised *Bildung*, as culture and creation, and insisted on the arbitrariness, artificiality and deviation of any process of *Bildung* or formation: 'A human being should be like a work of art which, though openly exhibited and freely accessible, can nevertheless be enjoyed and understood only by those who bring feeling and study to it' (Schlegel 1991, 67). Art, Friedrich Schlegel argued, is not the accurate presentation of the world, nor the natural expression of human life; art is essentially other than life: 'The need to raise itself above humanity is humanity's prime characteristic' (ibid. 96).

Nature may be creative, but it creates according to its innate tendencies; human creation has the capacity to be ironic: to present itself as other than what it *is*. Indeed, what it *is* has no being other than a capacity to create. Human life, as capable of *Bildung*, is *essentially* capable of being other than any fixed *essence*. This is why human life is ironic. On the one hand, *all* life is creative and must 'become' as part of an infinite process of natural production: 'No poetry, no reality' (Solger in Schlegel 1991, 70). On the other hand, humans have a capacity to create in such a way that they *reflect* this creative process: 'A beautiful spirit smiling at itself is a thing of beauty; and the moment when a great personality looks at itself calmly and earnestly is a sublime moment' (Schlegel 1991, 69). And once humans recognise natural production or creation, they can create another nature, a non-natural or super-natural nature, a creation of will and art

rather than unselfconscious or blind production: 'Every good human being is always progressively becoming God. To become God, to be human, to cultivate oneself are all expressions that mean the same thing' (ibid. 55). In poetry, for example, we do not just *copy* nature. Like nature, we *create*, and the poem is evidence of this creation; the poem is mimetic but it does not copy a thing so much as a process. It creates just as nature creates, and in so creating itself we have the power to see the world in its *becoming*, not just its inert *being*: 'In all its descriptions, this poetry should describe itself, and always be simultaneously poetry and the poetry of poetry' (ibid. 51).

There is a problem, however, with expressing or realising this process of creation. Once we create a poem we are left with a created object, just as once we form or define ourselves we are left with static forms and definitions. Romantic irony must tackle this process of the *fall* of creative life into inert objectivity; it does so by recognising that creativity or the human spirit must always be other than any of its creations, definitions or manifestations. Far from seeing this fall, in pseudo-Christian terms, as a loss of a pure origin, the German Romantics embraced it as a *felix culpa*, or fortunate fall. It is only in *not* being at one with itself, in not being self-identical, that life can become and create, or can recognise itself *as life*, even if that recognition will always be partial or ironic. For there will always be a potential for (future) life and becoming not exhausted by actual and existing creations. Creation is not the deviation from some proper and complete past, as it had been in Platonism with its notion of original forms. Creation is a release of the dynamic potential of life. Indeed, we only have a sense of the infinite, or what is *not* finite, from various created finite viewpoints. Romantic irony therefore reverses the relation between origin and effect, between origin and fall. It is not that there is an original paradise or plenitude from which we are separated. On the contrary, it is only in diverse life itself, in all its difference and fragmentation, that we get any sense or idea of some whole or origin. The origin or foundation is a created effect of life, not its preceding cause. Far from finite daily life being a fall from an original infinite plenitude, it is only the fragmentary, the finite and the incomplete that can give us a sense of the infinity that lies beyond any closed form. An ironic 'fall' realises, therefore, that there was no paradise before the sense of loss. The idea of an original plenitude is an image created *from life*: 'All life is in its ultimate origins not natural, but divine and human' (Schlegel 1991, 102). The idea of a fall is, however, essential to irony and life as irony. It is in creating images of a lost paradise that we create ourselves *as fallen*, and thereby create ourselves at all. For to be selves or personalities we must be limited or delimited from some grander whole.

This is why, for the Romantics, the poem is so important. The poem is a fall from the pure flow of creative life into some determined and limited object. Such an understanding of the poem was explicitly related to the Ancient Greek notion of *poiesis* as the distinct object or end of a creative act or *praxis*. But unlike other created things, which simply *are* and retain no evidence of their becoming, true poetry presents itself *as fallen*, that is, as other than or detached from the process that generates it. In contrast with the theological notion of a fall from some divine and eternal origin, the fall of irony embraces rather than mourns its finitude, difference and non-identity. It is in *not* being complete, in affirming one's difference and distance from some pure and undivided ground, that one also attains character and consciousness. The self is necessarily fallen: not fallen *from* some origin, so much as producing a lost and other past in the very act of falling. It is the fall itself, the creation of oneself as a speaking and finite being, that creates the idea of the unfallen origin.

Further, for the Romantics, this fall is one of 'buffoonery'. German Romantic irony was defined through a constellation of concepts, including, in addition to buffoonery, humour, wit and satire. The joke or *Witz* undoes the mastery of the subject, as laughter and nonsense disrupt logic and sense. Irony is related to buffoonery not just because subjective mastery is undermined; buffoonery falls, enjoys the humour of the fall, laughs from on high at the falling buffoon, and remains implicated in the fall. One can never master the ironic process, never recognise or stand above one's finitude: 'Irony is the clear consciousness of eternal agility, of an infinitely teeming chaos' (Schlegel 1991, 100). The minute we see ourselves as *other than* what has fallen, as beings who can overlook and describe the fall, we fall further into smug self-recognition: 'One can only become a philosopher, not be one. As soon as one thinks one is a philosopher, one stops becoming one' (Schlegel 1991, 24). Irony must recognise that we can never overcome singular viewpoints and achieve a God-like point of view; we are always subject to a cosmic joke. For any idea we have of our selves or our world will be part of a process of creation and destruction that we can neither delimit nor control. If humour often relies on a feeling of superiority or elevation above life's misfortunes, irony recognises – but never fully realises – the implication of all life in this chaos. The ironic attitude must not just take a delight in seeing the clown slip on a banana skin; it must not just laugh at this fall from human coordination into an animal or thing-like buffoonery. It must recognise that we are all part of this falling; we are always dupes and effects of a life with a power well beyond our control and recognition.

IRONY AS A STYLE OF EXISTENCE

Romantic irony, therefore, does not see either irony or tropes in general as purely literary devices. On the contrary, all life is ironic or subject to the conditions of trope and metaphor. To speak or see the world *as* something is already to differ from the literal world itself. Indeed, the very idea of a basic, foundational or literal world is itself a specific image or figure, described through a certain style. The ideas of ground or foundation, for example, rely on spatial metaphors, while the notion of the *literal* can only be thought through the concept of writing, literariness or script. Instead of poetry being a special or marginal aspect of a language and experience that would otherwise be straightforward, poetry, or the creation of distinct images, is the condition for all experience: 'a poem is only a product of nature which wants to become a work of art' (Schlegel 1991, 2). Romantic irony therefore extends both irony and poetry to include all life and perception:

> There are unavoidable situations and relationships that one can tolerate only by transforming them by some courageous act of will and seeing them as pure poetry. It follows that all cultivated people should be capable of being poets if they have to be; and from this we can deduce equally well that man is by nature a poet, and that there is a natural poetry, or vice versa.
>
> (Schlegel 1991, 89)

If we could secure a stable context of human recognition then irony would be a device or event *within* life and language; irony would be a deviation from the proper and common sense. There would be a literal language and a present world of truths and facts, which could then be ornamented or arrived at through irony. If, however, all life were instability, process, becoming and creation, then irony would be the very truth of life. Life would be *poetic*, a process of becoming and creation, and the only speech adequate to life would be ironic. Philosophical or theoretical propositions would aim at a world of facts and eternal truths; but ironic speech would refer to the instability of language: 'Where philosophy stops, poetry has to begin' (Schlegel 1991, 98).

For this reason, German Romantic irony explored a potential in Socratic irony that had, by and large, been neglected: irony as a style of existence rather than a rhetorical figure. Irony for the Romantics was the only true mode of life. To live as if one were a fixed self who *then* used language to represent a world would be to deny the flux and dynamism of life. It would also be a mode of subjectivism: positing some ground – the subject – that could act as the basis for judgements and predications. Irony transforms subjectivism: the subject is no longer a ground that precedes and underlies judgements. The subject 'is' nothing other than an ongoing process of creation. Instead of transparent self-consciousness, where language is used to reflect upon and know the self, the Romantic ironic subject aims for self-destruction. The ideal is one of anti-self-consciousness (Hartman 1970, 298–310), where language and poetry transform the self from an identity within the world, to an unreflective, spontaneous and open existence. The self is no longer a thing, but a process of creation and expression that can be intuited in the *act* of language or speech, but not as something spoken about or represented. Any fixed, bounded, determined or created self must at once signal its fragility, destruction and de-creation: 'Sacrifice of the self is the source of all humiliation, as also on the contrary it is the foundation of all true exaltation' (Novalis 1997, 26).

For the Romantics this potential for the self to be other than any fixed or created term was hinted at in Socratic irony and the genre of dialogue. Socratic dialogue was exemplary precisely because it was open and dramatic, presenting voices and personae rather than fixed propositions or a single *theoretical* viewpoint. The Greek word *theoria* was tied not just to looking, but to an elevated look that could grasp the Ideas themselves: those forms or essences that could always be seen in any singular particular and which allowed for any particular instance to be what it is.

By contrast, *poiesis* is anti-self-conscious; *poiesis* is the creation of some term (such as a poem) that is other than the act. Unlike *theoria*, which aims to see life as it is and to be at one with the essence of life, *poeisis* allows the fall of life into fragmented, detached and finite productions, such as the various works and voices of culture. Instead of the aims of philosophy as theory, to achieve an all-inclusive and transparent knowledge, the Romantics asserted *poiesis*: life is not a thing to be known, but a process of creation whereby what is created is always other than the power to create: 'Poetry elevates each single thing through a particular combination with the rest of the whole . . . Writing poetry is creating. Each work of literature must be a living individual' (Novalis 1997, 55). For this reason, life is not just ongoing activity (*praxis*) directed to some functional end; it also creates products that become disengaged or split from any conscious intent (*poiesis*). Speech is not just the purposeful expression of our intentions; it also contains an unthought or 'dead' element that is not intended. (Think of all the letters, syntactical con- straints, and grammatical idioms within which thought must move, but which are not thought itself. For this reason much Romantic poetry described fragments, ruins, inscriptions, monuments and myths: all the ways in which the thought and activity of the present must work with received and inherited elements.) According to the twentieth century French philosophers Phillipe Lacoue-Labarthe and Jean-Luc Nancy, 'Each fragment stands for itself and for that from which it is detached. Totality is the fragment itself in its completed individuality' (1988, 44).

This brings us to the heart of irony and dialogue. To acknowledge *poiesis* is to acknowledge that the creativity of life can never be encom- passed or reflected in an overarching point of view. Conscious activity is never at one with the forms it creates. The Socrates of the dialogues is a poet rather than a theorist; he creates masks, personalities and positions rather than offering *a* position or viewpoint. His irony disrupts agree- ment and complacency; it is unsettling and directed towards strangeness rather than recognition and consensus. The Socratic personality was ethical precisely because it was neither fully presented nor at one with itself but in a state of constant presentation. Indeed, contrary to both traditional and modern readings of Socrates, the Romantics also stressed the *contradictions* of irony and Socratic irony (Albert 1993). Irony was not just signalling the opposite of what was said; it was the expression of *both sides or viewpoints at once* in the form of contradiction or paradox: 'Irony is the form of paradox. Paradox is everything simultaneously good and great' (Schlegel 1991, 6). And any reader who feels that 'behind' the irony there is *a* hidden sense has fallen into the very simplicity and singleness of viewpoint that irony sets out to destroy. For Schlegel, therefore, the dissimulation of Socrates was not in the service of *intending* another higher or non-contradictory idea that the privileged few might understand and that might resolve the dialectic; it was about *allowing* – almost involuntarily – both sides of a tension:

> Socratic irony is the only involuntary and yet completely deliberate dissimulation. It is equally impossible to feign it or divulge it. To a person who hasn't got it, it will remain a riddle even after it is openly confessed. It is meant to deceive no one except those who consider it a deception and who either take pleasure in the delightful roguery of making fools of the whole world or else become angry when they get an inkling they themselves might be included. In this sort of irony, everything should be playful and serious, guilelessly open and deeply hidden . . . It contains and arouses a feeling of indissoluble antagonism between the absolute and the relative, between the impossibility and the necessity of complete communication. It is a very good sign when the harmonious bores are at a loss about how they should react to this continuous self-parody, when they fluctuate endlessly between belief and disbelief until they get dizzy and take what is meant as a joke seriously and what is meant seriously as a joke.
>
> (Schlegel 1991, 13)

CONTRADICTION: DOSTOEVSKY, BLAKE, SWIFT

From the beginnings of philosophy (Aristotle's *Metaphysics*) to the twentieth century (Edmund Husserl's *Logical Investigations* [Husserl 1970]) one of *the* incontrovertible principles of logic is the principle of non-contradiction: one cannot assert both that something is and that it is not. You cannot say that it is raining and that it is not raining. Now, this principle relies both on a logical present: a thing can be and not be at two separate moments and is only contradictory if asserted as being and not being at the same time. The principle also relies on an *ideal* logical subject. There may be those who indeed assert that something is and is not, but this would be a logical error and their judgement would have to be rejected as invalid. We say that *logically* one cannot say that something is and is not; logic assumes an ideal subject of correct judgement. Even explanations of irony work on this principle. If I say, 'Another day in paradise!' and it is blowing a blizzard out there you assume that I *cannot* mean that it is paradise, so I must mean the sentence ironically. You assume this because you assume I would not say that something is the case, when it is not the case. Now this is a case where I am contradicting what I see, not what I say. So the contradiction is still not logical; there is nothing logically wrong with being in error about the weather, but one can only take this as an instance of irony if we assume that we agree about the outside world *and* assume that we would not contradict ourselves. We reach agreement, not by you correcting me and telling me that it is raining, since that would be too literal. Rather, you assume what a reasonable subject would say, hear that I am saying the opposite – which I cannot assert – and so you assume that I am saying one thing, but mean its opposite. Irony seems to rely on us both agreeing about the world *and* assuming that when we speak we do not contradict ourselves, that we hold to what we say.

Now, Romantic irony rejects this principle of non-contradiction: the very principle that supposedly underlies all speech, argument and even disagreement. All argument, assertion and agreement relies on the distinction between what is and what is not; if it were possible for something to be true and false at the same time, then we could not speak with notions of agreement, force or judgement. This is why, if we spot a contradiction in what someone is saying, we feel that we have invalidated what they are saying. This principle applies to all argument, including the very basis of logic itself. If I want to *argue* against the principles of reason or argument then I am already, supposedly, undertaking an argument and deploying reason. If, for example, I were to argue against the principle of non-contradiction I would have to make a case against it; I would say that it was *not* universal or necessary. But in doing so I would be employing the principle; in saying that the principle did *not* hold I would rely on the opposition: either the principle of non-contradiction holds or it does not. Similarly, if I want to argue that all arguments are relative, with no universal logic, then I have to employ the principle. I am saying that there are *no* universal logical principles; again, I am opposing the logical universal to the absence of logical universals. This is the principle of non-contradiction: we cannot say or think 'a' and 'not-a'. Any argument against the principle already relies on it. For to be against the principle is to see something as other than, or not, the principle; the principle cannot be both true and untrue.

But what if we adopt a genre quite different from argument? Perhaps this is just what literature is, a way of saying that something both is and is not the case, of asserting both things at once. And perhaps *this* is irony: not saying something other than what is meant in the form of a simple opposition, but saying something while allowing the possible validity of its contrary. Contradiction works at two levels: logically and socially. *Logically*, we could argue that there could be no thinking, no sense that something *is* at all, or truth, without a sense of the true and the untrue being contradictory or unable to be held together. *Socially*, we could argue that in order to have a world at all we have to adhere to what we say, and not assert its opposite. Insofar as we speak there is a common assumption that we mean what we say; without this assumption communication, reason and argument would not be possible. It would be a 'performative contradiction' to speak and *then* claim that one did not mean to speak, be understood or claim some common ground (Apel 1998). Fyodor Dostoevsky's *Notes from Underground* is just such a 'performative contradiction', where the narrator continually declares that he does not want to be read, does not care whether he is believed or not, and does not want the reader's, or humanity's, understanding: 'I, however, am writing for myself alone, and let me declare once and for all that if I write as if I were addressing an audience, it is only for show and because it makes it easier for me to write. It is a form, nothing else; I shall never have any readers. I have already made that clear' (Dostoevsky 1972, 45). Imagine someone who said, 'Don't understand me.' Like 'I don't care what you think' these sorts of utterances cannot really mean what they say. Why would I speak to you if I did not want some sort of communication to take place? Could I really say, *and mean*, 'Don't listen to me!' In *saying* this I am, implicitly, asking you to listen to me. I, at least, want to have the minimal recognition that I do not want to be recognised. It is just this disruption of common sense, communication and assumed coherence that Romantic irony sets out to achieve.

I think perhaps the 'clearest' exponent of this sort of paradoxical irony in English Romanticism is William Blake (1757–1827). His poems both present a message or moral *and* show that moral to be pernicious and symptomatic of fallen conscious. His *Songs of Innocence* assert the beauty and value of a state of childhood innocence *and* they show that innocence to be naive, lulling and paralysing. His *Songs of Experience* present a world as fallen, using the poetic voice to attack modern corruption and industrialism; at the same time, these poems are also critical of the accusing, pessimistic and negating voice of judgement. They criticise criticism, saying and not saying that one must criticise. Consider his very famous poem 'London' (1794) from *Songs of Innocence and of Experience*:

I wander thro' each charter'd street,
Near where the charter'd Thames does flow.
And mark in every face I meet
Marks of weakness, marks of woe.

In every cry of every Man,
In every Infants cry of fear,
In every voice: in every ban,
The mind-forg'd manacles I hear

How the Chimney-sweepers cry
Every blackning Church appalls,
And the hapless Soldiers sigh,
Runs in blood down Palace walls

But most thro' midnight streets I hear
How the youthful Harlots curse
Blasts the new-born Infants tear
And blights with plagues the Marriage hearse
(Blake 1957, 216)

On the one hand, this is a classic indictment of poverty, urban abjection and the absence of spirit and hope in modern life. It is a classically

'Romantic' poem in the everyday sense: a rejection of the city, a condem-
nation of institutionalised religion, and an attack on political oppression,
militarism and poverty. On the other hand, the poem can be read
ironically, and, precisely because it is a poem, detached from any present
speaker or consciousness. As a 'Song *of* Experience', the poem is uttered
from a bleak point of view. The voice is all-condemning: '*every . . . every
. . . every . . .*'. Nearly all of the songs of experience present a consciousness that is totalising in its despairing view of the world, recognising
no hope, no joy and no desire, and seeing itself as elevated above a closed
and fallen world: 'The mind-forg'd manacles I hear'. Perhaps this poem is
not about the misery of the world; perhaps it is the ironic repetition of
a voice that can see nothing but misery. Perhaps Blake is ironising the
moralising and condemning voice of humanist despair: the voice that says
that all we can do is offer charity, pity and amelioration without any
radically utopian hopes, a judgemental voice that also sets 'Harlots'
opposite new-born infants. How would we decide between the ironic and
sincere readings? Surely, we cannot decide. The poem *both* manages to
express its lament *and* suggests that this lament is part of the problem. It is
'guilty' of contradiction. It says and does not say that London is utterly
miserable. It both says and does not say that the voice or point of view
that sees misery everywhere is a symptom of our loss of joy. The poem
achieves the force of both speech acts; it presents a London worthy of pity
and shows or performs just how limiting the attitude of pity may be.

Whereas in logical discourse a contradiction leads to nothingness,
insofar as we dismiss contradictions, in poetic discourse contradictions
are productive and ironic. They allow any voice to be doubled by the
suggestion that what is said is both meant and not meant. This Romantic
irony becomes much more complex and undecidable in Blake's later
prophecies where he produces the figure or character of Satan. On the one
hand Satan is heroic: rejecting authority, anything that is other than his
will, and anything that would limit his power. On the other hand, Satan's
voice is also the (ironic) mirror of the tyranny he would denounce. 'I must
be free' is at once the most liberating *and* enslaving of all speech acts; it
is an assertion of the self, a subjection to a principle (freedom) and an
imperative or command to anyone or anything that stands in one's way.
In demanding one's freedom the voice of revolution can also produce
itself as one more law *and* the negation of anyone else's freedom.

The contradiction of Blake's work operates at a social and performa-tive level. We have to take 'Blake' as both saying or articulating a voice of despair *and* not saying or agreeing with what he says. The tradition of irony has also deployed logical contradictions, where it is not just that we assume a difference between what the speaker says and what she means, such that the speaker may be taken as asserting both 'a' and 'not a'. There are also logically contradictory speech acts, such as Nietzsche's claim that there is no such thing as truth or that truth is a fiction (Nietzsche [1873] 1979, 84–5). One *cannot say* logically that it is true that there is no such thing as truth (Lacoue-Labarthe 1993, 4). If, like Nietzsche, one does say this, then one expresses a contradiction.

Before Nietzsche, Jonathan Swift had performed, rather than stated, a logical contradiction in his attack on reason. *Gulliver's Travels* (1726) is the ironic travelogue of the gullible Gulliver who moves through a series of fantastic lands all of which provide material for him to reflect upon, criticise and celebrate his original home of England. In the final book, however, Gulliver arrives at what he tries to present as a utopia: the land of the Houyhnhnms who have horse-like bodies but possess powers of speech and reason and who take Gulliver to be a Yahoo, the human-like 'animals' devoid of all speech and civility. In Gulliver's description, the reasoning Houyhnhnms indulge in such a mania for logical purity that they become irrationally enslaved to principles of reason; their refusal of ambiguity, deception, corruption and distortion is presented as a repres-sion of the body, of texts, of difference and history. They acknowledge only one point of view, so clearly true that it requires no argument, interpretation, inscription or alteration, 'because *doubting* or *not believing* are so little known in this country, that the inhabitants cannot tell how to behave themselves under such circumstances . . . the use of speech was to make us understand one another, and to receive information of facts; now if *anyone said the thing which was not*, these ends were defeated' (Swift [1726] 1967, 286).

The narrative concludes with Gulliver being so enamoured with pure reason, and so disgusted with the bodies of his fellow humans, that he is left no other option but to converse 'rationally', without any possible dissension, with his horses. For only the Houyhnhnms represent a reason beyond conflict and beyond even the possibility of coercion. What is more violent than an act of force which disavows all force, which does not take responsibility for its attack on others precisely because anything other than the rational is deemed to be beyond consideration? '[For] they have no conception how a rational creature can be *compelled*, but only *advised*, or *exhorted*, because no person can disobey Reason, without giving up his claim to be a rational creature' (Swift [1726] 1967, 328). So compelling is Houyhnhnm reason that it is presented as entirely other than force. The proposed extermination of the Yahoos, then, would not be compulsion or violence so much as the unquestioning extension of pure thought.

Swift does not *say* that reason is violent, for that would be a reasoned attack on reason; he shows the contradiction of a reason that violently presents itself as other than violent. Swift shows the effects of this principle of pure reason by presenting the Houyhnhnms as both violent and seductively persuasive. It is perfectly 'rational' to wish for the extermination of deceit, confusion, misunderstanding and error, even if this leads to the conclusion, which Gulliver adopts, of willing human genocide. Swift does not offer an argument against the tyranny of right reason; rather his narrative describes, performs and enacts the encounter between an incontrovertible reason and the horrific conclusions it is led to adopt when it encounters an irrational body.

The sense or force of *Gulliver's Travels* is therefore essentially literary: one could not translate what it wants to say into philosophy or a discourse of reasoned argument, precisely because it is presenting the very violence of reason. One *cannot say* that one rejects, or wants to argue against, rationality; for to make this accusation against reason one must employ reasoned arguments. One either remains at the level of manifest contradiction, as both Blake and Nietzsche do, who happily speak in self-refuting, impossible and contradictory aphorisms, or one performs rather than states the contradiction. Blake constantly attacked law, system, truths and principle: but he was also aware that the expression of this attack on law was itself a law. He both worked against and embraced this contradiction. His poetry displays both a need to form some statement or principle that attacks principles – for without such a statement or attack on reason one falls into passive acceptance – at the same time as he destroyed and contradicted these principles: 'I must create a system or be enslav'd by another man's' (Blake 1957, 629). Is this a 'principle' or an attack on principle? 'One Law for the Lion & Ox is Oppression' (Blake 1957, 158): is this the *one* law that will free us from the tyranny of law?

Far from eliminating contradiction, Romantic irony tends to emphasise the equivocity of voice. And Romantic irony is not just limited to the contradictions of speaking positions. Romanticism is often attacked for a certain incoherence. Many poems are about the inexpressible, unimaginable or unrepresentable origin of life and consciousness. But how can we speak about the unspeakable? The minute we say, for example, that such and such a term is not translatable into our language, we have already contaminated it, included it, and presented it *as* untranslatable. Romantic irony embraces this dead end and contradiction, its poems often being about the impossibility of sincere, pure or authentic poetry.

GERMAN ROMANTIC IRONY: CONTEXTS AND DIFFERENCE

In order to understand the force of German Romantic irony we need to see the *problem* of irony. How can we mean something other than what we say? This would be possible if there were persons and meanings *behind* language or saying; language would work like a container for our ideas. Irony would occur when we put the opposite idea into a different word: we could use 'clever' to mean 'stupid'. But how could we *know* the person or sense behind words? The first solution is Platonic. There simply are true ideas, such as justice, beauty, or the good, and when language appears as unreliable, limited or unstable we can appeal to the idea behind the word. It is because all the sophist's definitions of justice are so unworkable that we know that there must be a justice *beyond definitions*. On this account, Socrates' irony would lead us to recognise this other and higher idea. If, however, as the twentieth century has tended to do, we find the existence of real and eternal ideas or essences to be mystical, we will want to offer an explanation of meaning from within human language.

Concepts do not *label* ideas; we form ideas or generalisations from frequent and conventional use of concepts. A concept is nothing more than a constitutive rule: we do not recognise and submit to the rule of a concept; it is in speaking and interacting that certain regularities are formed and from there we might come up with some general pattern or concept. 'Justice' is the way we use a word, and if we use the word in a way that does not work, then we are either not recognised as competent users *or* we have to ask if the word is uttered ironically, metaphorically or unconventionally. If concepts seem to have a certain law or essence this is not because ideas exist which govern our language; it is because our language is a regular practice.

If I said, 'That's true justice!' when a wealthy and manifestly guilty media tycoon was acquitted of libel in the course of a high-cost legal battle, you would *know* I was being ironic, not because of some ideal essence of justice, but because 'we' recognised that this is not what 'we' take to be justice. We assume that there is a common sense of justice that we all recognise, and that this case is one that flouts that common sense: this is *not* the impartial and general application of rules that we have come to know as justice. We can say something other than what we mean, not because there are separate and hidden meanings, but because in using a word unconventionally, or against expectation, you assume that I am using language differently. Irony, here, refers to groups of speakers in shared contexts who use language to maintain that context of actions and mutual recognition. Irony is explained by how 'we' use language, and without this assumption of a 'we' no strict border between the ironic and the non-ironic would be possible.

Now, the German Romantics saw a problem at this point. The German enlightenment philosopher Immanuel Kant (1724–1804) had already argued that judgements appealed to a *sensus communis* (Kant 2000, 173–6). If I make a claim that is not empirically or objectively verifiable, such as 'This is beautiful', then I make an implicit appeal to others who would also recognise beauty. I am not just saying 'I like this', for this would be saying that the object is merely agreeable; it tastes nice to me. When I cite this as beautiful, I say that it would appear as beautiful for any experience. Such a community of consensus may not be given, and indeed we do argue about the beautiful, the aesthetically valid, and what we ought to do. However, we can only have these *arguments* if we agree that there is something to be argued about. All discussion, even a violent disagreement, therefore relies upon a 'we', some *ideal* of humanity. It is not that ideals, such as the good, justice, the beautiful, *exist* above and beyond language; they are assumed goals or ideals towards which, and on the basis of which, discussion and dialogue proceed. We may not be able to define such concepts in strict terms, but we nevertheless know how to argue *about* them.

It is this approach to language, that extends from Kant to the twentieth century, which in various forms has been dominant. Meanings are generated from interaction and use. Concepts are the forms and regularities that our discussion takes; they cannot be intuited in some pure and ideal form. Contra Platonism, there is no beauty in itself; it is from the continued recognition of particular beautiful things that we form a rule of the beautiful.

The German Romantics also recognised the problem of positing ideas above and beyond language. We only have concepts, selves and speakers through language. *Poiesis*, or the creation of forms through which we think, is not a peculiarly literary event; it is essential to all thought. Any sense of what is other than language can only be generated from language. As we saw in the *Symposium*, Plato is only able to express his idea of pure truth above and beyond dialogue through the use of dialogue and irony. We could conclude, then, that there simply is no truth or meaning outside human speech and communication.

The German Romantics who gathered in Jena from 1796 and who influenced, and were influenced by, other Romantic movements, took the insights of Kant and idealism to turn *poetry* rather than knowledge into the absolute principle of subjectivity, and they did so through irony. To begin with, they had a transcendental understanding of poetry going back to the Greek word for *poiesis*: the creation of some external form. 'Poems' or literary objects were specific instances of a far more general 'poetry', which included the creation and formation of concepts, selves and fixed objects. All life is 'poetic' insofar as it is creative and productive. However, poems as such reflect upon and are aware of their status as detached creations, as other than the force of life that brings them into being. German Romanticism's criticism of the closure of philosophy is still relevant today. Friedrich Schlegel used the notion of irony to criticise the assumption that language, the effects of language and the forces of texts could be reduced to conscious intent and the self-conscious will of the subject. To this extent, the notion of German Romantic irony provides a way to think beyond many of the contemporary assumptions regarding language.

We can begin with the contemporary account of meaning from contexts. Any self, world, object or value can only be given through some shared system of conventions and differences; any reference to what lies outside a context of language can only be given from that context. It makes no sense to refer to meanings or ideas in themselves; meanings are just what we posit from acts within a context. Insofar as we speak we remain committed to rules and conventions; without the lawfulness and regularity of contexts there would be no language. One has to *mean* what one says; all language involves commitment and sincerity. There could not be a universal practice of speaking without meaning what one says:

> the retreat from the committed use of words ultimately must involve a retreat from language itself, for speaking a language . . . consists of performing speech acts according to rules, and there is no separating those speech acts from the commitments which form essential parts of them.
>
> (Searle 1969, 198)

To be committed to a meaning, to speak at all, is just to behave in ways that could be expected or made sense of from one's context. Any interpretation or explanation of a meaning would itself be another act in a context. It makes no sense to ask what the world is *really*, outside our concepts or context, for any world that we experience as other than our concepts is only thinkable from concepts; we are always already in a context. That is just what having a world is.

German Romantic irony, by contrast, reverses this order between concept and world. It is not that we have a world, life or subjectivity seen through language and concepts; texts, concepts and language are effects, fragments or poems thrown out by an infinite life that goes well beyond any context. This life may not be *knowable*, for knowledge and theory are indeed conceptual, but it can be *felt* through irony. If, for example, we are presented with a tragedy by Shakespeare, a philosophical fragment or an ironic poem, then we are not presented with the experience of the whole of life; but we are given a sense of this wholeness through its very absence. An irony of this form would not gesture back to some norm or idea to which it was inadequate; it would be *necessarily fragmented* or incomplete. Consider the following poem by William Blake, again from *Songs of Innocence and of Experience*:

> Tyger Tyger, burning bright,
> In the forests of the night

What immortal hand or eye,
Could frame they fearful symmetry?

In what distant deeps or skies
Burnt the fire of thine eyes!
On what wings dare he aspire?
What the hand dare seize the fire?

And what shoulder, & what art,
Could twist the sinews of thy heart?
And when thy heart began to beat,
What dread hand and what dread feet?

What the hammer? What the chain,
In what furnace was thy brain?
What the anvil? What dread grasp,
Dare its deadly terrors clasp?
(Blake [1794] 1957, 214–15)

Now, on the one hand we might want to say that there is a clear irony lying in the absurdity or limitation of the speaker's voice. The speaker addresses God as a mechanical creator and then wonders how anything so complex as the world might have been put together. We might say that Blake is ironising eighteenth-century natural theology, or the idea that from any ordered creation we should assume some rational and ordering principle. For the dissecting intellect of natural theology, we do not need startling revelations, angels or miracles to disclose God, for God is just the principle of the world's natural harmony. Blake ironises this argument by showing that if God were nothing more than a rational creator or divine watchmaker we would have to be mystified or terrified by something so arbitrary or irrational as the tiger. As long as we talk and think within the bounds of 'reason', what cannot be explained will appear as incomprehensible or terrifying. However, this irony does not offer a better, more rational or more coherent way of comprehending divine creation; the problem – and what is ironised – lies in the will to know, encompass and comprehend as such. What the poem produces, through irony, is a sense of the limits of the defining intellect. The poem does not offer a more coherent image of God, for the very problem lies in our attempt to reduce God and the creative force of life to some single image.

By producing poems Blake displayed, expressed and constantly activated the creative power of life; he never reduced that power to a single voice or image. Indeed, it was the very idea of an image or personification of God that he constantly ironised in the fatherly figures of Urizen (Blake 1957, 222–37) or 'Nobodaddy' (ibid. 171), the grand old maker who sits in the sky measuring out the mathematically ordered and closed universe. Blake's Romantic irony is therefore quite different from the tame notion that irony signals an other *meaning*, or that irony demands that we assume some more coherent sense. There is no single coherent voice in Blake's work. Like the Socratic dialogues invoked by the German Romantics, it is in the multiplicity of voices that life is opened up for question, no longer reducible to any of its expressions.

A text, such as a text of logic, which presented itself as a closed set of propositions, would have to exclude or repress the process that created those propositions. An ironic text, by contrast, gestures to its own incompleteness. Ironic texts, for the Romantics, were marked by several tendencies. First, they were fragmentary: by not being closed or complete they gestured to a process of creation that is always coming to completion. Think of S.T. Coleridge's (1772–1834) *Kubla Khan* (1816), which not only describes its interrupted process of composition as having been induced by a dream-like state, but also ends with the intention to produce further work and art: 'I would build that dome in air' (Coleridge 1951, 45).

Second, ironic texts were not *works*: not purposive or intentional objects generated from a single consciousness with an intention to communicate some content. Truly ironic texts often convey a sense of the incoherence of voice, or that one *cannot* say what is being said. The speech act of irony is one that fails to work. Irony is often self-undermining or internally contradictory. Critics have often commented on Milton's desperate attempts in *Paradise Lost* (1667) to avoid attributing contradiction to God. How could God grant Adam and Eve the freedom to choose evil, and yet hold them ultimately responsible for evil? The Romantics who followed Milton embraced this contradiction. From Blake's character of Satan in the prophecies to P.B. Shelley's (1792–1822) *Prometheus Unbound* (1820), the Romantics asserted the pain, the subjection and the worth of freedom:

> torture and solitude,
> Scorn and despair, – these are mine empire: –
> More glorious far than that which thou surveyest
> From thine unenvied throne, O Mighty God!
> Almighty, had I deigned to share the shame
> Of thine ill tyranny, and hung not here
> Nailed to his wall of eagle-baffling mountain
>> (P.B. Shelley 1971, 208 [*Prometheus Unbound* 1.14–20])

Freedom is *both* a subjection to fate, for our decisions are constantly thwarted, and only possible through fate. If one were absolutely free – if our decisions met with *no* resistance or conflict – then they would not be decisions at all, just the course of the world's events or, as Shelley refers to it, divine tyranny. Freedom is internally contradictory and ironic. To declare freedom is to posit oneself in opposition to life; but if there is a life other than oneself, then one is never absolutely free. Mary Shelley's (1797–1851) monster in *Frankenstein* (1831) objects to his creator, in the name of freedom, that he did not ask for freedom, will or creation. He expresses the irony of existence and freedom; only in freedom can one experience the limits and failures of freedom. The one thing we are not free to choose is freedom itself: 'Increase of knowledge only discovered to me more clearly what a wretched outcast I was' (M. Shelley 1992, 127).

In addition to being fragmentary and contradictory, ironic texts are *critical*. Art is no longer a presented and beautiful *thing*; it includes a reflection on its own origin *and* acknowledges a distance or difference from that origin. It is never at one with itself. Romantic poetry, especially, is not only temporal, in that it moves from premises to a conclusion, but also destructive of a single line of time and origin. John Keats's (1795–1821) *Ode on a Grecian Urn* (1820), for example, posits the timelessness of art in opposition to the fleeting joys of life: 'Ah, happy, happy boughs! That cannot shed/Your leaves, nor ever bid the Spring adieu.' It then 'concludes' with a reflection on the impossibility for art and representation to grasp those pleasures that are essentially fleeting and temporal: 'Cold Pastoral!' Here, it is not only the fixing of beauty that allows for truth; there is also a truth in beauty or the fleeting itself: 'Beauty is truth, truth beauty.' The 'conclusion' seems to turn back and retract its original elevation of eternal art over the flux of life; but such a retraction occurs in a poem, an art object *about* the failure of art to deal with time, and that does so through a temporal development. In its central statement or proposition – 'Beauty is truth, truth beauty' – it displays the very problem of propositions. There cannot be an identity between truth and beauty. For truth, as eternal, would always be other than any of its temporal or artistic representations; but this can only be known *through* those representations. At the same time, beauty can only be *truly* beautiful or known *as* beautiful if it has already lost some of its beauty, if it has been frozen or fixed into a form, such as the poem, or urn, for reflection. These three features of Romantic irony are themselves contradictory or difficult to sustain in one and the same text. Irony is both fragmentary in being aware of its incompleteness and critical in acknowledging the failure of any poem or fragment to be fully aware of its own origin; but irony is also opposed to the notion of a work that would achieve effective closure and completeness. Irony works against its own striving or intention for completeness, aware that such a striving can only fail, but that the failure is itself a moment of partial illumination. In the case of Keats's 'Ode' the poem both works with the desire for art as a closed and complete object, and celebrates the failure of that desire by producing a poem about the self-sufficient urn's cold and distant beauty. A desire for complete beauty is articulated, presented as impossible, and then celebrated in its very impossibility or failure.

THE FRACTURED ABSOLUTE

German Romanticism's paradigms for irony ranged across literature and history, testifying to a tendency in life itself: a tendency to *create* in order to recognise the freedom, disruption and purposelessness of creation. Socrates was, for the Romantics, one such paradigm. But theirs was not a Socrates who used irony to arrive at truth. Their Socrates was a character in formation, who was nothing behind the masks and personae he created. Another Romantic paradigm, alongside Socrates, was the Latin rhetorical tradition: the Ciceronian orator who presented himself as an ongoing work of beauty and creation, presented to, and through, the public and political life: 'To live classically and to realize antiquity practically within oneself is the summit and goal of philology' (Schlegel 1991, 37). Neither Socrates nor the Roman orator presented *norms* or examples of human nature, since freedom, irony and *Bildung* (or creation) lie in the spontaneous or unintended difference from nature.

Indeed, nature itself began to be defined ironically: not as a world of forms or ends which come to inevitable completion, but a dynamic process of formation that can always result in accident, disruption, loss and fragmentation. Such a power for formation can only be given ironically, after the event of having formed. The very power of life can never coincide with or see itself *in formation*, for it will always require some formed medium upon which it can work and come to realisation. 'We' form ourselves through voice and language, and such media are themselves already formed and irreducible to our intent. There is, therefore, always a fragment of death, loss or mourning in life, always a past medium that can never be rendered fully present. Romantic irony also, therefore, celebrated the notion of antiquity and the ruin (Spencer 1954; St Claire 1972; Levin 1931). We never create ourselves from a pure origin or *ex nihilo*; creation always begins from elsewhere, from the fragments or ruins of the past. The ironic self is never a single and self-conscious origin so much as a process of creation that reflects upon the disparity and multiplicity of voices that it brings into being: 'Irony is the clear consciousness of eternal agility, of an infinitely teeming chaos' (Schlegel 1991, 100). Not surprisingly, then, the drama and the novel, as displays of divergent voices, were crucial for Romantic irony: 'Many of the very best novels are compendia, encyclopaedias of the whole spiritual life of a brilliant individual' (Schlegel 1991, 10). Novels were the modern manifestation of the tendencies formerly expressed in ancient dialogue or classical oratory, 'Novels are the Socratic dialogues of our time' (Schlegel 1991, 3).

Romantic irony, therefore, claims an absolute status for both art and romanticism, for romanticism is that moment when the various artistic deviations from nature are recognised *as art*, as events that can never be at one with the absolute they express. The absolute reveals itself only in *not* being closed, finished or at one with itself. Poetry is absolute because all life is formation and externalisation of a hidden creative power. All art is 'Romantic' precisely because it is in Romantic irony that art reaches what it was all along: 'Romantic poetry is a progressive, universal poetry' (Schlegel 1991, 31). Art is not the poetic presentation of an otherwise inert and objective world; there is no world without the forming power of art. Irony is the only authentic and true mode of art. It is art aware that the power that produces the work always remains beyond the work. The self represented in art is never coincident with the self *who* represents. And the self who represents is not so much a *self* – not a being, persona or individual – as an impersonal and transcendental power *to become*. Such a power must always go through its becoming belatedly, drawing upon already formed genres, styles and forms.

But if the Romantics looked back to all earlier art as ultimately tending towards the 'truth' of irony, how can we read the pre-Romantic expressions of irony on their own terms? One of the common political objections to Romanticism is its incapacity to be critical. Romantic poetry is a retreat from the difference and conflict of political life, and Romantic irony collapses all political and concrete differences into an absolute of poetry, imagination or inwardness. From the Romantic point of view, any outer, real or material world can only be known and mediated through poetry and spirit. What is lost in the elevation of irony to the very spirit of life is any sense of those conflicts and questions that can *not* be harmonised by, or reduced to, the life and becoming of the subject.

Karl Marx (1818–83) followed the German philosopher G.W.F. Hegel in arguing that if there appeared to be mystical forces beyond human control, then human knowledge and practice needed to expand its domain of power. For this reason, many critics today of Marxist orientation regard irony, or the sense of some immutable otherness beyond human intent, as a reactive and failed politics (Eagleton 1990; McGann 1983). Theory, it is argued, should have no 'outside'; what appears as other than knowledge can only be, and should be, dealt with through knowledge. Romantic irony, today, has been defined as both reactionary (McGann 1983) and revolutionary (Handwerk 1985). The Romantic assertion that we can only speak ironically, that the subject can never turn back and know its own world-forming activity has been affirmed as a harbinger of postmodernism, as one of the first attempts to think beyond a totalising and all-consuming subjectivity. Indeed, some writers have claimed that German Romanticism goes further than contemporary post-structuralism; it not only destroys the primacy of 'reasoning man', it also sees art as a way of creating new and less tyrannical understandings of life (Bowie 1997). But Romanticism has also been criticised as an ideology: the representation of a specific and historically contingent political impotence as a universal and absolute predicament. Jerome McGann has therefore insisted that we see Romantic irony, not as an essential condition of a speaking subject that can never fully know itself, but as symptomatic of the abandonment of a public and critical assessment of the social forces of language. *Good* irony, according to McGann, is thoroughly demystifying: 'The romantic ironist is a satirist because part of his business is to arraign our foolishness about all sorts of order – cosmic, personal, and literary' (McGann 1983, 294). McGann therefore presents Byron, rather than Wordsworth, as an exemplary Romantic.

While early Romanticism affirmed and mourned some pre-linguistic force that remained ever out of reach, Byron's poetry looked at how this unrepresentable origin was invented and sustained by a literary industry that mystified language and creativity. According to McGann, Byron's irony is directed against cant, or an unreflective use of language. The purpose of irony is to repeat and parody the language of a context in order to expose the possible *re*-creation of context: 'The satirist as ironist is nearly as duplicitous as his canting opponent, but, unlike his opponent, he makes certain that the membranes are thin enough for us to hear the deep utterance underneath' (McGann 1983, 276). Irony is not a gesturing to some ineffable and mysterious chaos beyond language; it is the use of language to expose the force of language. We will look at these claims in more detail in the following chapter when we examine the relation between irony and satire in Byron's *Don Juan* (1821) and Swift's *Gulliver's Travels* (1726).

4

BEYOND IRONY AND SUBJECTIVITY

Byron and Swift

THE IRONIC SUBJECT

For the German romantics, and the contemporary theorists of irony who affirm romanticism, the concept of irony is tied to the concept of the subject. On the one hand, all speech, language, text or poetry implies a subject or origin *who speaks*. On the other hand, the subject cannot be reduced to what has been said or written; nor can the subject control or fully determine the speech which both has an origin before the subject and a force beyond the subject. The notion of the subject is derived from the Latin *subjectum*, referring to a ground, basis, or what exists independently (Heidegger 1967). The notion of the subject goes beyond its modern associations with persons to include anything that exists in itself or precedes various qualities and accidents. There is a subject or basis for predicates, or a subject that underlies or remains the same with changes of quality. The idea of the *human* subject is usually defined as a specifically modern notion; it is only in modernity that we have the idea of human knower as the basis or centre of all inquiry (Heidegger 1967).

It is often argued that pre-modern cultures had a notion of 'man' defined as a rational animal among a world of other beings, so that 'man' would only differ by degree from all other living beings. But only modernity thinks of a human subject as an entirely different mode of being (Foucault 1970). The subject is not a being among others, not just an animal with reason, but the very ground or condition for there being anything at all. There can only be a perceived world or beings if there is some consciousness or subjectivity that allows that world to be thought. The modern subject, then, is what allows the world to be presented, but cannot itself be presented. Any description, definition or representation of subjectivity determines the subject as a thing or substance, but the subject is not a thing so much as the process through which things are given, represented or synthesised.

This is what led the German Romantics to adopt irony as the only true style for thinking. Any *described* subject is always other than the subject who is doing the description. There is always a gap between the subject *who speaks* and the represented subject *spoken about*. Instead of striving for ever more accurate descriptions or definitions of 'man', the ironic response acknowledges the limited nature of any definition. The process of poetic creation will always be other than any created poem. Subjectivity can *never* be typified or exemplified in any literary character. There can be no ideal self precisely because subjectivity is the process that produces character and is always other than any presented persona. The self that lies behind masks and personae can only be known as different from what is presented, never presented 'itself'. The Romantics could therefore 'turn back' to Socrates and pre-moderns like Shakespeare and argue that a divine irony was produced through the *absence* of Socrates and Shakespeare, in their disappearance behind the characters, positions and masks they created. For the Romantics, it was Shakespeare who typified the idea of the absent author: 'Shakespeare's univerality is like the center of romantic art' (Schlegel 1991, 52):

> there probably is no modern poet more correct than Shakespeare. Similarly, he is also systematic as no other poet is: sometimes because of those antitheses that bring into picturesque contrast individuals, masses, even worlds; sometimes through musical symmetry on the same great scale, through gigantic repetitions and refrains; often by a

> parody of the letter and an irony on the spirit of romantic drama; and
> always through the most sublime and complete individuality, uniting all
> the degrees of poetry, from the most carnal imitation to the most
> spiritual characterization.
>
> (Schlegel 1991, 53–4)

It is difficult, today, to question whether such discoveries of pre-modern
irony are historically accurate, for the very notion of distinct, bound and
authentic historical epochs is itself Romantic, as well as being intertwined
with the concept of the subject. While the writing of history and notions
of human nature have been in existence since Plato's day, the notion of the
subject – particularly the ironic, absent and unrepresentable subject –
radically alters how we think about history. Irony brings in *both* a notion
of eternity *and* the possibility of thinking in terms of historical contexts.
Consider the character of Socrates. Even on a traditional reading, Socrates
is seen as one who refused the given, contextual and politically accepted
definitions of human life – what we are – and instead asked how we
ought to live. In so doing he adopted an ideal of human life: one should
not just exist; one should question how one ought to live. At the same
time, however, he refused to present a *definition* of such a life. His irony
lay in questioning norms and opinions by invoking what would be true
regardless of context (what is true eternally). For Socrates and Plato the soul
of man cannot be determined or valued as yet one more thing within the
world, for it is only through reflection and cultivation of one's soul that
one can know how to order, value and manage the affairs of the world.

We need to distinguish, though, between this Platonic emphasis
on the Socratic soul, which was other-worldly, and the modern subject,
who is the condition for any world or thing being represented. Despite
modern mobilisations of Socrates for a theory of the ironic subject, the
Socratic soul was not yet a theory of *subjectivity*. Socrates presented
and performed a good life; he did not argue for some unrepresentable,
ineffable and transcendental 'subject'. Only later, in modern philosophy
and the attempt to provide some ultimate condition for truth, knowledge
and representation, was it possible to think of the subject as a necessary
condition before all speech, thought and activity.

Instead of accepting that there is a world with man as a rational animal
within the world, philosophers from René Descartes (1596–1650)

onwards argued that the world was produced, known or represented through the subject. The subject is, therefore, not to be confused with any specific personality, character or self. Subjectivity is the principle or process – the peculiar immaterial or transcendental process – through which things, persons or a world are synthesised.

Once the notion of subjectivity is accepted and pushed to its radical conclusions, crucial consequences follow for the relation between philosophy and literature. If it is the case that subjectivity cannot be known in itself but only in and through its produced representations, then the old notions of philosophical 'theory' become untenable. Consciousness cannot contemplate itself in a moment of pure thought or self-reflection, freed from all worldly distortions and figures. Consciousness only knows itself through its products. Only ironic writing, a writing that does not pretend to be the full and transparent representation of 'thinking man', can lay claim to any rigour or authenticity. Romantic *poetry* supplants philosophy as the primary discourse because, while philosophy can only make literal claims about what *is*, poetry shows language in its formative, synthesising and productive process. Poetry does not present an ideal definition of man or humanity; it does not fall into the illusion of taking 'man' as yet one more definable substance. In presenting distinct and singular *characters*, literature no longer presents human life as some general unchanging essence. Literature displays each character as singular and *other than* the subjectivity that lies at the origin. (So, when Wordsworth refers to the 'still sad music of humanity', he is not referring to an observable human *nature* with distinct tendencies, as Alexander Pope (1688–1744) did in his *Essay on Man*; 'humanity' for Wordsworth is a lost and ineffable origin known only *as lost*.)

In English Romantic poetry this emergence of the subject has explicit political and historical consequences. First, there is now no notion of 'man' who *then* differs historically or culturally, with some basic underlying nature. Instead, the Romantics had a strong sense of radical historical difference: a difference, or power to differ, without any underlying substance. The Romantics looked back to both ancient and medieval 'worlds' in which the entire structures of perception and value were different. Indeed, they saw the idea of 'man' as a repressive abstraction imposed upon life. Wordsworth, in 'Intimations of Immortality', gazes nostalgically upon the infant who has not yet adopted the social conventions of 'man'. Blake celebrates a 'soul' or imagination in opposition to 'natural man'; and even Byron, in *Don Juan* (1821), while acknowledging the tendencies of the human body, will also look fondly on the love of Haidée and Don Juan that eclipses all knowable and perceivable forms.

Don Juan, which we will examine more fully in Chapter 6 as a satire opposed to English romanticism and irony, also indulged in its own Romantic yearnings. This is not surprising given the fact that Byron's epic covered nearly every available style and mode of desire, but it is also evidence of Byron's fondness for the idea of an emotion unencumbered with the norms and conventions of everyday life. The early love scene between the youthful and exiled Don Juan and the Greek Haidée, who finds him after having been cast on an island after a shipwreck, plays with the notion of an experience that is not already reduced to the received forms of language. It is precisely because Juan and Haidée do not speak a common language, do not have a ready-made context of conventions, that we see the capacity for love and spirit *before* it has fallen into language. Byron's description of this scene is ironic in two senses. It gestures to a feeling or 'reading' of the body that is other than the physical, for it is the unseen or 'surmised' that engages the lover's gaze. But *Don Juan* is also written with an ironic awareness that we only know or represent this unrepresentable love through the conventions of love poetry. The narrator refers to a music that is sweeter than anything heard, but in doing so invokes the Romantic (and often-heard) image of 'unheard music'. The poem celebrates what lies before all convention, but does so through conventional images, such as young lovers and warbling birds, and then reinforces the very matter of poetry with the heavy feminine rhyme at the end ('better/letter'). This is a poetry that intimates what lies beyond the letter, but does so through the letter:

> CLI
> Now Juan could not understand a word,
>   Being no Grecian; but he had an ear,
> And her voice was the warble of a bird,
>   So soft, so sweet, so delicately clear,
> That finer, simpler music ne'er was heard;
>   The sort of sound we echo with a tear,

Without knowing why – an overpowering tone,
Whence Melody descends as from a throne.

. . .

CLXII
And then she had recourse to nods, and sighs,
    And smiles, and sparkles of the speaking eye,
And read (the only book she could) the lines
    Of his fair face, and found, by sympathy,
The answer eloquent, where soul shines
    And darts in one quick glance a long reply;
And thus in every look she saw exprest
A world of words, and things at which she guess'd.

CLXIII
And now, by dint of fingers and of eyes,
    And words repeated after her, he took
A lesson in her tongue; but by surmise,
    No doubt, less of her language than her look:
As he who studies fervently the skies
    Turns oftener to the stars than to his book,
Thus Juan learn'd his *alpha beta* better
From Haidée's glance than any graven letter.
                      (Byron [1821] 1973, 139–42)

For the Romantics, it is only if we can *think* a subjective power other than
any general definition that we will be able to look to a creative and
dynamic future. At the same time, any representation of this unexpress-
ible power would have to rely on some medium of expression. Byron's
'solution' in *Don Juan* was to affirm all those powers of love, heroism,
over-reaching and 'surmise' that lie beyond the fixity of conventions, at
the same time as he showed how conventional or fixed the representation
of those powers had become. *Don Juan* oscillates between cynical defla-
tion, where poetry appears as all too rigid, and the yearning for a power
beyond already-recognised conventions. Irony, in its various romantic
modes, was crucial in expressing this inexpressible power. For this reason
Byron has been at the centre of a critical debate regarding the status of

irony, romanticism and politics. According to Anne Mellor's *English Romantic Irony* (1980), we can read Byron as a liberating exemplar of German Romanticism; Byron affirms the chaos that exceeds any definition of self or any described world. According to Jerome McGann (1976) Byron's irony was satirical and political in contrast to Romanticism's penchant for the ineffable. Byron – as we already see in the Haidée section just quoted – was aware that any emotion posited outside language was posited and determined through language. Responsible poetry does not attempt to step outside language, but acknowledges its force and form. McGann's reference to Byron's use of satire against Romantic irony suggests a distinction that we will explore further both in this chapter and Chapter 6. To see Byron as a satirist is to emphasise the debunking, critical and politically self-aware modes of *Don Juan*. Satire rejects any elevated or ineffable subjectivity that lies beyond located human speech and action. Romantic irony, by contrast, suggests that the limited and finite forms of human speech lead us to think or imagine that which lies beyond all limit.

In this sense, we can see a tension in the ethic and ideal of irony: a tension between irony in its full Romantic sense, and irony as a satirical and debunking technique. On the one hand, irony could be as it was for the Romantics: a refusal of any voice, authority or definition of the self, an appeal to an infinite beyond all form, language and context. On the other hand, as demonstrated in the critical moments of Byron and other Romantics, this very appeal to an infinite beyond language must itself adopt a language. Irony, in its distance from any law or self, should not become one more privileged voice or law.

These two possibilities within irony, as both the debunking of law and as an intimation of what lies beyond all law, can allow us to read tensions in many of the classic Romantic texts that both affirm the human spirit but are wary of falling into a doctrine of defined humanism. Blake, for example, showed how the received moralising voices that claim to speak for 'us', or 'man' in general, were actually particular, stylised, interested and repressive. He did this, not by giving a more authoritative and *proper* voice, but by presenting voices in their effects. The clearest case of this is his *Songs of Innocence and of Experience*. The poems of innocence present the voice and style of trust, charity, benevolence, pity and optimism. Frequently the speakers posit or assume an all-powerful, fatherly, distant but sympathetic creator. Now Blake does not say that such a point of view is *wrong*, nor does his irony consist of simple contradiction or the implication of opposites. He repeats the voice of innocence in all its charming naivety and beauty, but we are also at the same time aware of its limits. The very idea of an all-trusting, benevolent and supremely fatherly God in heaven reduces us to passive lambs. The very sing-song rhythm of the poems, their repetitiveness and blind optimism preclude all possibility of change, disruption, action or complaint: 'So if all do their duty they need not fear harm' (Blake 1957, 118).

By contrast, the *Songs of Experience* express judging, despairing, condemning and faithless voices that confidently see the whole of the scene and eliminate any notions of mercy, grace or the reception of goodness. If innocence is closed because it defines itself through an external and unchanging God and nature, experience is closed because it steps outside nature and sees only meaningless, futile and purposeless change, a mechanistic and Godless nature: 'It is eternal winter there' (Blake 1957, 212). The truth lies in neither innocence nor experience but in the conflict and contradiction between the two. One must *both* (as in innocence) have faith in a spirit beyond human life and matter *and* (as in experience) doubt and challenge any image of that spirit. There can be no definition of the world through an eternal and fixed image of God, nor through a meaningless and mechanistic reduction of man to matter. There can be no universal image of reason or man, only the poetic celebration of the spirit from which images emerge. Blake is ironic, not because he *says* something other than what is presented, but because he presents as conflicting and limited all those voices that would claim to speak for, and define, life, and displays their style, imagery, inscription and effects. What is *other* than the voices of innocence and experience is their relation of conflict, and not any existing proposition or position. If innocence and experience are the 'two contrary states of the human soul', imagination is *other than* any state: 'The Imagination is not a State: it is the Human Existence itself' (Blake 1957, 522).

Even though Romanticism was critical of any defined or static subject, and used various voices to preclude any normative definition of man, it still held on to a subject that was always more than any of its effects or definitions. Blake also made pronouncements about the creative or spiritual power, as did the German Romantics. Although both the Romantics and Blake stressed the ineffable nature of the spirit and imagination, they nevertheless frequently referred to the soul or spirit's power and ineffability. Unlike later modern ironists, Romantic irony still put forward some voice of its own, was still capable of making first-person and sincere pronouncements. Alongside Blake's repetition of the voices of human moralism – those that felt they could speak for and define man in general – he also strove to express the 'divine' power of poetry, just as the German Romantics had also argued for irony as the only style adequate to the synthesising spirit of subjectivity. This raises one of the central paradoxes of irony and its relation to politics. If we accept the Socratic and enlightenment principle that one ought to decide one's values for oneself, rather than merely receiving or repeating already determined doctrines, then the articulation of the principle *as a principle* leads to paradox. How can I tell you that you ought to obey no external principle? How can I form a proposition that argues against a morality of received propositions? Socrates' answer was to live the ethical life as a question, without offering a moral theory.

Since Socrates it has often been stated that there can be no *theory* of irony. Irony is the resistance to a single fixed point of view. The minute one speaks about the ironising spirit one has fallen back into literal pronouncements and definitions. If Socratic irony could still appeal to Ideas beyond human action and definition, modern irony can have no such ground. The enlightenment rejection of all received and already defined principles and the emphasis on self-formation and self-definition must refuse any fixed principle. But how do we articulate or express this refusal to be anything other than self-determining? If there can be no general rule for moral and political life, and only ongoing participation and decision, then politics and ethics might require a new style. No longer offering theories of human nature or general propositions, one would speak in such a way as to disrupt all notions of generality. For the Romantics only literature could produce such dynamic and creative, rather than propositional and didactic, styles.

SWIFT AND UNREASON

Swift's response to this problem of articulating a principle of reason, or a principle attacking rigid principles, in *Gulliver's Travels*, was to present the rational and certain Houyhnhnms ironically. The various books and lands encompassed by *Gulliver's Travels* seem to lead inevitably to a perfectly rational conclusion: Gulliver arrives at the land of the Houyhnhnms, who are unaffected by political squabbles, differences of opinion, deceit, dissimulation or ambiguity. They have a perfectly rational language without any word for that which is contrary to law. Prior to arriving in the land of the Houyhnhnms, *Gulliver's Travels* uses a number of varying ironic and satirical techniques. Sometimes the voice of Gulliver unwittingly exposes the absurdity of the culture he describes; sometimes his voice is self-incriminating and absurd; at others, his reflections self-consciously expose the limits of human nature. But it is the conclusion of *Gulliver's Travels* that presents the paradox of reason. The earlier chapters describe and lampoon all the delusions of reason: the scientific, political and religious theories that have led human life into futile and violent endeavours. Well before the paradoxes and irony of Romanticism, Swift presented the paradox of a critique of reason, and he did so not by expressing some ultimate 'subject' beyond reason but by displaying or performing the conflicts of reason from within the voice of reason itself.

The Enlightenment had stressed that true reason cannot be a law that we simply obey; reason must be the refusal of any imposed law (Kant [1784] 1959). Any general principle that would organise morality would impede the moral power of human life to deliberate and decide for itself; one can only present moral principles negatively, as the refusal of received norms, notions, superstitions or dogma. Reason is not a represented rule or law; it is the criticism of fixed representations, which is why Kant describes enlightenment as 'freedom from imposed tutelage' (Kant 1959). However, when expressed as a theory or principle the pure form of enlightenment leads to a contradiction: 'Obey no one!' is itself an order demanding obedience. Far from stating this as a principle, or presenting a counter principle, Swift presents an image of a reason that has taken itself as a law. The narration of *Gulliver's Travels* implies, ironically, that the all too reasonable Houyhnhnms are far from rational. *Their* reason is an unquestioning belief in the rationality of their own nature; their reason is a substance: they see their own bodies as the very embodiment of reason, their own laws as incontrovertible, and their own species as exemplary. At the end of Gulliver's encounters with various forms of human failing, absurdity and frailty we are presented with a race who feel so confident of their moral beliefs that there is no disagreement, no conception of evil, and no word for 'pride' (Swift [1726] 1967, 345). The Houyhnhnms have no conception of themselves as moral agents or deciders; what is good is simply what they are. This is so much the case that their only conception of evil is not what they judge to be detrimental but what is other than themselves: 'the Houyhnhnms have no word in their language to express anything that is *evil*, except what they borrow from the deformities or ill qualities of the Yahoos' (Swift [1726] 1967, 323). They are supremely confident of their moral knowledge and reasoning – so much so that they do away with books and insist that their lore is transmitted unambiguously, immediately and unproblematically through tradition (ibid. 321). They have no writing, no medium that allows for interpretation; indeed, they regard reason as pure, immaterial and incapable of error, difference, alteration or corruption. Reason is not a power to question; it is a rectitude that has lost all need of inquiry.

Even though Gulliver has spent most of his travels observing the human body's capacity to stray from, distort and pervert reason and principles, he easily submits to the pure reason of the Houyhnhnms. In so doing, however, he not only presents their reason as a tyrannical *doctrine*, he also performs or displays the contradictory nature of a reason that acknowledges no possibility of otherness. There is an irony here, for *Gulliver's Travels* manages to say that reason is insufficient without actually stating what the text means explicitly. But the technique or irony that exposes the insufficiency of reason by using reason's own voice does not suggest – as Romantic ironists would do – some ultimate principle beyond all reason.

On the one hand, Swift seems to be in line with the enlightenment critique of reason: once reason has become a rigid law or principle it has lost all its reasoning power. On the other hand, it is just this belief in a disembodied and pure power of reason that allows the Houyhnhnm belief in the value of eliminating distortion, tradition, writing and otherness: anything that corrupts the ability to detach oneself from the body and passions. Indeed, theirs is a body or nature that is uncorrupted by nature or embodiment:

> As these noble Houyhnhnms are endowed by Nature with a general
> disposition to all virtues, and have no conceptions or ideas of what is

evil in a rational creature, so their grand maxim is to cultivate *Reason*, and to be wholly governed by it. Neither is *Reason* among them a point problematical as with us, where man can argue with plausibility on both sides of a question; but strikes you with immediate conviction; as it must needs do where it is not mingled, obscured, or discoloured by passion and interest.

(Swift [1726] 1967, 315)

Gulliver's Travels does not just present a voice of pure reason that has fallen into corruption, it also displays the tyranny of believing in pure reason in the first place. To believe in a power of reason that is *nothing* other than the capacity to question and free oneself from imposed doctrines is to create a mythical site of original and uncontaminated purity; all impure or contaminated forces must then be attributed to reason's other. It is because the Houyhnhnms have no word for evil that they must posit another body, the Yahoos, whom they use to refer to all negative, evil and irrational qualities.

Gulliver's Travels is more than a satire on the tyrannical purity of reason and its inherent xenophobia. Swift's ironic style precludes the satire from having a distinct and locatable object. For most of the narrative, Gulliver faithfully repeats the ideals of his former English home in such a way as to unwittingly disclose their contradictions: 'There are some laws and customs in this Empire very peculiar, and if they were not so directly contrary to those of my own dear country, I should be tempted to say a little in their justification' (Swift [1726] 1967, 94). We may say that the irony lies both in Gulliver's sincere, but self-betraying, repetition of English humanism, and in his wondrous descriptions of all those foreign practices that are more intense versions of the absurd rationalism he has left behind. But beyond the satirical *content*, the absurd depictions of science, literalism, politics, vanity and the human tendency to take one's own self as the measure of all things, the style of *Gulliver's Travels* also displays the violence, risks and tyranny of language and description. This is not just a satire that belittles human nature; the voice itself is a display of that nature. Gulliver is never outside or distinct from the follies he describes; either the descriptions he gives are self-betraying *or* the absurdities he views in other lands are allegorical doubles of his own culture. Gulliver is self-betraying when his attempt to explain the glories of gunpowder to the king of Brobdingnag is met with horror, a horror which Gulliver's homeland, and Gulliver, tellingly lacks. Any broad-minded reason would be able to calculate the efficiency of such means of violence. This is a form of irony that has no sense of the meaning of what it is saying. The voice of Gulliver is presented as blind to its own violence:

> A strange effect of *narrow principles* and *short views*! That a Prince possessed of every quality which procures veneration, love, and esteem; of strong parts, great wisdom and profound learning, endued with admirable talents for government, and almost adored by his subjects, should from a *nice unnecessary scruple*, whereof in Europe we have no conception, let slip an opportunity put into his hands, that would have made him absolute master of the lives, liberties, and the fortunes of his people.
>
> (Swift [1726] 1967, 175)

The object is not just England, nor Europe, nor the tendencies of human nature, but also a tendency of speech itself. For there are other passages where Gulliver, well before he meets the Houyhnhnms, praises a purely literal language which, like gunpowder and the later plans for Yahoo extermination, would eliminate distortion, ambiguity, conflict and dissent: 'Their style is clear, masculine, and smooth, but not florid, for they avoid nothing more than multiplying unnecessary words, or using various expressions' (Swift [1726] 1967, 177). It would seem, then, that if we read Gulliver ironically, as an object of derision, his commitment to abstractions and transcendentals would place him laughably below the literal Brobdingnagians, whom Gulliver at this stage sees as impoverished precisely because they 'only' have the discourses of morality, history, poetry and (useful) mathematics; they lack abstractions:

> The learning of this people is very defective, consisting only in morality, history, poetry and mathematics, wherein they must be allowed to excel. But, the last of these is wholly applied to what may be useful in life, to the improvement of agriculture and all mechanical arts; so that among us it would be little esteemed. And as to ideas, entities, abstractions and tran-scendentals, I could never drive the least conception into their heads.
>
> (Swift [1726] 1967, 176)

It would seem, if we take Gulliver's commitment to abstractions as the object of irony, that Swift's narrative would place a positive value upon a pure 'masculine' language. Much of *Gulliver's Travels* does, indeed, lampoon the absurd and overly speculative projects of redundant science and unfounded theories and suggests that learning and language need to be recalled to life and the body. Most of the irony is in the service of satire, attacking any elevated notions of humanity or reason that have supposedly liberated themselves from desire. But the irony is far more complex than this. The elimination of ambiguity and 'useless' language, or the commitment to complete literalism is both absurdly impossible and contradictory. The attempt to eliminate the body or physicality of language – to speak the world *itself* – only multiplies the number of objects or bodies required for communication. Gulliver describes the absurd projects of the people of Lagado who try to reduce language to mathematical formulae or dispense with language altogether. But Gulliver's very description exposes the inherent irony of language. For it is the very nature of language – as sign – to be at once a physical body and a sense *other than* that body. A pure language would be both thoroughly immaterial (pure ideal and sense) and thoroughly material (the thing itself):

> For, it is plain, that every word we speak is in some degree a diminution of our lungs by corrosion, and consequently contributes to the short-ening of our lives. An expedient was therefore offered, that since words are only the names for things, it would be more convenient for all men to carry about them such *things* as were necessary to express the particular business they were to discourse on.
>
> (Swift [1726] 1967, 230)

The desire for a pure or literal language, a language devoid of ambiguity or figures, produces a chaos of things, an outrageous and insecure collec-tion of signifiers with no coherent sense. And the failure of that language is attributed, by the literal minded Gulliver and the Lagado scientists, not to the essential feature of language to work only if it refers to more than one thing across time and context – only if there is a general sense – but to the irrational bodies of others. The paradox of language is the paradox of the pure body. The body itself, the pure literal and uncorrupted thing

– nature before all reference or culture – can only be known *in itself, before all relations*. But the very nature of language is relational – circulated, communicated, translated, and transported from one body to another. Any science built on knowing, retrieving or sustaining this pure body must therefore create some system of signs or language that is not the pure body or pure nature itself, a language that allows that nature to be known and secured. A purely literal science would have to eliminate its very status as science – as the creation of a body of knowledge, meanings, sense and tradition. Pure reason defines itself against the corrupt and irrational bodies of others, those who allow language to circulate without attachment to the proper body of the referent: 'And this invention would certainly have taken place, to the great ease as well as health of the subject, if the women in conjunction with the vulgar and illiterate had not threatened to raise a rebellion, unless they might be allowed the liberty to speak with their tongues, after the manner of their forefathers; such constant irreconcilable enemies to science are the common people' (Swift [1726] 1967, 230). There can be no pure science – no pure grasp of the object itself – without some relation to that object. Language, and its distance from the literal or pure referent, is not an accident that befalls reason and thinking.

This is why the Houyhnhnms' reason ultimately inhabits a contradiction, which is also the very contradiction of language. Pure thought and truth should require no force, rhetoric, image or persuasion, and so Houyhnhnm reason presents itself as freed of all books, signification or material supports; the Houyhnhnms have no libraries, texts or myths. At the same time, their reason is nevertheless passed from body to body in the form of tradition: all the features of writing and myth – the institution of a common system, language and frame of reference – are already present in Houyhnhnm reason, but repressed or denied. By the time Gulliver meets the Houyhnhnms, they merely intensify a propensity that all Gulliver's encounters and narratives have displayed: once a system of reason is formed, it lulls thought into a comfortable arrogance and self-belief. The tyranny of the Houyhnhnms' reason lies in its very structure; it is unambiguous, pure, committed to absolute consensus, and devoid of any aspect of self-reflection. They have no word for pride precisely because they are unaware of the vanity and self-regard that allows their own discourse to take itself as definitive.

Gulliver is able to be gulled by this discourse precisely because he has always seen human tendencies and follies as objects of satire; he confidently separates himself, and reason, from the corruptions he views and satirises. He readily submits to a received voice of authority, and can do so because he never questions the value or possibility of authority – how it is that certain voices are instituted as rational and authoritative. It is Gulliver's submission to reason that discloses *both* a denial of his own complicity and humanity *and* a readiness to accept an external and inhuman voice in response to his misanthropy. What his travels *ought* to have taught him is that satire can have no fixed object; viewing the world, or worlds, from different perspectives, precludes one from *knowing* human nature. But Gulliver submits all too readily to a voice of reason that *knows* Yahoo/human nature definitively: 'I write for the noblest end, to inform and instruct mankind, over whom I may, without breach of modesty, pretend to some superiority from the advantages I received by conversing so long among the most accomplished Houyhnhnms' (Swift [1726] 1967, 342).

Gulliver's Travels moves from satire – where human bodies, vanities, judgements and conventions are described directly or allegorically – to irony. The final book on the Houyhnhnms and Yahoos no longer takes human nature as an *object*, but adopts a voice that would seek to set itself above humanity. Gulliver speaks as though he has heard the voice of an inhuman law, a reason *not* susceptible to the vanities he has witnessed in his travels. Far from offering a criticism or argument against reason (which would require the very language of reason), *Gulliver's Travels* displays the force of reason, or the way in which voices of rectitude, rationality, order, cleanliness and consensus can only assert their purity through the repression and extermination of the forces and tendencies that would disrupt reason.

Gulliver's Travels concludes with the voice of observation and reason becoming a hysterically violent anti-humanism, showing that the very belief in the possibility of a pure rationality must repress the body and its tendencies. Swift does not just satirise the violence and tyranny of reason. He diagnoses this repressive tendency as part of the human condition. *Gulliver's Travels* reflects incessantly on the enjoyment in observing, recounting and speculating about violence. There is a tendency, both observed and displayed by Gulliver, to loath the body, to recoil with disgust from the human condition. By presenting the pernicious effects of a politics directed to purity, and the absurdity of 'our' attempts to divorce ourselves from the body, Swift does not just *use* satire as a vehicle. The very style of satire – the capacity of human speech for invective, ridicule, disgust, distancing and elevation – is shown in both its positive effects and its risks. On the one hand, satire allows us to view the human condition: Gulliver's travels present him again and again with the follies of human vanity and endeavour – all the ways in which 'we' allow our bodily and particular desires to be dressed up as reason and knowledge. On the other hand, we also see the violent tendencies of the satirical impulse, the capacity for misanthropy and disgust that ultimately leads Gulliver into abandoning human speech and dialogue altogether (Rawson 1994, 41). We could say that Swift is both satirical – making human nature and society an object of derision – *and* ironic: speaking satirically but providing stylistic clues to indicate that Gulliver's disgust, for example, is *not* meant – for the text implies a position other than that of Gulliver, a position that views Gulliver's gullibility.

Swift's writing is certainly ironic in the pre-Romantic sense. Swift adopts a voice, such as the voice of the traveller who faithfully recounts what he has seen and learned, in order to show the limits of such a voice. It is because Gulliver is *so* faithful to what he observes that he loses all judgement. Gulliver dutifully accepts the Houyhnhnms' definition of reason – as true, unerring, unambiguous and non-contradictory – and from there concludes that the irrational (and disturbingly human) Yahoos ought to be exterminated or, at the very least, castrated. Swift repeats the voice of dutiful belief and commitment to finding the truth in order to show just how blind and unquestioning such an 'enlightened' observer might be. Gulliver, at the end of *Gulliver's Travels*, is clearly gullible. We *know* that Swift is *not* saying what Gulliver's tale proposes: that it would be rational to sympathise with the extermination of human life because of its moral corruption. So Swift uses irony, or the repetition of a certain image of reason, to demonstrate its absurd conclusions. But he can do so only because we view Gulliver as *not* what we ought to be thinking. Swift's irony is a rhetorical device directed *against* a certain identifiable type or structure of reason. So Swift's irony, or his use of voices and positions, has a target. Swift's satire is directed against those who feel they know the truth or reason of the human soul. Against the pure reason that

Gulliver adopts from the Houyhnhnms, where there is no disagreement, deceit, ambiguity, pride or sentimental attachments, Swift sets the noise of language and the desires, smells, passions and excrescence of the human body.

Irony can show the limits and blindness of reason, but this does not lead us to some ultimate principle. Irony can debunk our high ideals of reason and purity, but for Swift this only brings us back to human nature and its tendencies, its irrational attachments and uncontrollable tendencies. Whereas Romantic irony stresses human becoming and history, or the power of self-creation, Swift's pre-Romantic satire focuses on what resists reason and purpose: all those bodily and material tendencies that are neither creative nor productive, but often pointless and destructive (Boyle 2000, 35).

Whereas the Romantics saw irony, or the adoption of masks and voices, as the appropriate response to the difference and becoming of life, Swift's emphasis on human nature and the body suggests that there is an underlying *matter* or nature. Any attempt to think of a reason or culture which is purely civilised and self-creative, *without* being determined by the body, is precisely what *Gulliver's Travels* sets out to satirise. We can think of Romantic irony, then, as post-satirical. Swift still holds to a human nature, with a body and its tendencies; and he sees any belief in a reason that could free itself from this body as a dangerous illusion of purity. It is only by projecting corruption, error, embodiment and desire onto the Yahoos that the Houyhnhnms can erect a disembodied and timeless reason. Swift uses irony in the last book of *Gulliver's Travels* to present the tyranny of pure reason, but what this irony unwittingly discloses is reason's dependence on the body. Romantic irony, by contrast, presents the limit of reason; but what is other than reason is not the finite human body, but an infinite process of creation and difference.

IRONY AGAINST SATIRE: BYRON

Romantic irony, far from being reflective on the 'human' condition or body, far from having a resistant notion of 'man', suggests that life is nothing other than self-creation and becoming. Any voice or position is not the expression *of* a subject or the representation *of* a world; the 'subject' just is the process of expression or writing. This leads to two

broad interpretive possibilities, which we can see fleshed out in two dominant readings of Romanticism. The first, put forward most explicitly by
Anne Mellor, in *English Romantic Irony*, argues that Romantic irony
oscillates between the formed self in the world and the transcendental
process of life as de-formation. Byron's *Don Juan*, according to Mellor, is
Romantic because it presents the loving, believing and creating personality of Don Juan *and* the cynical, faithless and satirical persona of the
narrator (Mellor 1980, 49). The epic oscillates between the will to create
and give form, and the recognition that any such act of form will always
be overcome by the flux of life, chaos and history (ibid. 57). Romanticism
is ironic, for Mellor, precisely because it refuses all definition of man and
nature, recognising that any image we have of man is just that: an image.
Romantic irony would, then, be a way of understanding history; each
epoch and culture would be one more finite expression of the flow of life
(ibid. 73).

On the other hand, and in direct opposition to the de-politicising
definition of Romanticism as above and beyond any commitment to a
form or context, Jerome McGann has read Byron, Romanticism and
irony in terms of a quite specific context – with much more emphasis on
satire. McGann's *Romantic Ideology* (1983) attacked Mellor as typical
of a broader tendency in literary criticism whereby the manifest values of
romanticism are repeated in our own definitions of art as timeless and
happily apolitical. We should not, McGann insists, use Romanticism's
own theory of irony (or the 'Romantic ideology' that rejects all worldly
forms and definitions) to read and understand Romanticism. Rather, we
should see Romanticism *in context*, and see Byron's Romanticism as a
criticism of early Romantic irony's decontextualising gestures. *Don Juan*,
far from positing a receding creative principle that we can only view after
the event, commits itself to specific, material, located and worldly acts
of language. Byron is critical of a Romanticism that would elevate itself
above and beyond life. Most importantly, Byron turns back to the pre-
Romantic tradition of rhetoric and satire. By foregrounding the rules,
conventions and genres of classical rhetoric, Byron attacks the Romantic
ideal of a 'view from nowhere'. Far from being beyond the world, poetry
should be an ongoing event of worldly engagement. Irony is not, as it was
for the German Romantics, a transcendental principle of life that could
recognise itself only through its creations. Irony in Byron is a worldly

rhetorical tool, directed against those who would turn language into mere cant or mysticism.

Language, according to McGann, should be recognised as a social and political act – as a relation to other speakers, with a specific use and force. The Romantic and ironic ideal of an elevated and absent poet merely reinforces a fallen political condition. It is when language becomes detached from life, debate and action that it becomes vapid Romantic verse or unquestioning political cant. The key point of McGann's reading of Byron and Romanticism goes well beyond these specific issues and opens the question of the politics of irony and literary history.

The German Romantics, Coleridge, and many contemporary Romanticists regard the ironic position of elevation above context as the only possible ethics. Because there can be no final definition of 'man', poetry should present the creative and transcendental power of the imagination, a power that will always exceed any closed context or culture. In 'Kubla Khan' (1816) Coleridge presents an act of creation, the decree of a stately pleasure dome, and then the destruction of that creation; the lyric voice of the poem is not a character so much as an observer who views the dissolution of physical monuments and thereby presents itself as other than any fixed creation. The same applies to P.B. Shelley's 'Ozymandias' (1817), also a poem that presents a fragment of destroyed art and enables the poem to be other than the actual and limited object its describes. Wordsworth's *Prelude* (1805), more explicitly, adopts the voice or 'I' of the poem to describe his own life; but unlike Don Juan the character of the *Prelude* is not a physical self with qualities, tendencies and identifiable features so much as a capacity to observe and reflect upon the spirit or power of which he is an expression. Mellor's Romantic irony, which defines Romanticism as a creation of selves that also recognises a power of creativity irreducible to the self, fits such exemplary Romantic poems perfectly. Poems are Romantic if they affirm a life above and beyond any specific or finite expression. According to McGann, this is just the problem; we define irony through an unreflective notion of Romanticism and then hail as typical only those poems that fit the paradigm. By contrast, McGann argues that we should see this appeal to a pre-contextual 'life' as the effect of a specific context: the failure of concrete political revolutions prompted the Romantics to mystify the human condition, creating an inner paradise in the absence of worldly hope. We should not affirm Romanticism on its own terms; we need to see it in context and *as* a context. This is precisely what Byron, according to McGann, managed to do. To celebrate a Romantic irony of ineffable subjectivity is to merely repeat Romanticism's own political failure, a failure Byron was already satirising.

There are two ways to understand context and its limits. McGann insists on what he refers to as a speech-act theory of contexts. We can only speak, act and have a social world because of shared conventions; any attempt to think outside those conventions would itself be a move within a context, and would be recognised as other than conventional only from the point of view of convention. We can challenge a language, discourse or context, but we do this not by leaping outside a context or appealing to some ineffable and ironic 'beyond' but by reflecting upon, diagnosing and speaking about our context and other contexts: this is the point of Byron's *Don Juan* which ranges across history, genre and locality (McGann 1968, 288). Against the use of 'romanticism' as a label to cover everything from Jane Austen (1775–1817) to Blake, McGann suggests that we should ask how the very idea of the 'Romantic' has been used to mystify a range of texts and their social emergence. Against Mellor, and the American twentieth-century construction of Romanticism as a general and apolitical body of poems, McGann refuses to see Byron as intimating a general flux, chaos or fluidity beyond defined terms and contexts. Rather, *Don Juan* is the presentation of various contexts, ranging from contemporary political rhetoric and poetry to myth and history.

Far from irony being the sense of some transcendental 'beyond', McGann insists on Byron's irony as thoroughly *human* (McGann 1968, 290). Whether there be any transcendental power or not, all we have are human contexts and specific speech acts. Byron's irony does not detach itself from life and the human world; it shows the force of different styles and contexts in relation to each other (Garber 1988, 209). *Reading* literary history should, according to McGann, not take on the Romantic elevated point of view that looks at the timeless creative spirit. It should look at how speech works in contexts: what words and texts mean in relation to each other, and the social acts with which they are contiguous, including the European revolutions which marked the nineteenth century and the local parliamentary issues of Byron's own time.

The problem with McGann's politicising of Romantic irony lies in his commitment to context. We should not, he rightly insists, see Romantic irony as *the* truth of all literature, such that we take the Romantic ideal of a timeless imagination and use it to avoid all questions of what poems do, and the local contexts they criticise and serve. But in order to criticise the Romantic ideology, McGann himself has to appeal to a general theory of language – language as politically effective and forceful *act* of exchange and communication. It is as though McGann wants to turn back from Romanticism – the epoch that recognised all historical periods as located within a flow of creative and destructive time, with language as an almost mystical medium – and retreat to an eighteenth-century understanding of *man*, when human life was nothing more than its political and worldly relations. McGann explicitly favours Byron and Byron's own celebration of the tradition of Augustan satire, particularly Alexander Pope (1688–1744): a tradition that itself had turned back to Cicero and the notion of language as public and political engagement. Cicero himself had, as we have seen, already regarded Socrates as a 'fall': with Socrates, language and philosophy become disengaged reflection rather than active and involved praxis. Cicero's engaged and contextually aware rhetoric was already an appeal to a more integrated and engaged model of language and theory; it was already dependent upon a loss of origin. There was a time – this narrative of the fall suggests – when language was not a mystical and uncontrollable force, but a self-conscious political action whose effects we could manage and negotiate. The Romantic awareness of language as the outgrowth of a creative process that can only be known after the effect creates an ineffable origin beyond conscious political decisions and contexts. McGann's appeal to Byron as an engaged and social satirist, rather than a Romantic poet aware of 'language', has to place itself and the texts it reads within a specific historical narrative, and it has to lament a certain point in that narrative: the point at which a contextual or political understanding of language is lost. Once 'we' have become ironic in the Romantic sense – recognising that any definition of the human can never exhaust just who or what the human *is* – then it is difficult to turn back to a determined notion of the human. But this is just what any criticism of Romantic irony, such as McGann's, seems forced to do.

On the one hand, we might want to acknowledge the force of McGann's critique. By elevating the creative imagination or spirit as a forming power, Romantic irony does not allow for historical difference: all contexts become examples of the productive power of 'life'. But McGann's reference of these contexts *back* to human language is also a transcendental gesture; instead of being outgrowths of the imagination texts are events within the context of human language, where man is defined as a political animal. McGann's criticism of Romantic irony leads to a double bind. McGann is rightly critical of the universalising and de-historicising effects of Romantic irony. The elevation of *poiesis* as *the* process that creates historical epochs, discourses and contexts posits some ultimate but unrepresentable condition; what the Romantics do not question is the political and historical location of their own explanation of history. McGann therefore refuses the transcendental strivings of Romantic irony. Romanticism's attempt to feel, imagine or intuit what lies beyond representation can never detach itself from a context of representation. The problem with McGann's anti-transcendentalism is, however, that 'context' becomes one more transcendental condition. Not only must McGann himself use a narrative to explain context – he refers to language as a system of conventions grounded in human action – he also privileges a certain norm of language. Language explained contextually is a language of purpose, communication, recognition and convention. What has to be excluded from a contextual explanation of language are all those linguistic features and events that have no basis in praxis – the accidental, unconventional, singular or incoherent forces of a language. It was precisely this dimension of language – what is beyond *both* self-conscious intention *and* purposive and creative life, which was the focus of Derrida's deconstruction.

5

IRONY OUT OF CONTEXT
Derrida, Nietzsche and de Man

POST-STRUCTURALISM: DERRIDA

One of the great achievements of Jacques Derrida's post-structuralism was its capacity to forge a path between these two styles of irony: a satirical irony that attacks the conventions of a specific context, and a broader Romantic or transcendental irony that aims to think beyond context. Derrida acknowledges *both* that each speech act is always located, specific and never detached from the forces of the world – never fully transcendental or pure. At the same time, certain located speech acts *within a context* can prompt us to think the very emergence or creation of contexts. One of Derrida's most well-known examples is the concept of writing (Derrida 1974). This concept seems to have been repressed or marginalised in western thought, but Derrida argues that this is for essential and necessary reasons. There is an irreducible tension at the heart of the very relation between writing and thinking. One cannot reduce meaning or truth to the physical script which allows that truth to be transmitted; nor can one think of truth or sense without some system of differences. Writing is necessary both for truth and meaning, but also precludes the possibility of a *pure* truth or meaning. Philosophers privilege pure concepts and logic and are suspicious of the ways in which writing, or any form of copying technology, can detach words from their origin and allow them to circulate without their original sense.

Derrida's earliest work examined the origins of geometry and was critical of reducing the truth of sciences to their merely written symbol, for the truths of mathematics remain true regardless of their context or the signs used to convey the sense of these truths through time (Derrida 1989a). But Derrida also insisted that one can only have a science or pure reason through some system of writing; logic cannot be reduced to writing but it cannot be freed from it either. Further, this context or system of mathematical truth prompts us to think what is true in general, what must remain true *regardless of context*. For this reason, writing becomes a double concept in Derrida. On the one hand it refers to actual writing in the form of marks, script, texts and material symbols, and in this sense all speech and thought is marked by some specific and actual writing; all thought must take place in some physical context. On the other hand, there is a more general writing, for we can only have specific texts, systems and marks through the possibility of writing in general: we can think or imagine other systems, other languages and other contexts only because we have this concept of writing as such that is not reducible to this or that instance of writing.

All those features that we normally attribute to language and writing – writing as a system of differences without any stable ground, end or limit – characterise experience in general. To experience something *as something* it must be marked out, determined, located or identified. This requires some system or marks of traces that enables a perceiver to see perceptions, in all their flux and difference, as somehow the same through time. All experience, then, must give form to the world or synthesise the world, but it can only do this through some pre-given system such as language or concepts. All thinking must, therefore, both inhabit a context but also be *more* than any context. For Derrida this enables a new approach to politics, where politics is not the gathering of persons in a common context. We need to see any manifest political context as the effect of a multiplicity of forces, forces that will have effects beyond any recognised and intended context; this in turn expands the domain of responsibility and how we can read a text. For we can now attend to all those forces and effects that are unintended and which destabilise contexts. In the following passage Derrida answers John Searle, who had attacked deconstruction for its attempt to consider language out of context:

> We said: *independently of all determinable contexts.* Does one have the right to read like this? No, certainly not, if one wishes to imagine a sentence or a mark in general without any context, and readable as such. This never occurs and the law remains unbreachable. But for the same reason, a context is never absolutely closed, constraining, determined, completely filled. A structural opening allows it to transform itself or to give way to another context. This is why every mark has a force of detachment, which not only can free it from such and such a determined context, but ensures even its principle of intelligibility and its mark structure – that is, its *iterability* (repetition *and* alteration). A mark that could not in any way detach itself from its singular context – however slightly and, if only through repetition, reducing, dividing and multiplying it by identifying it – would no longer be a mark.
>
> (Derrida 1988, 216)

We must understand the signs or marks of our language not just as physical tokens but as *signs of* some present and coherent world. For this reason, Derrida remarks, we must work with a necessary but impossible distinction between the ironic and the non-ironic (Derrida 1988, 114). For a language to work as a language, I have to accept that its signs *intend* some meaning or sense that is not the sign itself. I have to have some idea of a proper sense, which we would all recognise, and which is more than or in excess of the sign itself. I have to assume a common and sincere meaning that would remain stable across different uses. There could be no such thing as a *language* without a notion of proper meaning. At the same time, any such proper meaning is necessarily absent, anticipated and deferred. Writing and language, therefore, are always structured by the problem of irony: we must have both a secure contextual sense *and* understand any specific use of a word or concept as having a force beyond the present context. A word can only have meaning, or work in a context, if I recognise its continued sense beyond what is said here and now. Language is not something that we make up as we go along; it must have a pre-existing order, but each conversation also alters and defers that order.

The ironic implications of Derrida's work are summarised in one of his key ideas: necessary impossibility. Derrida's deconstruction works, on the one hand, with the necessity of language as law and system. In order to speak or intend, our utterances and experiences must be submitted to some law. This is necessary, for there would be no being, presence or reality without this commitment to identity or *what is*, above and beyond singular differences. On the other hand, such lawfulness is never achieved and is strictly impossible. Each inscription of a lawful language is particular, and each instance of a concept fails to fulfil the concept in general. Like Socratic irony, then, Derrida's deconstruction is both committed to the necessity and lawfulness of concepts, and aware that no contingent use or definition can speak for the totality of the concept. We might also say, then, that language is necessarily fallen: never at one with the origin or presence it seeks to name. But we might also see this positively, and this is where deconstruction differs from the negative accounts of language that preceded it. We can only have the notion of the origin or the presence that lies before language from the productions of language. It is only with the notion of language *as fallen from presence* – only with the process of language as mourning – that an 'original' presence is effected (Derrida 1989a, 37). Derrida recognises the productive impossibility of his own position. One of Derrida's ancestors in the destruction of presence was Friedrich Nietzsche, who saw truth as a particularly persuasive fiction: 'Truths are illusions which we have forgotten are illusons' (Nietzsche [1873] 1979, 84). And it is by moving beyond Nietzsche, and Nietzsche's irony, that Derrida also allowed for an affirmative dimension of deconstruction.

NIETZSCHE

All language, Nietzsche recognised, is other than the thing itself. In 'On Truth and Lies in a Non-Moral Sense', Nietzsche describes the sense impression of a leaf, which is then translated into an image and which is then again referred to the concept 'leaf' (Nietzsche [1873] 1979). By the time we get to the word there has already been a series of unjustifiable 'leaps'. Literal or original language is merely a metaphor or figure that has repressed the ways in which it produces, rather than names, the stability of concepts. Nietzsche, however, was caught in a paradoxical position. To say that language is *not* the thing itself, or is *not* literal – even to say that language can never be truth – still allows for some ultimate truth or presence which language fails to grasp. Indeed, Nietzsche's explanation of the emergence of the fiction of truth both presents itself *as true* and gives a highly physical and literal explanation – just the sort of final scientific authority Nietzsche is criticising: 'To begin with a nerve stimulus is transferred into an image: first metaphor. The image, in turn, is imitated in a sound: second metaphor. And each time there is a complete overleaping of one sphere, right into the middle of an entirely new and different one' (Nietzsche [1873] 1979, 82). Nietzsche explains the emergence of metaphor as a departure from 'nerve stimulus'. All language, he insists, is other than the thing itself, other than the truth. But he wants to present this frozen or fixed 'image' – this illusion of truth – *as* illusory, as other than the pure world. To say that there is no truth itself becomes a truth, and to continue speaking of language as *metaphorical* or other than the real chaos of life, still places some reality outside language. Nietzsche dealt with this paradox in a number of ways, one of which was to write ironically. Nietzsche's irony was not the Romantic irony of celebrating the creative self above and beyond any of its created forms. Nietzsche's irony attempted to affirm the forces of life and will that extended beyond any creative self. He may not have been able to name or speak about the forces that lay beyond language and the human viewpoint, but by writing aphorisms, contradictory observations, retractions and manifestly absurd histories he showed that language was not master of itself.

A key example was Nietzsche's use of history and scholarship. His *Birth of Tragedy* (1872) recounts how the spontaneous and active Greek imagination of the tragic theatre 'fell' into a rationalising, parasitic and dissecting intellect: 'let us imagine a culture without a secure and sacred primal site, condemned to exhaust every possibility and feed wretchedly on all other cultures – there we have our present age, the product of that Socratism bent on the destruction of myth' (Nietzsche [1872] 1993, 110). The problem, however, is that writing a history of this fall from primal life into rationality itself deploys all those means of argument and rationality it would denounce. Nietzsche's histories were ironic precisely through these contradictions. Indeed, Nietzsche referred to them as 'genealogies'. Instead of believing that there is a past that one can narrate, one recognises that any past is traced back from the present. One should, therefore, write histories that destroy, rather than stabilise, truth. In the *Genealogy of Morals* (1887), for example, Nietzsche describes the origin of truth: truth was invented by those who were simply too weak to affirm their will *as will*. The *Genealogy* therefore offers itself as the truth of truth, as the paradoxical claim that if we look at the past honestly and without all the deceptions of morality, we will perceive an 'original' will to deceive (Nietzsche [1887] 1969a, 150–1). Far from being embarrassed by such contradictions Nietzsche's aphorisms maximise conflict (Kofman 1993). One cannot *say* that there is no such thing as truth without involving oneself in contradiction. But the style of contradiction can itself be employed in order to show, if not state, that any true world – any world that supposedly does not conflict with what we say – can only be produced through a repression of the force and will of language. According to the Yale school critic Paul de Man (1919–83), this leads Nietzsche beyond a critique of the subject to a critique of the performative: the self that precedes and governs language is an illusion, but the idea of language as *act*, as something that is done, performed or controlled is no less illusory. For the very distinction between self and world, active and passive, act and effect is produced through language:

> By calling the subject a text, the text calls itself, to some extent, a subject. The lie is raised to a new figural power, but it is nonetheless a lie. By asserting in the mode of truth that the self is a lie, we have not escaped from deception. We have merely reversed the usual scheme which derives truth from the convergence of self and other by showing that the fiction of such a convergence is used to allow for the illusion of selfhood to originate.
>
> (de Man 1979, 12)

Nietzsche's irony was also crucial in attacking one of the concepts that had been central to the definition of Romantic irony: the concept of the subject. The Romantics had argued that the notion of the subject was unavoidable and impossible. Any event of speech or writing, any experience, presupposes that there is a subject *who* speaks, writes or perceives. If we have a world of forces and relations, then there must be some ground or subject – or some point of view – who brings these forces into relation and into a perceivable world. Nietzsche, by contrast, argued that the subject was an effect of force. It is not that there are subjects who *then* synthesise the various forces of life and becoming into an organised world. Rather, there are forces and fluxes that, through collision and conflict, create subject positions. The subject, for Nietzsche, was an effect of grammar. The will, in all its human and inhuman forms – what Nietzsche referred to as will to power – is an eternal or boundless site of force and conflict. Certain forces produce points of relative stability. Language, for example, is a mode of force, life and action that produces regularities. By speaking in propositions it takes the flux of life and orders it into subjects and predicates. Instead of thinking of pure actions – dancing, for example – our language creates a subject *who* dances. Poetry, and other forms of non-propositional writing, aim to disengage thinking from the logic and politics of the subject. Instead of imagining that there is some ultimate human or subjective ground which then engages in action and conflict, Nietzsche insists that there are just contrary forces *from which* we assume some preceding subject (Nietzsche [1887] 1969a, 119). We should use language ironically, being aware that it creates an illusion of relative stability. But we should not think that there is a truer world *behind or before* language, for it is only through language that we can have any priority of before and after, original and secondary, literal and figurative, subject and predicate.

DECONSTRUCTION AND AFFIRMATION: DERRIDA

Derrida, similarly, but in quite different ways, also performs, rather than states, the limits of truth. Nietzsche saw metaphysics as the means by which weak wills enslave the strong. Socrates' genius lay in this production of a style of speech that presented itself, *not as a style*, but as a selfless presentation of the truth. In effacing itself, or in presenting himself as absolutely selfless, Socrates produced one of the most powerful forms of self: 'The moralism of the Greek philosophers from Plato downwards is pathologically conditioned: likewise their estimation of dialectics. Reason = virtue = happiness means merely: one must imitate Socrates and counter the dark desires by producing a permanent *daylight* – the daylight of reason' (Nietzsche [1889] 1968, 33). Nietzsche's own project was both to admire and reverse this strangely self-denying 'will to truth'. And this could only be done by producing a style other than that of true discourse, such as the masks, aphorisms, genealogies and fictions of Nietzsche's own work. In *Thus Spoke Zarathustra* ([1891] 1969b) Nietzsche writes an almost novelistic narrative, with the central 'character' Zarathustra being an enigmatic figure of magisterial pronouncements rather than a coherent psychological type. By creating characters and voices, rather than a reasoned argument, Nietzsche presents forces of language that cannot be reduced to reason or some pre-linguistic truth. Derrida, by contrast, recognises that while 'truth' or concepts such as presence may have emerged from will and rhetoric they can, once produced, have an extra-rhetorical ethical force or power. The concept of reason, for example, may have a specific textual and technical history but, once such a concept emerges, it can enable us to think of that which lies beyond all textuality and determined history. Derrida himself produces what he refers to as an 'aconceptual' concept – *différance* – which names that process of producing names, a process which is both unnameable and unconceptualisable (Derrida 1982, 7).

Whereas concepts strive to give a sameness of sense thorough time and across differences, *différance* tries to name that which is always singular, non-identical and incapable of being sustained in any general identity. Derrida often seizes on how a text's differential features work against what it wants to say. A famous example is analysis of *pharmakon* in the dialogues of Plato, where the word refers both to cure and poison. Now, a common-sense reading would suggest that we sort out such conflicts of meaning by reference to context. It seems perverse to look at what a word *can also* mean when one meaning or another is clearly what the author wants to say. It would be perverse or an act of wilful misunderstanding for you to read all my mentions of the author 'Swift' as also having the meaning of swift as an adjective (as fast); it is purely accidental that in English this author and this adjective share the same sound and mark. Such accidents are effects of difference, or the physical features of a language that we do not intend. But by focusing on just these accidents, such as the ways in which *pharmakon* refers both to cure and poison, Derrida can look at the relations a text produces, the forces and connections it allows, and then ask *why* and *how* we decide *not* to read this way. There is always an excess to the meaning of a text; *différance* refers to those marks which enable us to speak and write, but which also go beyond and disrupt sense.

We might say that *différance*, or the production of specific differences, has the power to create concepts but is itself always belied by any concept. Before there can be a concept – a sense of that which remains the same – there must be the tracing or marking out of the same, some *differentiation* of what is or remains present:

> there is no life present *at first* which would *then* come to protect, postpone, or reserve itself in *différance*. The latter constitutes the essence of life. Or rather: as *différance* is not an essence, as it is not anything, it *is not* life . . . Life must be thought of as trace before Being may be determined as presence . . . It is thus the delay which is in the beginning . . . To defer (*différer*) thus cannot mean to retard a present possibility, to postpone an act, to put off a perception already now possible. That possibility is possible only through a *différance* which must be conceived of in other terms than those of a calculus or mechanics of decision. To say that *différance* is originary is simultaneously to erase the myth of a present origin. Which is why 'originary' must be understood as having been *crossed out*, without which *différance* would be derived from an original plentiude. It is a non-origin which is originary.
>
> (Derrida 1978, 203)

Here, Derrida uses the concept of origin – what exists first – in order to destroy or 'cross out' the idea of origin: if we ask what is truly original, then we are forced to think of a process of dividing, delaying and differentiating. Derrida's method might be construed as both ironic and counter-ironic. He uses a concept, such as origin, but in such a way as to render that concept impossible. To begin with, he insists that deconstruction is not a method. Rather than adopting a position of reading outside or before a text, Derrida himself inhabits or ventriloquises the text in order – like Socrates – to allow a position's limits to be revealed from the position itself. An example is his criticism of structuralism. If it is the case that meaning is produced through a structure or system of differences, then the very concept of structure will itself be an effect of difference and cannot be used to explain difference. From its own point of view, then, structuralism is impossible; its own acknowledgement of the production of meaning – that meaning is produced through a structure – itself relies on a structure. What structuralism cannot explain is how structures emerge; it can explain this or that structure, but not 'the structurality of structure' (Derrida 1978, 280). It must always use one structured term to account for the emergence of structures. Further, like the sophist, the structuralist may try to avoid metaphysical commitment to ultimate concepts, foundations or truth; she might insist that all we can have are languages or systems without any grounding term. Against this, Derrida shows how structure itself becomes one more elevated concept or origin, one more metaphysical ground that explains and reduces the force of concepts (Derrida 1978, 26).

Derrida takes the ironic method further, and beyond, the traditional ironic or Socratic technique of insisting on the implied truths and commitments of his opponents. There might be another thought of structure *as text*. Here, instead of seeing various systems within which thought is located, we might imagine a dynamic, mobile, playful and decentred structurality or *différance*. Reading a text would not be about discerning its oppositions, system or values; it would look to all those unintended, accidental, inhuman – but nevertheless *productive* – moments that exceed all organisation or active intent. Texts have a force beyond their intent. Beyond what they want to represent, mean or communicate – the constative – texts also produce effects or 'perform', and this is due to their textual condition (Derrida 1978, 292).

Instead of seeing structures as systems that enable meaning and limited contexts, Derrida looks at the ways in which structures can produce unintended conceptual forces. The concept of reason, for example, may have a specific history – and reason may have been used repressively and for particular intentions. Nevertheless, the very concept of reason – the idea of what must remain true regardless of who speaks or from what position – is also what allows us to challenge any closed structure or context (Derrida 1978, 58). That is, a context is 'closed' if we simply accept it as the system of signs and conventions within which we think and speak; a context can be 'opened' if we acknowledge that the conditions that make a context meaningful, such as the signs of a language, are not themselves meaningful or capable of being decided from *within* a context. We could, for example, have a discussion about the relative merits of human rights, but the discussion could also be opened if we began to interrogate the very concept of the human – whether we can think in ways which do not presuppose a common humanity. We could also try and explain the concept of reason by looking at its definitions in various contexts, but we could also appeal to an ideal of reason that could open a context: is this context, this language, this way of thinking *reasonable*? Such a question asks us to think of reason beyond any specific context or structure. We could always open a structure by asking: *is it rational? Ought we to think this way?* The context or closed system of a language therefore allows us to think what lies beyond or exceeds any closed context.

Différance – as a non-concept or aconceptual concept – takes this even further. Derrida also looks at the non-meaningful effects of texts. Not only must any discourse or concept adopt a specific tone or material voice, such tonalities can also disrupt or solicit a text. Imagine that a philosopher uses a word with an intended sense, such as the concept of communication. She might want to argue that all language is communication: the meaningful, intentional and active exchange of signs for the purpose of a common understanding and consensus. But 'communication' also has other senses; we can speak of the communication of vibrations or tremors across space, or the communication of passageways or viruses. Today, when we talk of communications we also refer to flows of data or signs that are never read and have no human intention: think of all the networks of exchange and data that are processed without any monitoring or sense. There can be communications that are undecidably poised between both senses: when viruses are communicated from one computer to another, when we speak of diseases being communicated, we would seem to be referring to a sense of communication which had nothing to do with language. But Derrida insists that language often does communicate in this way; texts circulate, are reprinted, copied, and contaminated in ways that produce senses and meanings that are unintended. Any philosopher who tried to talk of communication in a purely human and intended sense would have to eliminate all the suggestions, connotations or tremors produced by the word communication; she would have to rely on the word *not* communicating other senses. But, as Derrida so frequently insists, if we are to use a word successfully, if it is to be meaningful and understood by others, then it must have a force beyond our private intent; it must already be capable of distribution beyond any single point of control. Once we inhabit a structure we are bound not just to the identities and meanings produced by structure, but also to its accidental, unintended and productive effects.

It may seem that one of the consequences of Derrida's emphasis on *différance*, or those radically singular forces that act before all intent and identity, and before any conceivable notions of a 'before' and 'after', would be a total dissolution of all notions of personal and political responsibility. The contrary is actually the case. Contextual accounts of meaning focus on the ways in which speech acts are grounded in common human expectations. Derrida, however, insists on looking at the ways contexts themselves are both generated and destabilised through the very sign systems that make them possible. We can only have a shared context through some system of language, and such a system must necessarily transcend the intent of any single speaker. The structure of signs that makes intention possible is itself irreducible to intention and has its own communicative force – the effects of which can be neither controlled nor determined in advance. Far from reducing the world to mere 'play', Derrida's insistence on textuality actually intensifies both political and personal responsibility. Because a context has a specific force we cannot simply accept 'the' political as the common arena of human speech. We need to look at all the effects and forces that are *not* intended.

Consider, for example, the key concepts of democratic discourse: concepts of autonomy, activity, reason, self-determination and right. It may well be that when we use this discourse we have thoroughly open, ethical and inclusive intentions. But it is also the case that such words have a textual and systemic history that we cannot control. Can the notion of the detached rational subject of democracy be divorced from values associated specifically with white Western man? Is the idea of a reason that must eliminate all ambiguity, partiality and difference not tied to a specific *political* community? Such determinations of political discourse are unavoidable, for we could never speak from some position devoid of force, but we also need to acknowledge all the ways in which ethical discourse produces divisions, determinations and hierarchies.

Not only, then, does Derrida's emphasis on the forces that lie beyond context intensify political responsibility, it also foregrounds the responsibility of any decision. Derrida insists that a decision is undecidable. If there were some ground, rationale or determination for a decision – such as a context that allowed us to *know* what we ought to do – then we would not really be making a decision. Because of textual undecidability, all our decisions are singular: 'there is no other decision than this one: decision in the matter and form of the undecidable' (Derrida 1997, 219).

Not only does this heighten personal responsibility, by impelling us to consider the force of what we decide, it also increases the power of irony and interpretation. We cannot decide the meaning of a text on the basis of some context, for we would still have to decide *which* context we were using *and* just what that context itself meant. Far from irony being a special case of meaning that departs from stable contextual recognition, we would have to say that all language must mean more than it says, must always exceed the simple determinations of context. Whereas ironic texts seem to foreground the difference between the stable use of language in a context and the ironic uses which are contrary to recognised meaning, Derrida's deconstruction insists on looking at the way in which *any* text has a force to disrupt what we take to be stable and decided. All meaning is potentially ironic. It is always possible to ask of *any* text or utterance: what is it *really* saying (regardless of intent or origin)? In so doing, deconstruction intensifies and criticises the Socratic critique of sophistry. A concept is always more than its accepted definition; it can always be questioned, and used to solicit a context. But the supposed meaning of a concept that would lie beyond the context is always generated from contexts.

One of the main effects of Derrida's emphasis on textuality is that, far from the world being seen as an effect or construction of language, we recognise that there are forces of differentiation and implication well beyond the speaking subject. Language is not a structure of *meanings*, so much as a mobile, complex and productive text: creating effects of presence, sense and reference. At the same time, one can never speak or write from a position of pure play; some position of sense or decision will always be produced in any engagement with a text. The subject of speech and interpretation is, therefore, a necessary effect (rather than a transcendental ground) of textuality.

ALLEGORY AND IRONY: PAUL DE MAN

The key implications of Derridean post-structuralism for poetry and irony were spelled out by Paul de Man, one of the Yale school theorists who re-read Romantic poetry in the light of deconstruction. At first glance it might seem that de Man is a far more conservative thinker than Derrida, particularly in his commitment to irony (Gearhart 1983, 77). Derrida's main objection to structuralism was its linguisticism; far from thinking difference radically, structuralism merely explained differences as effects of some general and homogenous system of signs. Against this, Derrida looked at texts in terms other than those of signification. The force of a text is not just its sense – the meaning that we must assume it intends – but connections, connotations and productions that are unintended.

De Man's emphasis on literature and the inescapability of irony would seem to fall back into a Romantic notion that language is a subjective medium, and that we can only think what is other than language from some ironic awareness within language. But this would deny de Man's stress on the concomitant impossibility and necessity of irony. On the one hand, irony does seem to expose the naivete of an 'allegorical' account of language: the idea that our language seems to double or correspond to some world. On the other hand, any self-conscious irony that felt it could step outside all allegorical illusion by seeing the world and self as an effect of text and language would itself be subject to a far greater illusion. There can be no point of ironic self-destruction – where 'we' realise that our identity and our world are textually produced. Any such realisation would have to *repress* a necessary allegory. This would not be a naive allegory that posited a real world behind signs, but an allegory that recognised that all we can do is to write allegorically. To write, or narrate, is necessarily to produce a gap or distance between a text and what it signifies. At the same time, this signified or referent is only given from the position of the signifier or text. Our nature is always an inscribed and textual nature; our identity is always a type of character or fiction. Without the function of allegory – without the narrated or imagined difference between a world and its symbolisation – there could be no ironic self-realisation. We can never arrive at some point of pure ironic self-coincidence, where we see ourselves and our world as mere textual effects. For we can only think ironically *after* the creation of ourselves through allegory, or through the imagined difference between a literal world and a signified world.

The problem or difference of allegory and irony relies on the irreducible function of narration. On the one hand, there can be no world, self or experience without some allegorical narration: some sense of signs as being other than or different from an original reality. On the other hand, one can also recognise – ironically – that this supposedly original and unattainable reality can only be perceived *as original* through some narrative that produces itself as allegorical, as *not* the thing itself. De Man's emphasis on literature and irony, rather than philosophy and reflection, is crucial here. Philosophy would see language as a medium for reflection; we can speak in order to recognise ourselves as above and beyond the signs we use. Literature, by contrast, abandons this aim of circular self-coincidence. Any language we might use to reflect upon and know ourselves actually produces the self it supposedly names, and does so through narration – through naming what *must have been*.

For de Man, time is not a coherent medium of a before and after that we then name (and then reflect upon ironically). Time is given or distributed through narration. Only with the minimal narration of a past and self who will speak could there be the essential function of allegory of signs being different from the world – and the no less essential but impossible irony that strives to think this narration:

> Irony divides the flow of temporal experience into a past that is pure mystification and a future that remains harassed forever by a relapse within the inauthentic. It can know this inauthenticity but can never overcome it. It can only restate and repeat it on an increasingly conscious level, but it remains endlessly caught in the impossibility of making this knowledge applicable to the empirical world . . . Allegory and irony are thus linked in their common discovery of a truly temporal predicament.
>
> (de Man 1983, 222)

In Paul de Man's terms: it is only through narrating the self that there is a self at all. We cannot think of selves *who narrate*, precisely because selves are formed through narration. But we could also never arrive at a 'theory' of this process of narration: 'any theory of irony is the undoing, the necessary undoing, of any theory of narrative, and it is ironic, as we say, that irony always comes up in relation to theories of narrative, when irony is precisely what makes it impossible ever to achieve a theory of narrative that would be consistent' (de Man 1996, 179). To think of the self as created *through* narrative is itself narrative. De Man turns back to Romantic irony and gives it a post-structuralist twist. The spirit or imagination that is belied by any of its forms or definitions is created through those secondary definitions. For de Man, only literature can be authentic (Gearhart 1983, 80); only literature acknowledges that it creates through narrative, rather than presenting narrative as the representation of some mythical prior reality. Romantic irony is, therefore, all-consuming. Any attempt to think a position or self outside literary voices must itself adopt *some* literary style. Philosophers, historians or scientists who speak with an authority that is supposedly above and beyond stylistic variations have merely repressed the stylistic dimension of their own discourse.

De Man's elevation of literature, as the only authentic rhetoric of temporality – because it reflects on the way it produces a before and after, an origin and fall, an authentic and inauthentic voice – is also an insistence on the impossibility *and inescapability* of the subject. To assume that subjects are effects of forces is to disavow and repress the subjective activity – the narration – that explains those forces. At the same time, while we can only think and criticise our thinking from some subjective point of view, that 'subject' is an effect of narration. While the modern lyric seeks to reflect upon and destroy this narrative illusion of the subject, by turning back on itself and describing the process of its own creation, de Man nevertheless insists that one cannot escape this condition of impossible irony and allegory. De Man maintains, extends and criticises the German Romantic tradition. He recognises the ethical and political predicament of Romanticism – that its gesture to a pre-subjective absolute does seem to abandon our responsibility or our role in the creation of this absolute. But he also recognises that ethical authenticity – the attempt to take control of the ways in which our narratives produce us and our origins – must always be contaminated by inauthenticity. We write and think belatedly, from a textual condition we can neither master nor abandon. The attempt to think beyond the ethical dilemmas of Romanticism would need, therefore, to think beyond the logic of authenticity and originality. It may be that the pre-linguistic origin is an effect of language and narration, and can therefore never be grasped. But does this mean that we should remain in a position of necessary impossibility or ironic finitude? Perhaps we need to think beyond irony and the questions of originality and subjectivity.

6

SATIRE AND THE LIMITS OF IRONY

From Byron and Swift to Butler

One might want to object that just because we cannot *think* or *speak about* what lies beyond style and language, or just because we cannot think outside our own historical context, this does not mean that there is not something – some reality or matter – that underlies history and language. We might want to say that Romantic irony makes the mistake of seeing the thought and expression of the world as exhaustive of the world. For the ironic tradition has always regarded what lies outside language as created through language; what is other than the speaking subject is nevertheless known only in its relation to subjectivity or in its potential to become known by the subject. There is no radically meaningless or purely objective outside. For Plato's Socrates, everyday language is transcended by *ideas*, so what is other than human speech is nevertheless an idea, form, concept or essence. For the Romantics, what precedes subjectivity and speech is nevertheless a creative, active and constituting process – known only as *other than* the subject position it engenders.

THE LIMITS OF LANGUAGE

Irony from Socrates to Romanticism is critical of theoretical knowledge: a knowledge that would simply be given or viewed, without the knower being implicated in the articulation of that truth. Irony draws attention to the gap between saying and said, between speaking position and posited truth. Those who feel that they simply *know* the ultimate truths of life have forgotten or repressed their own location and position *within* life. Instead of a style of speech that simply asserts the truth, Socratic and Romantic irony emphasised the processes of dialogue, thinking and expression from which truths are given.

One tendency in irony is its criticism of *knowledge and authority*. The world is not something there to be known and represented by already existing subjects; subjects and world are created through the activities of speech and writing. However, we could also say that this emphasis on the *creation* and *production* of truth once again returns us to some ultimate authority. In Romantic irony it is poetry, literature or creativity that is posited as the productive principle from which any position or voice emerges. In order, then, to think beyond irony and its elevation of creation as the truth of life, we might need to step outside its metaphors of activity, production, generation, writing and expression. There has been a long-standing tradition critical of the elevation of irony, a tradition going back to Cicero that emphasises the locatedness of speech. Far from ideas or concepts existing in some realm above human speech, the tradition of satire emphasises the meaningless, material and inessential emergence of ideas from life. While irony insists on a sense or 'said' behind what we 'say', satire points to the meaningless conditions of speech: all those experiences that are not yet organised into concepts or ideals. To begin with, we can look at how satire debunks all the high ideals of rational human aspiration, and this is certainly how Swift uses the mode of satire. But we can also see how, after the intensity of Romantic irony, many writers try to work with both the satirical and the ironic tendencies.

Byron's *Don Juan* used irony to criticise Romanticism and Romantic irony. Byron's irony was satirical precisely because he retained the classical notion of irony as an identifiable figure with a specific contextual force. Byron quoted and parodied distinct styles and genres, and his attention was directed to historically specific contexts – rather than a general notion of 'life'. Further, Byron's use of irony had a clear object: the philosophical or metaphysical tendency to speak as if one were elevated above the forces of this world. While irony in the Romantic sense stresses an ineffable or immaterial creative principle that can only be recognised through its effects and productions, the satirical irony of the Augustans to which Byron appealed tended to focus more on man and human nature: on all those aspects of bodily and human life which contaminate reason, freedom and creation. Whereas the early Romantics had emphasised poetry as creation, freedom, fluidity and expression, Byron played up all those aspects of poetry that were *resistant* to control and creation: all the problems of rhyme, rhythm, received images and structure. Byron's use of feminine rhyme in the last couplet of his stanzas has a deflating effect; it emphasises the way in which the materiality, sound or noise of language forces the verse and content: 'And turned, without perceiving his condition,/Like Coleridge into a metaphysician' (Byron [1821] 1973, 68 [1.91]). Byron often ironically repeated the grand Romantic gestures, but did so in a mechanical or awkward manner – to show just how impossible it was for poetry to be *pure* creation or becoming: 'If you think 'twas philosophy that this did,/I can't help thinking puberty assisted' (ibid. 69 [1.93]). Instead of seeing all life as a process of poetic creation, Byron emphasised how often poetic ideals clash with life, or how the wonder that prompts romantic striving often leads to unintelligible abstraction:

> Young Juan wander'd by the glassy brooks,
>   Thinking unutterable things; he threw
> Himself at length within the leafy nooks
>   Where the wild branch of the cork forest grew;
> There poets find materials for their books,
>   And every now and then we read them through,
> So that their plan and prosody are eligible,
> Unless, like Wordsworth, they prove unintelligible.
>   (Byron [1821] 1973, 68 [1.90])

In this way, Byron combined irony and satire. On the one hand, he used satire to debunk all the high ideals of Romantic striving, all the ideals of an elevated poetry. On the other hand, he used irony against a certain satirical tendency. Irony could still create some heroic or poetic ideal, but it would not be one of unmediated creation and self-becoming, not a romantic irony that has nothing outside itself. The Byronic hero is created both as an impossible and as a desirable ideal. Byron retains the Romantic value of thinking beyond the given and conventional world, but remains aware that there is always a context, style and limit to this irony.

In order to look at this tension between ironic and satirical tendencies we first need to get a sense of satire and its involvement with irony. Swift is cited both as an ironist and a satirist precisely because he can at one and the same time be read as an exponent of the enlightenment – in his attack on conventions, authority and fixity of beliefs – *and* as an irrationalist. His commitment to the Enlightenment would explain his irony, or his distance from received dogma and opinion. But he also saw the limits of the Enlightenment in his satirical tendencies: we can never reach a point of ironic detachment where we would be purely self-determined. The image of the rational and purely self-determining subject can only exist through the repression and violent extermination of the body and its passions.

Swift's satire uses irony, or the limited and partial voices of his characters (Elliott 1960, 200), in order to focus on those aspects of life that are radically resistant to purpose, production, creation and reason. The humour and frustration of the early parts of *Gulliver's Travels* is achieved by displaying the human hypocrisy surrounding the body. The giant Gulliver in Liliput extinguishes a fire in the royal apartment by urinating, but this 'heroic' act eventually becomes the ostensible reason for his political persecution (Swift 1967, 107). The real reason for his expulsion and threatened extermination is political – the high cost of maintaining Gulliver, and courtly rivalry; but Swift shows the ways in which disgust is manipulated for interest. The body and its functions must be controlled, hidden and distanced from 'society'. The 'natural', or fully human, disgust with the body both leads to political tyranny – the use of the loathsome aspects of the body to expel certain political figures – and gives a perverse image of reason. Reason is achieved only through a blindness to, or repression of, the body. Swift's satire shows how both reason and polite political society achieve purity by denying the very life and body that make them possible.

We could also see the distinction between eighteenth-century satire with its emphasis on 'man', and nineteenth-century irony with its emphasis on the creative spirit or subject that refuses all human definition, as more than a historical distinction (Hazard 1954, 14). How we read Byron, Swift or any other voice in literary history depends on how we understand the very concepts of irony and history. Is irony always context-located, such that any use of voice must refer to a specific social context and what language acts *do*? Or, does the occurrence and question of irony destabilise the borders of context? Take the 'examples' of both Swift and Byron. One could read both these authors satirically, precisely through an appeal to context. *Gulliver's Travels* could be interpreted as a satirical repetition of modern discourses of discovery, science and reason. We could read Gulliver's disgust with the body as a parody of emerging enlightenment; his absurd and self-destructive loathing of humanity displays a tyrannical tendency of modern rationalism. Similarly, we could read *Don Juan* as the presentation of competing voices of its day, both the elevated idealism of romanticism and the moralistic cant of politics. But to read these texts *in* context, to see them as satirising specific discourses, is also to situate the satirical voice outside these contexts; the voice is directed against this specific context and therefore has a locatable force and identity. Reading satire in this way – as the repetition of a specific context or discourse that we can recognise and locate historically – also requires our own contextual limitation, for we must be other than the context viewed and satirised, and we must also have a sense or definition of who we are.

ROMANTIC IDEOLOGY: MCGANN

Jerome McGann, for example, insists that we should not read the Romantics Romantically; we should see Byron as challenging, not falling into, the Romantic world-view. We can only be other than Romantic, or recognise Byron's specific and directed irony, McGann argues, if we locate him in a historically specific context of political satire. McGann explicitly rejects the idea of a Romantic irony that dissolves fixed positions and hovers, chaotically, above all determination; this image of irony is, he argues, a specific Romantic evasion of concrete political contexts.

Such a gesture of determining Byron's proper context necessarily requires that we be able to think beyond our context: to see a text as located in a context we have to have a sense of that context, our own difference or distance from context *and* a thought of context in general. McGann's returning of Byron to context requires a notion of history, and McGann's ability to judge that history; it requires a trans-contextual point of view, even if one recognises one's position *in* history. The problem of irony is unavoidable. Once we locate a text historically, politically or discursively, we *also* open the possibility that it might be dislocated, read with an attention to other possible points of reference *and* read as if it were also capable of thinking beyond any specific context. To *not* read the text this way, to locate it within a context, is still an interpretive decision about just what constitutes its proper context.

One may never be able to adopt a context-free view from nowhere, but one can think, imagine or speculate – as Romantic irony sought to do – about the limits of one's context and try to form a concept of the becoming, history or temporality which allows varying contexts and concepts to emerge. Once we speak ironically we can no longer be sure just who is the object or subject or ridicule. Swift is not just satirising the Britain of his own day. The joke would be on us if we felt we were entirely other than Gulliver, or able to separate ourselves definitively from the context of rationalism. Swift ironises the purveying and detached Gulliver, the Gulliver who feels that he can objectify, satirise and contextualise humanity. It is Gulliver who finally recognises all of humanity as worthy of extermination precisely because it does not live up to the claims of pure reason. Far from merely satirising a particular context and way of speaking, it is possible to see a force in Swift's text that destabilises all notions of shared context and understanding. Language, in Swift, is *not* purposeful exchange or communication; it is often noise, distortion, and nonsense. Not only are many of the languages described by Gulliver unpronounceable, such as the Houyhnhnms, Swift also has a sense of the ways in which the matter of language, its sounds and rhythms, infect the understanding. If Gulliver is gullible – if one's proper name is also a pun – then the idea of a pure and intended language becomes problematic; we are never quite sure just what these words mean, whether they are *meant* to mean anything. The idea that all contexts can be translated, understood, rationalised and represented is precisely what leads Gulliver into an allegiance with the Houyhnhnms, or those who define themselves as pure, reasoning subjects.

Similarly, as McGann himself acknowledges, Byron's *Don Juan* is critical of the satire of invective and elevated cruelty that goes back to the Roman satirist Juvenal (AD 55–127). Byron may have ridiculed the Romantic irony of pure elevation, but he also saw a destructiveness in a position that was only negative or was unaware of the force and creativity of its own position. Byron does not just adopt a more lenient and complicit satirical tone, in the tradition of the other Roman satirist Horace (65–8 BC); he is also critical of the cynicism that would reduce human life to force, rhetoric and persuasion. In addition to the satirical impulse that ridicules the Romantics, there is also a sublime irony in *Don Juan*, a criticism of the knowing gaze and the objectification of 'man'. This is nowhere more clear than in Canto 5 where the very figure of looking and surveying takes on a complex layering. Juan has been sold into slavery, and the narrator presents the tyranny of the eye of imperialism that would look on bodies as mere commodities:

> As the black eunuch enter'd with his brace
> > Of purchased Infidels, some raised their eyes
> A moment without slackening from their pace;
> > But those who sate ne'er stirr'd in anywise:
> One or two stared the captives in the face,
> > Just as one views a horse to guess his price;
> Some nodded to the negro from their station,
> But no one troubled him with conversation.
> > (Byron [1821] 1973, 232 [5.54])

First we see the point of view of the slave-purchasers, quoted above, then the eye of Gulbayez, the Sultana, as she views Juan's body (Byron [1821] 1973, 245–46 [5.107–14]). The text, we might say, ironises the objectifying gaze of an imperialism that would reduce human life to so much knowable and purchasable matter. Once the slaves have been herded out of the palatial room, the narrator laments the *aesthetic* emptiness or soullessness of the scene, refusing any moral judgement: 'Perhaps there's nothing – I'll not say appals,/But saddens more by night as well as day/Than an enormous room without a soul/To break the lifeless splendour of the whole' (ibid. 233 [5.56]). But if 'we', the readers, feel we can be other than this detached gaze, then the irony is on us. The point of view and tone of the narration – the digressing, detached and uncommitted point of view that judges life only in terms of its pleasantness to the eye – is also exposed as blind, as not seeing the human suffering it unwittingly describes:

> This massy portal stood at the wide close
>   Of a huge hall, and on its either side
> Two little dwarfs, the least you could suppose,
>   Were sate, like ugly imps, as if allied
> In mockery to the enormous gate which rose
>   O'er them in almost pyramidic pride:
> The gate so splendid was in all its *features*,
> You never thought about those little creatures,
>
> Until you nearly trod on them, and then
>   You started back in horror to survey
> The wondrous hideousness of those small men,
>   Whose colour was not black, nor white, nor grey,
> But an extraneous mixture, which no pen
>   Can trace, although perhaps the pencil may;
> They were mis-shapen pigmies, deaf and dumb —
> Monsters, who cost a no less monstrous sum.
>
>   (Byron [1821] 1973, 240 [5.87–8])

Here the satire of *Don Juan* – its refusal of poetic inflation and high ideals – meets its ironic limit. The objectifying gaze that sees all life as so much matter, that refuses human judgement, is presented both as inhumanly cruel and narrowly aesthetic, capable of seeing the form and object of a scene but not its sense. Later, we are presented with Juan's heroic resistance to the objectifying gaze of Gulbuyaz; the very heroism that has earlier been satirised as a delusion of puberty is at once affirmed, and then deflated in the final couplet of submission:

> He stood like Atlas, with a world of words
>   About his ears, and nathless would not bend:

The blood of all his line's Castilian lords
    Boil'd in his veins, and rather than descend
To stain his pedigree a thousand swords
    A thousand times of him had made an end;
    At length perceiving the 'foot' could not stand,
    Baba proposed that he should kiss the hand.

(Byron [1821] 1973, 245 [5.104])

We could follow McGann and see an historical opposition between satire and irony. Augustan and classical satire was aware of the material and located conditions of speech and argument, aware that any elevated viewpoint would always be generated from specific forces and contexts. Irony, in its later Romantic form, by contrast, conceives of poetry as the refusal of closed context in favour of the thought, feeling and intimation of the creative power that produces contexts. This would also allow us to divide satire and irony according to a theory of man or a theory of the subject. Satire focuses on desires, bodies, the actual world and 'man' as a being whose thought is often led or circumscribed by his actual needs and interests. Irony of the nineteenth century no longer sees 'man' as a knowable object with specific contexts to be satirised, but affirms 'subjectivity': a power of creativity or becoming that exceeds any definition, style or context.

The problem with such a distinction is that it is already ironic; we have already created an overview of human history and seen satire as a position within that history. As both de Man and Derrida have tirelessly argued, any attempt to overcome the subject or reason by situating it within a historical narrative itself adopts a subjective or rational position above narrative. For de Man this is because of the inescapable problem of narration. The very act of speaking about the world creates a position other than the world, and only irony can reflect on this unthinkable gap. Beyond the locatedness of satire and the overview of irony, writers like Derrida and de Man have therefore stressed the necessity and impossibility of irony. We cannot avoid irony's elevation and questioning; nor can we achieve a pure separation from context. The task of a post-ironic ethics cannot be a return to satire, a return to the specific contexts of history within which 'we' are located. For the very thought of this located 'we' – this humanity that realises itself in various epochs – itself creates some trans-historical or trans-contextual community (Derrida 1973, 6). Rather, we need to acknowledge both the violence of the ironic viewpoint that judges contexts, and the violence that would simply resign itself to a context and refuse all question. As Derrida has argued, *not* to ask the question of one's context – to refuse or disavow the possibility of thinking – is the 'worst violence' (Derrida 1978, 152).

ETHICS AND POSTMODERN IRONY

In order to think of oneself as contextually located and immanent one must imagine that one is located in, or immanent *to*, some field. One can only assert that one's position is discursively constructed if one has assumed that *discourse* is some ultimate determining force; one can only assert that the world is known through competing perspectives if one has adopted the overarching notion of perspectives, viewpoints or ways of seeing as constitutive. In order to have a sense of oneself as located one needs to imagine a general field *within which* one is situated. Not only does one have to imagine some general horizon, such as history, discourse, culture or contexts, one also has to refuse or set oneself in opposition to any privileged or 'meta-contextual' position (Mileur 1998, 200). This is the paradox of postmodern and postcolonial political positions; the attempt to abandon the overarching point of view of Western metaphysics must itself step outside and delimit Western metaphysics, must see itself as *other than* the violence of hierarchies and transcendental elevations. It must reduce all cultures to relative terms in an undifferentiated field. Only through imagining an undifferentiated life that is then structured through imposed relations can one abandon judgement or the thought of intrinsic difference (Hallward 2001).

How can one offer a critique of judging reason without adopting a tone of judgment? How can one present the cruelties of morality without moralising? How can one criticise the rational point of view that detaches itself from all contexts, without such a criticism creating its own elevated context? Only irony can, at one and the same time, judge the tyranny and moralism of a certain context *and* display its own complicity in that tyranny. Canto 5 of Byron's *Don Juan* presents the imperialism of the over-arching gaze, *and* shows how our own reading of the other's tyranny is itself always at risk of being blind to its own elevation. One cannot avoid the *predicament* of irony. The attempt to think a context *itself* can only take place if one has a *sense*, definition or position in relation to that context.

The contemporary celebration of irony often fails to take account of this violent paradox at the heart of the relation between speech and context. McGann is quite right to note that the celebration of an irony that would affirm 'the' human spirit necessarily precludes consideration of the force of specific speech acts, and just whose 'humanity' is being generalised (McGann 1983). But it is also the case that one cannot return to the locality and immediacy of contexts. By virtue of the fact that texts are *read*, and are read *as past*, we have some sense of a meaning that is translatable across contexts. We cannot avoid the horizon of history in general, nor the assumption of a continuity of sense. To read is to assume that the text means something *for us*; the singularity or immediacy of the past is lost the moment it is seen *as past*. What we can do, via irony, is work with this inherent political tension: that any judgement that condemns the violence and closure of a context must in turn elevate itself above context. Without a notion of the subject who can think beyond the closure of context there would be no judgement, but the confident belief that such a subject exists or can be achieved closes off all possibility of self-judgment.

THE IRONIC SUBJECT AND HISTORY

Post-structuralism appears as one possible response to the predicament of postmodern irony. If postmodern irony affirms the equal validity and ultimately groundless nature of all discourse, post-structuralism recognises that one cannot speak from a position of groundlessness. Even the assertion that all values depend upon context constitutes itself as a position capable of revealing some trans-contextual truth. Richard Rorty, the contemporary American liberal pragmatist, has insisted that the value of postmodern irony lies in its ability to refrain from making such truth claims, but this does not allow for Rorty's own position. Rorty can only affirm the value of a postmodern refusal of truth claims because he has posited a better standard of truth (pragmatism) and a better standard of speech (as what is most open to renewal). Against a postmodern irony that claims to have freed itself from all hierarchies, grand claims and metaphysical posturings, post-structuralism of the Derridean and de Man variety acknowledges that one cannot avoid a position of judgement or subjectivity. The ironic subject does not just take part in the discourses and norms that are present; she can ask *whose* norms these are and whether they are valid. Irony allows for detachment and an 'eternal' point of view; the ironic self can question whether life might not be otherwise, whether 'we' might create ourselves differently. Indeed, irony detaches itself from any recognised 'we' in order to question and disrupt accepted norms. Irony is provocative, disruptive, but also hierarchical – setting itself above everyday life and opinion.

However, any expression of this ironic self as a *principle* – any appeal to this unrepresentable subject or process – would once again give substance and representation to what is essentially unrepresentable (before all ideas and constitutions of what 'is' or remains present). This ironic subject also places itself, again hierarchically, above the historical epochs it surveys. This is why any text can be read ironically. If it is the case that there is a power or potential of human subjectivity, which can never be exhausted by any image of the self or 'man', then it is also possible to see the entire history of literature and philosophy as a series of creations and productions behind which lies a creative 'spirit'. It is in this gesture, which is supposedly radical and anti-humanist insofar as it rejects any single norm or image of 'man', that irony can fall back into the very normalising morality that it sought to avoid. The essence of 'man' or 'subjectivity' is, supposedly, that he has no essence; he is nothing other than a power for self-creation, self-determination and active becoming: 'Man, since always, is his proper end, that is, the end of his proper' (Derrida 1982, 134). Such an ideal, as Derrida has noted, has an accompanying politics and cultural ideal, for it is Western rational man, and the modern Western state, that has more often than not represented this ideal of pure autonomous development, freed from all determined belief, tradition or ideology.

According to Derrida, Western metaphysics has been dominated by logocentrism, the project of grounding all life on what can be rendered meaningful, purposive, actual and present. Against this, Derrida argues that any *thought* of the forces that produce meaning can never entirely master those forces – and there will always be forces, both in language and without, whose effects may never be fully calculated. The potential or force of what we say may have consequences that go beyond what we intend and beyond what we recognise. This is what differentiates Derrida from both 'contextual' and 'pragmatic' accounts of meaning, or those who look at language in terms of what it does and how it functions. Derrida, in contrast with pragmatism, insists that language and differences have tremors, effects and ruptures well beyond social intent and recognition. In terms of irony, this means that a word can mean or do more than is intended; there can be a force other than explicit and literal meaning, but this cannot be reduced to an *other*, second or elevated meaning. We may 'use' language to speak and represent, but we cannot represent the differential process that produces or generates the system of signs within which we think. Nor can we ever fully think or calculate the forces of our speech. There are always effects that exceed speech and intention.

Not only can we not master the origins of what we say, we cannot control future effects. When Mary Shelley wrote *The Last Man* (1826), for example, she could not have calculated the possible meanings and resonances that such a text would have in an epoch of AIDS. Shakespeare would not have intended the staging of *Romeo and Juliet* as a tale of urban gang warfare, but this does not mean the text cannot have these meanings. One cannot determine in advance how the potentials of a text might be realised or actualised; one cannot reduce force to its manifest and present effects. Rather than grounding life on a subject that would determine, create or express itself in various forms, Derrida points to all those forces and differences that are ungrounded, unintended and unproductive – leading to uncertainty and ambiguity rather than sense and recognition. Far from the *subject* or consciousness being the origin of sense, the forces that produce the concept of the subject exceed and determine the subject. De Man's 'act' of narration that produces the self, from this inhuman point of view, would not be an 'act' so much as an event. Narrative is not something 'we' *do* in order to give ourselves an identity; narrative is an effect of a textuality that exceeds conscious action and intention.

Derrida is a profoundly ironic philosopher precisely because most of his readings of the history of Western metaphysics do not look at what texts *intended* to say manifestly, but what *is said or done*: the differences that texts create, the concepts and images that emerge, the alterations in a language. The idea that meaning lies 'behind' a text is itself an effect of text; we could not have the notion of meaning without certain figures or metaphors. Meaning lies 'behind', 'beneath' or 'before' a text: without these spatial or temporal notions we could not have any sense of meaning, but we could also not have time or space without a language that creates a before and after. Meaning is therefore both metaphysical and necessary. It is metaphysical because it is the very idea of what exists beyond the concrete or material signifier; and it is necessary, because without the idea of a sense or idea that remains the same – without the idea of presence or *what is* – we would not have a coherent and experienced world. We would only have a chaotic and anonymous flux of differences. One cannot, Derrida insists, use the notion of discourse or signification without also referring or intending a presence that lies behind or beyond that signification. The ideal of presence is not something one can simply decide to avoid in one's speech. By the same token, while this metaphysical commitment to presence accompanies our use of speaking and signifying, this presence can never be fulfilled, nor can it be freed from paradox.

In one of his longer essays on Kant, Derrida criticises the necessarily apocalyptic 'tone' of metaphysics. The Enlightenment attempt to reduce philosophy to pure argument and persuasion, without the imposition of a specific voice or received wisdom, is the desire to purify thought of all passively accepted images and inflections – the desire for an autonomous speech that would justify itself. But in order to speak and argue with clarity and purpose one *must* also adopt a tone, rely on a material system of marks and sounds that can never be fully one's own. The *idea* of the subject – of a reason that speaks and intuits before language – can only be effected through specific acts of language. Even so, one cannot abandon this idea. Without the idea of the subject, or a position of judgement or distance in relation to language, there would be neither thought nor criticism. It may be that we always speak from within a context and epoch, but each context also has certain concepts – such as the concept of the subject, the concept of irony or the concept of history – that allow us to think or anticipate what cannot be reduced to this or that context. At a certain point in history 'we' start to think historically, and this then allows for the possibility of a 'we' that is not just this or that community, but the whole of 'human' history, the very possibility of subjectivity in all its different periods. Concepts – such as the concepts of history or subjectivity – may be produced in specific languages. But once such concepts are formed they 'open' languages; they allow the thought of the very genesis of thinking and language. Without the *concept* of irony we could not think of a sense that is other than what is said. The thought of irony allows us to question not just the content of what is said, but whether the subject who speaks is *really* saying what is said.

The German Romantics had argued that the artist or ironist is one who recognises language in its effects, but always remains above and beyond language as essentially indescribable. English Romantics, like Wordsworth and Coleridge, did represent themselves as blessed with a divine insight – through poetry – into the very nature of nature, and its loss. The more politically radical irony of poets like Byron and Blake was critical of the image of the poet as elevated prophet or seer. For, to follow de Man, it is just at the point that one feels one has recognised irony, or recognised the way in which the self is created through poetry, that one is also most blind to irony. Any attempt to write a poetry that would grasp the very origin of poetry, any attempt to adopt a view from nowhere or speak as if one were no one in particular would merely repeat the illusion of allegory: the illusion that there is a point outside language to which language may be related or from which language may be viewed. It is for this reason that Blake and Byron *both* adopt the voice of the prophet, as one who denounces all given discourses and narratives *and* show how this voice above all language is itself one more particular style of language.

There would be a tyranny in thinking that one's voice or point of view were somehow above and beyond the world and all its differences. Byron does not just lampoon the image of the Romantic poet as elevated above the contingencies of everyday life; he also shows how poetry must of necessity speak through some particular style and system. There can, in short, be no artistic position above and beyond particular voices – only the recognition of the power of voices *to produce* various subject positions. For de Man, the difference between early Romanticism and 'modern' irony lies in just this destruction of illusion. Romantic irony remains committed to some inexpressible or ineffable self or subject forever betrayed by language; modern irony abandons the possibility of even thinking of such a pure self or ineffable subjectivity. Modern irony must destroy the production of origins and creative subjects, leaving nothing but the productive power of language spoken by no one: 'Modernity turns out to be indeed one of the concepts by means of which the distinctive nature of literature can be revealed in all its intricacy' (de Man 1983, 161).

PERFORMATIVE POLITICS AND GENDER: JUDITH BUTLER

De Man's own work was notoriously silent on the question of politics. He presented modern irony as *the* recognition of the power of narrative to produce speaking subjects, a recognition only enabled after the advent of structuralism. It is precisely because there can be no final recognition of irony that we cannot have an ultimate theory of narrative. Any description or account of the origin of meaning will itself be one more narrative and will have to install itself in the *illusion* of meaning: the allegorical illusion that language is the belated signification of some pre-linguistic identity. Poetry can work with this illusion – presenting it *as* illusion – only by presenting language itself, and not a language that is imagined as the sign of some world, or the expression of some subject. For de Man these structures of irony, and the impossibility of recognising irony, have to do with time (de Man 1983, 226). We can only have meaning – or allegory – if we imagine a self and world *before* signs. But we can also only have this difference between a before and an after *through language or narration*. This situation, for de Man, is transcendental and inescapable.

Some more recent writers have politicised this constitutive structure of language, the most notable being Judith Butler, whose *Gender Trouble*, published in 1990, revolutionised not just feminism but the very notion of discourse as grounded in a subject or identity (Butler 1999). Language is performative, according to Butler, because in speaking I produce myself as an 'I' to be recognised. For Butler it is not modern poetry with its reflection on language as such which can radicalise the illusion of a self before language; it is the political performance of gender. For the most part we live our gender and our social identity as the linguistic or social construction of our 'real' selves. We imagine, for example, that women are constructed *as feminine* through literary and cultural stereotypes and that there is a real sexual self somehow existing before cultural identity. But Butler, like de Man, wants to insist that this 'before' is an effect of language. The idea of a 'sex' or biology that is *then* overlaid with 'gender' or social identity is actually an effect of the performance of gender. Whereas de Man looks at the universal creation of 'a' subject, Butler focuses on the political identities of the selves produced. The self that is created through the performance of language is always the self of a certain gender. Language, through its system and regularities, creates or performs certain social roles. When I dress, move and speak as a woman I create myself as a woman. Our gender identity is not expressed in language but created and performed through language. But Butler wants to go further and say that language does not just perform and create identity; *it also creates the illusion of some subject or being that exists before language*. The performance of the self as gendered or as social, creates the illusion of a self or body that was there to be expressed.

Consider, for example, literary character. We can imagine that the images of women in novels somehow represent or reflect what women actually are; this would place language and literature as secondary. Alternatively, we could say that we only have ideas of 'woman' and femininity through the constructions of literature and culture; this would be a social construction argument. But Butler wants to take the next ironic or, in her terms, parodic and performative step. The assumption or performance of one's gender does not just construct identity, it *creates* the illusion of something that was there all along *to be constructed*. Performance creates the sequence of a 'before' and after, or a pre-linguistic nature that *precedes* a socially constructed nature. In being or acting as either male or female one presents oneself as a proper realisation of one's material body, and precludes matter from being anything other than what is recognised as either male or female (Butler 1993, 67). The 'heterosexual matrix' creates its 'before' through prohibition (Butler 1993, 95). To act and be recognised as a subject one must be either male or female; to *not* perform one's gender would be to deviate from the proper or natural body – the matter – that gender and identity presupposes. On Butler's account, we can only think of 'real' bodies who are subsequently constructed as women *because* language itself performs or creates the subject who precedes it.

Butler's radical proposal is avowedly political and ironic. It is only if we present identity *as* performed that we will recognise the ways in which it creates, rather than expresses, the subject. The subject 'is' nothing other than the illusion of a 'before' to language. The person who labels the homosexual as 'queer' has an allegorical notion of language: that there simply *are* homosexual identities, which can then be labelled and discovered. But the homosexual who, in a gay Mardi Gras, presents himself explicitly as an amalgam of performances, as nothing more than a series of camp gestures, allows the performance of identity to be presented *as performance*: 'the parodic repetition of "the original" . . . reveals the original to be nothing other than a parody of the *idea* of the natural and original' (Butler 1993, 41). The supposed pre-linguistic matter of the body that would issue in a secure male or female identity is thereby exposed as having potentials to act in multiple and incalculable ways, in 'alternative imaginary schemas' (Butler 1993, 91). By performing differently, by acting in ways that are not recognised as reducible to heterosexual norms, the illusion of matter as having a natural sex is undone.

Whereas de Man had argued that the power of language and narrative to create some originating subject was best recognised in modern poetry, Butler turns to the more public and politically charged examples of the destabilisation of identity. Both de Man and Butler, however, remain committed to the inescapability of the illusion of language, or language's power to create the subject who supposedly precedes it. Both remain committed to the performative function of speech: that the use of language *as language* creates us as subjects who supposedly, but not actually, exist before that language. Both de Man and Butler can be located within the tradition of irony: there can be no appeal to the world or body as such, in all its immediacy. The minute we speak or act with others we are already committed to a system or language whose origin we neither constitute nor control. And language must then have the function of a law: of a system that enables us to speak and act, but also precludes us from speaking or acting from some point beyond the system. We cannot elevate ourselves above this power of language; all we can do is destabilise the system from within by presenting it *as system*: as language.

Irony, even early Socratic irony, recognised that language has a force or power that limits what we can and cannot say. Socrates challenges the sophists who believe that rhetoric and concepts can simply be used and manipulated according to our individual wills. Concepts have a meaning, which lies above and beyond any particular speech act. The Romantics insisted that this Idea or sense, which Socrates constantly used to challenge the sophist's easy definitions, could never be presented. The Good, the Law, the Beautiful and the Soul are not objects that could be correctly labelled within language. It is because language is limited and always particular that we must imagine, but not articulate, that which precedes all limitation. For de Man, it is only after structuralism or the emphasis on the *system* of language, that we can see that what supposedly lies above and beyond language – the absolute – is actually an illusion created through language. For Butler, this is not just an illusion in literature; it has political consequences. The idea of a self *before* social performance has enslaved us both to notions of the essentially feminine, and allowed us to dismiss certain sexual identities as *unnatural*. By performing or drawing attention to the structure of gender *as* performance we will be liberated from a dogmatic politics or a politics that claims to *know* the real authoritatively. We cannot escape the systems of identity, or the illusion that there is a subject *who speaks*. But we can perform, repeat or parody all those gestures that create this subject.

Irony, for writers like Butler and de Man, is not a figure of speech that 'we' can choose to use or not use. There is no such thing as faithful and literal speech, which is at one with its world, and then ironic or distanced speech, which would speak with a sense of distance, quotation or otherness. In order to speak at all, 'we' must adopt a system that is not uniquely ours. Not only are 'we' therefore necessarily displaced from any unique or authentic self, we also only have this 'we' or 'self' through the very speech that appears to be Other. This also means that there can be no final achievement of irony. We cannot, as Richard Rorty suggests, adopt our language with a recognition that it is *merely* a language. Such a hope would rely on a notion of language as other than ourselves, as something we might have to use, but which 'we' would always recognise as provisional and arbitrary. Any thought of the 'we' or 'self' that may or may not be ironic, that would believe or doubt language, is itself an effect of language.

How, though, did this idea of the signifier or this impersonal notion of 'the' system of language emerge? Does it have a history? De Man insists that it does not. When the structuralists point out that language is an impersonal system that creates relations, and not just a collection of labels that 'we' attach to already differentiated things, they recognise a necessary and transcendental feature of language. It may be that we can only understand this structure from some particular point in history or language, but this does not detract from the necessity of structure as such. The pre-structuralist idea that language is something 'we' use is an illusion, and any attempt to think of a 'we' or world *before* structure, would itself have to use and be located within structure. We could only think the 'before' of a structure ironically, as itself an effect or illusion of structure. The attempt to give a history and origin to the notion of structure and to the concepts of the signifier and the subject was made by Deleuze and Guattari in their monumental history of capitalism, *Anti-Oedipus*, published in 1972. Not surprisingly, perhaps, Deleuze's criticism of the subject, the signifier and negativity was also issued in a critique of irony (Deleuze and Guttari 1983).

7

HUMOUR AND IRONY
Deleuze and Guattari

Against the elevation of the signifier and irony to a universal and inescapable principle, Gilles Deleuze and Félix Guattari have argued that the logic of the signifier and the idea of a necessarily imposed structure are strictly modern. Not only can we think of the emergence of signification, subjectivity and structure, we can also think beyond the logic of irony. Irony relies on the logic of the signifier: in order for a sign to *mean* it must have a lawfulness that transcends any specific speech act. It is not surprising that Gilles Deleuze's book on sense and nonsense, *The Logic of Sense* ([1969] 1990), was preoccupied with irony. Both in *The Logic of Sense* and in his writings with Guattari, Deleuze tried to free sense from the system of language, by arguing that human signification and the production of a speaking 'I' are effects of a 'milieu' of sense which goes well beyond the system of speech. Before I utter a proposition, for example, I must have a perception of this world and a desire to act in this world; there are problems, perceptions, desires, or 'planes' of sense that enable some system of logic to emerge. Deleuze and Guattari insist that there was a history and a politics before the logic of the signifier, before the notion of a necessary system, structure, subjectivity or law to which 'we' are all necessarily submitted.

Deleuze frequently refers to humour, and occasionally satire, as a tendency opposed to irony:

> The first way of overturning the law is ironic, where irony appears as an art of principles, of ascent towards the principles and of overturning principles. The second is humour, which is an art of consequences and descents, of suspensions and falls

(Deleuze 1994, 5)

Instead of thinking in terms of the concept as a law that governs what we say, humour and satire focus on the bodies, particularities, noises and disruptions that are in excess of the system and law of speech. The viewpoint of irony, or the viewpoint that surveys the totality of history as the history of 'man' – the viewpoint that sees itself as a point within a single plane of history – is challenged by Deleuze and Guattari's insistence that universal man and the speaking subject are modern Western illusions.

Far from structuralism (the recognition of language as an impersonal system) being a radical break with the traditional politics of the subject, Deleuze and Guattari insist that structuralism is an intensification of the modern tendency to reduce the differences and events of politics to one homogeneous and tyrannical logic (Deleuze and Guattari 1987, 237). Against the ironic view of the subject as the bland empty effect of 'the' structure of signification, Deleuze insists on a humour and a poetics that – far from producing the before and after of a subject who then speaks – *creates surfaces* (Deleuze 1990, 7). Before there is the linear temporality of a subject who experiences the world in terms of a before and after, within one universal history, various planes have to be differentiated – such as the inside/outside of a mind and world, or the various borders and territories that define organisms and communities. Humour beyond irony, or what Deleuze refers to as superior irony (Deleuze 1994, 182), is the art of surfaces, the art of thinking the noises, sensations, affects and sensible singularities from which bodies are composed, bodies that can then have relations: 'Humor is the art of the surface, which is opposed to the old irony, the art of depths and heights' (Deleuze 1990, 9). Against structuralism, which argues that an undifferentiated world is differentiated or carved up by the system of language, Deleuze insists on the singular pulsations of life, the capacity of life to become different, to destroy and prompt our concepts and categories. Any system is the effect of multiple and differentiating forces that create relations. Deleuze's irony insists on multiplicity. Instead of there being a unity, Idea or 'One' that is belied by the chaotic or undifferentiated nature of life, Deleuze insists that life itself in all its infinite variety produces Ideas – singular differences – which our languages and systems can only begin to grasp:

> Instead of the enormous opposition between the one and the many, there is only the variety of multiplicity – in other words, difference. It is perhaps ironic to say that everything is multiplicity, even the one, even the many. However, irony itself is a multiplicity – or rather, the art of multiplicities: the art of grasping the Ideas and problems they incarnate in things, and of grasping things as incarnations, as cases of solution for the problems of Ideas.
>
> (Deleuze 1994, 182)

Irony, traditionally, is temporal. It is through speaking that we have the sense of a subject who preceded speech and an original world that was there to be signified. We could only escape irony, and the point of view of the subject, if we could rethink this logic of time (and narrative). Deleuze and Guattari write a history of human culture which accounts for the emergence of the point of view of modern ironic 'man': the subject who is capable of thinking different cultures and epochs from his own human point of view. In order to have this ironic or detached notion of the subject, or the point of view that is always *other than* any particular quality, style or discourse, one has to produce a peculiar political and historical 'plane'. The 'subject' and the signifier, and the very ideas of meaning, context and sense, are effects of bodily, historical and political forces. For Deleuze and Guattari, then, politics is *not* primarily a group of persons coming together in a common language and arriving at consensus and recognition. Before the politics of irony, where 'we' are all subjected to the same system, there is a micropolitics, where passions, forces, events and differences collide *with no common ground*. Before the community of man, and before the production of 'a' context of speakers, there are just productions and disruptions of differences, which are not the differences *of language* or system but are singular (Deleuze and Guattari 1983).

Humour, according to Deleuze, is this art of singularities, of events that are not meaningful, not structured according to a logic of before and after:

> There is a difficult relation, which rejects the false Platonic duality of the essence and the example. This exercise, which consists in substituting designations, monstrations, consumptions, and pure destructions for significations, requires an odd inspiration – that one knows how to 'descend'. What is required is humor, as opposed to the Socratic irony or to the technique of ascent.
>
> (Deleuze 1990, 135)

Recall that Socratic irony was tied to the disjunction between what is true eternally and our contingent definitions: we can point to this or that instance of justice and beauty, but the *Idea* of justice or beauty exists above and beyond any of its single instances. For Plato, we could contemplate the *Ideas* of justice or beauty, but the Socratic dialogues suggest that we can only intimate or suggest such Ideas because our everyday definitions are inadequate. In contrast to those who claim to know or intuit ideas – the sophists who offer easy definitions – Socratic irony suggests that such ideas provide infinite ideals beyond everyday life, ideals towards which life can strive, but which can never be fulfilled.

The Romantics had seized on this negative dimension of irony and interpreted Socrates as nothing more than the performance of character. Instead of knowing the human soul and offering a theory of man, Socrates presented various personae that produced the soul as a power *to act*, rather than a thing to be observed. By being *other than* what he says Socrates is not a thing to be described by language so much as a demonstration of the creative power of language. Following the Romantics, de Man had insisted that the self or power *behind language* was an effect of the temporality of language. It is in the act of saying that a self *who has spoken* is produced. Irony strives to reflect on this necessary and fictional gap between a before and after of language. Any description of language as productive of the illusory real or 'before' that it seems to represent must itself rely on the temporality of language and narrative that it is trying to explain:

The reflective disjunction not only occurs *by means of* language as a privileged category, but it transfers the self out of the empirical world into a world constituted out of, and in, language – a language that it finds in the world like one entity among others, but that remains unique in being the only entity by means of which it can differentiate itself from the world. Language thus conceived divides the subject into an empirical self, immersed in the world, and a self that become a sign in its attempt at differentiation and self-definition.

(de Man 1983, 213)

Against this ironic account of narrative and subjectivity as unavoidable, Gilles Deleuze argues both for a different – non-linear and multiple – understanding of time *and* for a 'superior irony' beyond the subject. De Man follows a long tradition of philosophers (since Kant) in arguing that time is not possible without a subjective point of view: the idea of a before and after requires the perception of a series of sequence of events. Time *is* subjective, the creation or synthesis of an ordered world from some stable viewpoint: 'What all the figures of irony have in common is that they confine the singularity within the limits of the individual or the person' (Deleuze 1990, 139).

Irony, according to Deleuze, is a tendency in thinking, a tendency to not rest with the world in all its flux of differences, a tendency to posit some ultimate point of view beyond difference. The problem with irony, from Deleuze's point of view, is its elimination of all difference – its inability to admit what is beyond its point of view. And it is this ironic ascent that has dominated Western thinking: 'Classical irony acts as the instance which assures the coextensiveness of being and of the individual within the world of representation' (Deleuze 1990, 138).

HUMOUR

Deleuze's own philosophy suggests a contrary direction for analysis in the form of humour. According to Deleuze, humour descends. Both irony and ideas have traditionally been explained through metaphors of height. Ideas exist 'above' existence, giving the world form. Irony is the adoption of a point of view 'above' a context, allowing us to view the context from 'on high'. Deleuze sees humour not just as an opposite movement of descent; he insists that we need to consider just how this distinction between high and low has enabled us to think. Radical humour, or Deleuze's 'superior irony', dissolves high–low distinctions – such as the concept 'above' existence – in order to think of the play of surfaces. We tend to imagine life and narratives as relations among persons, their ideas and their intentions; and we understand irony as the elevation of an idea to an infinite principle – the words we say can have a meaning that goes beyond what we intend:

> For if irony is the conextensiveness of being with the individual, or of the I with representation, humor is the art of the surfaces and of the doubles, of nomad singularities and of the always displaced aleatory point; it is the art of the static genesis, the savoir-faire of the pure event, and the 'fourth person singular' – with every signification, denotation, and manifestation suspended, all height and depth abolished.
>
> (Deleuze 1990, 141)

Humour falls or collapses: 'down' from meaning and intentions to the singularities of life that have no order, no high and low, no before and after. Humour can reverse or pervert logic, disrupt moral categories or dissolve the body into parts without any governing intention. Humour is not the *reversal* of cause and effect but the abandonment of the 'before and after' relations – the very line of time – that allow us to think in terms of causes and intentions, of grounds and consequents.

If Samuel Beckett's (1906–89) theatre is 'absurd' it is not because life is rendered despairingly meaningless. Rather, we laugh when the order of time and explanation no longer holds. Consider a typically contradictory exchange from *Endgame* (1957): 'What time is it? The same as usual' (Beckett 1986, 94). The humour of *Endgame* lies in its confusion of logic and the order of sense. Concepts are used, not just in ways that suggest an unconventional meaning, but in ways that destroy the very convention of meaning. One cannot mean or say anything without some shared order of a before and after, a sense of what is and is not.

Beckett constantly presents temporal concepts as though they were spatial, as though it could be the same time as usual. His conditionals disrupt the logic of 'if . . . then': 'If I don't kill that rat he'll die' (Beckett [1957] 1986, 125). We laugh at the absurd order of this grammar; of course the rat will die if it is not killed, because it will die no matter what happens. What is presented as a causal relation is not only not causal; it also conflates cause and effect: killing the rat is also having the rat die. We do not spell out all these contradictions when we view the play; we laugh, as though the body responds when the mind is affronted.

Beckett also explores the humour of stupidity, where concepts are used in ways that contradict their meaning: 'Did you ever have an instant of happiness?' 'Not to my knowledge' (Beckett [1957] 1986, 123). Happiness is not something one *knows*. Unlike Socratic irony, which insists on what concepts must mean, Beckett's humour perverts conceptual meaning, saying what we cannot say. Similarly, in *Endgame*, a character repeatedly looks out of the window to see if it is 'still' the end of the world. The 'end' of the world becomes one object among others in an absurd time that can both continue beyond, and view, the end of time. If irony commits us to what we must mean, humour presents us with what we cannot say. And it is our bodies – in laughter – that explode or convulse at the point of humour.

In humour, the self appears less as an organised agent or organising subject and more as a collection of incongruous body parts. Think of the humour of the clown with outrageously large feet, or slapstick comedy where the body collides with a banana skin or entwines itself around the deckchair it attempts to assemble. Beckett makes use of this anti-subjective aspect of humour. In addition to conflicts of logic in his dialogue, he also writes classically comic movements of bodies: bodies that fall over banana skins, that struggle with ladders, tapes, dustbins and stuffed toys. The self is no longer a subject – an absent synthesising point of view – but an ad hoc, disconnected and disrupted connection of movements. The language of humour is less oriented to meaning – some sense behind the physical word – precisely because words are repeated as so much automatic or machinic noise. Humour takes the human subject back or 'down' to its corporeal origins. It is in this aspect that humour is the opposite tendency of irony, which strives to think the power of thought, subjectivity and synthesis beyond or 'above' any of its specific terms.

Just as traditional irony began with the capacity of the human being, as a political animal, to recognise the force of a concept above and beyond any of its single uses, so Deleuze also defines and goes beyond irony by stressing the political nature of human life. But for Deleuze politics is not the relation among human bodies who must then ask about the essence or concept of the human – what *is* the good, or what *is* the good life? For Deleuze, the political occurs when we create a notion or image of what it is to be human; politics occurs when life creates some norm or idea, such as the idea of 'man', towards which activity is directed. It is because human beings act and live together that they form concepts that organise and give stability to their world. The rich differences and fluxes of life are fixed into ever more manageable units. Traditional irony, for Deleuze, takes this tendency to representation to its infinite extension; instead of forming concepts of this or that thing, and instead of locating ourselves within the flows and durations of life, we try to think the viewpoint of life as a whole, the point of view of conceptuality in general. Irony does not just form a concept of this or that thing; it strives to create a concept of the subject as such – that point from which all concepts emerge. In so doing, irony is reactive; it takes one of life's creations – the concept of the subject – and views that particular event of life as some ultimate condition or origin.

By attacking the history of subjectivism, which posits a ground behind acts and forces, Deleuze provides a philosophy of time and history that is anti-ironic. While irony steps *above* the events and flows of time to ask about what *is* in general, Deleuze begins from the counter-tendency of humour. Deleuze sees laughter and humour as a destruction of subjective positions. Whichever direction we go in, irony or humour, Deleuze insists that both tendencies bring us to an ultimately inhuman unity: either the 'all' that lies beyond us, or the impersonal molecular singularities from which we move. We prefer humour, though, precisely because traditional irony has always seen the ultimate unity of existence as an already given absolute within which we are located. Ultimately, irony tends towards recognition; in seeing ourselves as effects of language and time we posit 'a' time or temporality of rhetoric from which we emerge. Humour, by contrast, descends to the depths of life, disclosing forces or powers that can never be exhausted by representation. Instead of seeing time as the sense or the synthesis that the subject makes of the world through language, Deleuze describes a pre-human time and perception that creates self and language and that extends well beyond the human viewpoint. This is not the narrative time of de Man, not a time that is produced through language; it is a time or becoming from which language emerges. It is a time before meaning and sense, a time of differing durations and perceptions.

For Deleuze and Guattari it is only by seeing literature as a becoming-animal, as destructive of some underlying notion of man or subjectivity without qualities, that we can liberate ourselves from the subjection of irony (Deleuze and Guattari 1986, 35–6). Consider Kafka's writing and its attempt to think of life as lived by a man-insect or a burrowing animal, or Melville's *Moby Dick* (1851), where Ahab no longer acts as an intending subject who views nature but pursues the whale even if this means losing his own self. Such forms of literature also destroy conventional narrative logic and point of view. If the lyric tradition in Romantic poetry creates an 'I' viewpoint that turns back to know itself in the very act of writing poetry, post-ironic literature, or the literature of superior irony, creates future and multiple selves rather than arriving at the original creating self. Deleuze's superior irony strives to think all the becomings that lie beyond the subject, all the points of view that lie beyond the grammar and logic of human representation. Plants, microbes, animals, body parts and particles are flows of becoming. Points of view are created from these flows.

Humour moves 'downward.' In opposition to the thought of a subject that must have preceded the act of speaking or narrating – a subject that can never be located in this world because he is the author of the world – humour shows subjects to be collections of sounds, gestures, body parts and signs devoid of any real sense.

SATIRE AND LITERARY HISTORY

Irony focuses on the *subject*, on the consciousness or power that lies above and beyond any specific character or utterance. Satire focuses on *man*: the human animal who may elevate himself through moral language but who, at bottom, is ultimately nothing more than a collection of desires and interests, a living and dynamic body rather than a timeless soul. If we turn back to Deleuze, this distinction between satire and irony can also give us some understanding of irony as an historical problem. For Deleuze and Guattari the 'subject' is an historical and political phenomenon that extends the concept of man, and does so through a peculiar understanding of language or the signifier. 'Man', they argue, occurs when, instead of regarding each other as desiring bodies who form political relations or 'assemblages', we imagine that there simply is some common nature which allows us to gather together and communicate; language is then seen as the way of *expressing* or representing who we are, and not as a system that produces a common 'we'. The 'subject' occurs when we no longer see ourselves as speaking because we have a common bodily human nature, but because the act of speaking – the power to signify or mean what is not present – produces a point of reason or humanity, which cannot be reduced to any physical or bodily commonality. It is only with the idea of the *signifier*, or a language system to which we are all subjected but which none of us owns or invents, that we have the subject (Deleuze and Guattari 1983). The subject is, for Deleuze and Guattari, a political and historical effect. Capitalism is a tendency towards subjectivism and the tyranny of a single but absent and empty axiom. Each agent is nothing more than a power to exchange and communicate, not a body with specific desires, but simply the desire to operate in systems of relation. The original collection of desiring bodies eventually understands itself as the expression of a 'subjectivity', which is nothing more than the capacity to relate and exchange.

Deleuze's distinction between humour/satire and irony allows us to make some observations about two distinct tendencies. As an attitude to existence, rather than a figure of speech, we can say that irony *elevates*, because it takes any specific style of language, or any specific image of the self, and presents it as finite and therefore limited in relation to an infinite power of ideas or subjectivity. We could say that Byron's *Don Juan* was ironic because it tends to list one moral position after another, one historical event after another, one style or poetic mode after another, with the author concealed behind a detached persona. Byron uses specific or stylised speech acts in order to be *other than* any of the voices or styles presented. Byron could be read as an exemplary Romantic: by presenting various voices as finite and limited; *Don Juan* has no expressed poetic voice, only the principle of creation or synthesis that must be presupposed but never presented. If earlier poets such as Wordsworth mourned the unrepresentable earlier self prior to social determination and identity, Byron celebrated the power of poetry to produce any number of selves, none of whom could be identified with the poet who creates.

Byron can also be read satirically. Indeed, passages in *Don Juan* present the Romantic discourse of ideas and poetic elevation as a way of repressing the desires of the body; Don Juan's lofty meditations and musings are described as an effect of an adolescent influx of hormones, with 'love' being a delusion of the body. Instead of creating a subject who exists above and beyond any of the presented poetic voices, Byron demonstrates that 'life' is nothing more than the adoption or creation of different moral positions serving different desires. The epic opens with Don Juan's overly zealous moral upbringing, motivated by jealousy and resentment; only those whose desires have been thwarted feel the need to speak of values that are 'higher' than desire. Morality and subjectivity are fictions that our passions require in order to cope with the chaotic, and almost inhuman, flux of desire. To be truly satirical, Byron's work would need to deflate or reduce all our elevated ideas and see them as caused by human nature or desire. For if satire descends, it does so by recognising the life from which elevated concepts or ideas emerge.

Satire recognises the lowly animal being behind all our ideas of self-creation. Satire is *immanently* historical; looking at the ways in which ideas of 'man' have been produced from the flow of life. By contrast, irony is transcendental; any history of ourselves must be narrated by some historicising subject. Irony presents the subject as the absent ground that allows us to think of or represent any nature or history; satire shows that such a presupposed ground is merely a way of disguising or denying the conflicting forces that produce us. Satire shows the ways in which we do *not* author ourselves, through the presentation of puns, humour, hypocrisy and stupidity.

We can explore the question of just how we read a text – whether ironically or satirically – by looking at literary history and literary character. According to Deleuze and Guattari's history of the subject in *Anti-Oedipus* (1983), 'life' begins with inhuman and pre-personal perception – interacting 'flows' of genetic, biological and animate material which form organisms, including human and animal bodies. Humans gradually perceive other bodies and form groups or territories by collective perception. A tribe, for example, is formed as an identifiable territory when it creates common marks – through tattooing, painting, scarring – across its social body. These marks are not *signifiers*; they do not represent a common whole or shared meaning. The whole is formed or collected only through the rituals of marking. An assemblage is created through collective perception; each body perceives the other perceiving body as similarly marked, and as also perceiving and sharing this process of marking. An assemblage is a collection of bodies that creates its own connections through difference – by producing or creating marks on otherwise radically different bodies. An assemblage is not a collection of bodies grounded on a notion of prior sameness. Some idea of 'man' can only be formed if an even greater assemblage of bodies recognises some common body as its organising image. The body of white, speaking, bourgeois man, for example, acts as the perceived image that identifies the whole. A body is no longer perceived as like one's own because it is marked out or rendered common through a perceivable inscription. Rather, one imagines that one can see and relate to others *because* deep down we are all human. Western history moves from the organisation of body parts and desires – tribes that collect around specific markings – to some concept of man in general. Instead of viewing bodies as collections of parts, desires and fluxes of singular or non-generalisable differences, one sees the body *as the sign of* some underlying and general humanity. We imagine some identity, some human nature, which provides a timeless, contextless and necessary ground. The political, or the creation of collectives, is no longer active, with different bodies gathering through some event and forming a notion of the human. The political is passive; we speak and act together *because* we are human.

According to Deleuze and Guattari political wholes and social identity are produced *from* desire and investments (Deleuze and Guattari 1983). It is the display of an external body – such as the body of the torturing despot, or the forgiving king – that creates the social body. The collective is produced when desires of bodies act in relation to an other body, seen by all, and seen to be visible by all. The king or despot that oversees punishment or torture is regarded with fear or terror; it is this collective perception of a body that organises and constitutes a political whole. Such an investment becomes more subtle when 'we' all invest and obey, not the actual body of the king or despot, but the concept of 'man' or subjectivity; we are gathered around the image of a speaking, reasoning, disembodied soul of common sense. Irony, too, can be related both to this production of terror and the enjoyment of cruelty. Irony produces a viewpoint that surveys the whole, that derides or chastens everyday life and desire. Further, the enjoyment of this 'high urbanity' could not proceed without the powerlessness, blindness or exclusion of those who are ironised. Irony is only possible with the idea of a subject who views life and its differences from on high, a subject with the power to be other than the struggle of bodily existence.

What Deleuze and Guattari's history of the subject in *Anti-Oedipus* sets out to demonstrate is that this elevated disembodied subject has emerged from a process of cruelty and terror. It is only with the organised torture of bodies that one can imagine a 'law' to which such bodies are subjected. The subject is an effect of terror, for it is only through terror that we produce a law to which we are all subjected, and the idea of a universal and dutiful 'we'.

Literature, according to Deleuze and Guattari, can reverse this historical and ironic tendency by re-living the cruelty and terror *from which* the law is imagined. Kafka is often read as an ironic or negative author because the 'law' always remains beyond any image or figure of the law – all we encounter are judgements and prohibitions, never the law itself (Derrida 1989b). Deleuze, however, sees Kafka as anything but negative and ironic. Kafka's fathers and judges in *The Castle* (1922) or *The Trial* (1925) are not *signs of* a hidden law. Rather, the weak but punishing father is imagined as that which stands in front of a law forever out of reach. Our subjection to law is an effect of irony. Because all we have are partial images, we imagine some law above and beyond our own life. Kafka exposes the law as a fiction, as nothing more than a series of authorities who have such a lack of force and power that they must present themselves *as signs* of some greater law. But there is nothing behind the father, the judge, the court or the priest. We need to see such fictions as signifiers, pure affects or sensations with no underlying or hidden reality. The subject, or the self subjected to an unseen law, is one fiction or image among others. By creating endless images of the law Kafka shows the law to be nothing more than the performance or image of power, with power itself being the power of images (Deleuze and Guattari 1986, 55). Before the modern notion of the subject there were just political acts of force, cruelty and terror; it is only in modernity that we imagine power or force to have a ground: the man or humanity which might act as some way of judging and organising force.

THE LITERARY SUBJECT AND THE EMERGENCE
OF IRONY

Much work on Renaissance drama has argued that selves are produced through the display of power. Far from there being some idea of the subject as pure consciousness above and beyond any social role, there was in the Renaissance just the performance of social roles, with selves being regarded as public effects and creations of social exchange (Greenblatt 1980). To read Shakespeare as expressing something like the 'human condition' or to regard Shakespeare as ironic – as a creative principle above and beyond the work – would be to miss the way his plays were events of display and performance that *created* a common social body. There was no idea of man in general, only the social performance and production of roles – with political power being clearly presented as the creation of an effective persona. The Renaissance did not yet have a notion of 'man' – a common self within us all. Rather, Renaissance drama presented social power as a complex network of bodies, actions and perceptions with notions of some ultimate meaning or morality being clear effects of this system.

The later idea of 'man' could only emerge through a different style of politics and social investment. Instead of displaying the performance and power of bodies, there would need to be a notion of character that expresses some underlying nature. If Shakespeare's scenes of public and kingly power show the ways in which a social body is created by the common perception or investment in a desired and powerful body, his soliloquies create the notion of an underlying and hidden self. Indeed, his plays themselves reflect on this historical transition and problem. Richard II believes in divine kingship and cosmic justice; he does not realise that power must be performed and created, that one must present the illusion of being a divine king. *Hamlet* also presents the problem of such illusion being recognised; if all we have is the social display and production of a moral order, how do we act in the absence of all illusion? Who are we really? It is not surprising that with the public production of effective selves in Renaissance drama, there was also an emerging genre of character. In the Renaissance one's political identity was produced through the public performance of power and the creation of an empowered body around which the social whole is organised, but there was also a tendency to move from public character to an underlying, hidden or intrinsic self.

Early novels, accordingly, produce 'man' not as an imposed political display or performance, but as a being whose identity is private, lying behind and motivating his actions. 'Man' is seen as having a human nature: a tendency to labour, acquire wealth, form families and enter into exchange. In Daniel Defoe's *Robinson Crusoe* (1719), for example, Crusoe encounters a man – Friday – with whom he has neither historical nor cultural connection. But he inevitably recognises Friday as a man and as the *same* – as capable of labour, production, acquisition and society. Modernity, and modern fiction, operate through this assumption of a common human ground, a presupposed humanity. For this reason, modern literature can be satirical by reflecting on those tendencies of human nature that 'we' all share. Whereas irony, classically, delimits human life by positing an elevated concept that is *not realised*, satire examines life and its inherent propensities. Socratic irony had posited a concept or idea that judged life, whereas satire displays life itself; the judgement occurs not because we are placed above life but because we recognise that the described life as also like our own. If irony, in general, posits some 'higher' or examining point of view in a text, modern *satirical* irony allows for no view above and beyond the human.

Characters who feel that they are elevated or above the trials of common life are frequently the objects of satire. The irony of a text like *Gulliver's Travels* or even *Pride and Prejudice* (1813) is satirical. Gulliver has no sense of his implication in the contingency of human life; his blindness lies in his belief that he adopts a position outside or above life.

Not only does Jane Austen (1775–1817) parody the way in which we take our local sentiments for universal truths, she also displays the blindness of those characters who believe themselves to be in simple possession of either a moral law or a social code. Her novels not only portray the vanities and tendencies of human nature, they also present characters who arrive at fulfilment only through knowing and reflecting upon the social nature of man. One cannot disengage oneself from human life and nature. For Austen, the art of fiction and the art of satire is also an art of recognition: examining the follies of others with a full perception of our own weakness. Satire assumes the common ground of 'man' and therefore works against the traditional aim of irony, an elevated or 'urbane' point of view above and beyond natural life.

The German Romantics had seen both the novel and Shakespeare as exemplary of irony. They recognised no literary-historical distinction between the many voices of a novel and the absence of authorial intrusion in Renaissance drama. But their conflation of both types of text as ironic relies upon including both Shakespeare and novels within a single movement that expresses subjectivity. Shakespeare, they argued, in *not* being present creates an absent point of creativity, just as novels with their many voices and characters also allow for a common ground of 'life'. Insofar as any text, modern or pre-modern, suggests a point of creation not presented in the text, then it is an instance of irony. Against this Romantic conflation, we can look at how literary texts in specific historical contexts create different notions of just what a creative context is. For novels, for example, one assumes that all events take place on the common ground of a presupposed human nature, with plots being the unfolding and development of this nature's possibilities. In pre-modern texts, by contrast, such a universal humanity is absent. If Shakespeare's plays are 'ironic' in the German Romantic sense – if they adopt no single or clear expressed position – then this is precisely because they contest and play with the very notion of what can count as human. We might say that the Renaissance begins to form some sense of a universal human point of view, some negotiation of various historical and cultural contexts, but has not yet formed a clear notion of *man* as universally shared nature. Shakespeare's Caliban in *The Tempest* is not included in the 'human'. Because he is outside the interaction of court life and power he remains inassimilable. Unlike Crusoe's man Friday, he is not a potential human nature awaiting recognition; Caliban is asocial and therefore inhuman. There is, in the Renaissance, no full sense of a 'man' in general who can be recognised, studied and communicated with across cultural and political boundaries. One is human only through one's political activity.

We can say, perhaps, that there is a literary-historical trajectory towards irony: from bodies collected in social space, to a sense of 'man' or human nature as underlying those bodies, until, finally, the notion of the subject who recognises himself as having existed all along in various historical contexts. In forming the concept of the subject as *other than* any expressed body, self or humanity, the Romantics also allowed for the possibility of reading literary history: not just reading texts from the past, but in reading those texts *as past*, as different expressions of a constantly differing subjectivity. We can only form a notion of *the subject* through reflection on the various modes of life through which that subjectivity is expressed. According to Deleuze and Guattari, it is the creation and perception of a common body that produces a social whole. It is the creation of 'man' in general, or the white, rational body of reason and good sense, that produces a universal community which then leads to the ironic notion of the subject: that point of view elevated above life and detached from any specific body (Deleuze and Guattari 1983).

JOYOUS STUPIDITY

Irony detaches itself from any specific time or culture and can imagine itself as a point of view that surveys 'life' or 'history' as one unified plane. According to Deleuze and Guattari, we can both chart the creation of the image of 'the subject' in history and see how this very concept of subjectivity produces history as a single horizon. Their counter-ironic task is not to produce a point of view above and beyond life, but to see life itself as a humorous or joyous multiplicity of incommensurable perceptions (Deleuze and Guattari 1987, 194). This would be directly opposed to the tendency of Romantic irony and subjectivity, which ultimately recognises all life as the expression of an absent or presupposed ground. For Deleuze and Guattari the creation of *a* history is itself an historical event: a convergence of multiple lines or planes of becoming that occurs through a later act of interpretation. We recognise the past as the creation of the present; we recognise other cultures as different expressions of our own, and we think ironically, with each event being interpretable from some ultimate human standpoint. We can, therefore, see literary history as the creation, rather than expression, of the plane of human history, with texts reading the past and other cultures as different expressions of the one human life. History has moved progressively towards capitalism, towards an ever-expanding political body through the production of an increasingly homogenised or universal notion of 'subjectivity' that 'we' all share. It is in capitalism that social connections need to be all-inclusive, with every body being human insofar as it is capable of labour and exchange

(Deleuze and Guattari 1983). 'Man' is created as a common power behind exchange and production.

Eighteenth-century literature, through its narratives of travel, everywhere finds the same common body, a body with a tendency to acquire wealth, exchange property and form families and societies in response to the needs of life. Whereas earlier social formations and literary productions had placed the social body first, such that Renaissance tragedies depict the havoc that ensues with the disruption or transgression of political order (Moretti 1988), eighteenth-century literature begins with individuals, often infants or foundlings, who produce social relations because of the nature of man. Swift's *Gulliver's Travels* is a satire in two senses. First, its object is man. Despite the travels to absurd and impossible lands, Gulliver discovers the same human desires that dress themselves up pompously as ideas. The object of satire is not a particular moral or political discourse so much as 'man' and his capacity to allow his acquisitive desires to be hypocritically masked by a politics that presents itself as pure law. Second, not only does Gulliver recognise the same object across his travels – man and his bodily desires – the narrative traces the emergence of Gulliver's ideas from his own body. Gulliver eventually refuses the humanity of his body, the bodily forces of urination, consumption and defecation that have been displayed as so compulsive throughout the narrative. Gulliver's final position of disgust with the human body is satirised, not just because he absurdly sees himself as other than human while occupying the very body he loathes, but because the position of bodily disgust, of inhuman loathing of the human, is itself seen as all too human. Swift constantly describes the human body's capacity to loath its own nature, and the tyrannical effects of this loathing. To deny or repress human nature is to set up a purifying and exterminating 'reason': a reason that is itself hypocritically embodied. If we read literary history 'backwards' we could see Swift as anticipating the problems of irony; to adopt a position of subjectivity above and beyond life is not only the creation of an image of reason, it is also a reaction against the forces of bodies. Instead of allowing the ironic Romantic subject to incorporate and re-read the past as its own, we could see the past as an anticipation and rejection of the modern ironic, elevated and disembodied subject.

Deleuze suggested not just that one could write a history of the body and its production of 'man' and then 'subjectivity'; he also suggested that there was something ethically affirmative in moving away from irony and its creation of a 'subject'. The idea of a subject who is a point of nothingness outside the actions and events of history creates a principle outside life. Irony has traditionally set itself up in judgement of life, whereas humour allows for the joyous eruption of life. Irony is, from a Deleuzean way of thinking, reactive rather than active. Instead of living forcefully and moving with life, and assessing the very force of life, irony imagines some principle beyond life, such as the law, that might judge life. Irony takes one of life's active creations, such as a concept or an image of 'man', and allows that creation to enslave or control life. Irony is reactive, also, because it produces life as fallen. From the German Romantics through to Paul de Man, irony recognises that any expressed self or character can only be a fallen limitation or determination of the infinite and undetermined subjective power; indeed, the subject is for de Man nothing other than this sense of what must have fallen. Even traditional irony – the sense of a 'said' that is other than the actual or manifest 'saying' – posits a concept or meaning above the actual speech acts of life. We imagine that there are ideas – such as justice or the good – that we can never fully instantiate.

Politically, according to Deleuze and Guattari, the tendency towards the subject and irony is life-denying. The key political question should not be how we manage our desires in order to achieve the law, but how it is that we have enslaved ourselves to laws that deny our desires (Deleuze and Guattari 1983). For Deleuze and Guattari the answer to this political question, which is the question of fascism, is that bodies have a tendency to create images that enhance their power; but these same images can also become separated and appear as external laws towards which life ought to strive. The image of the subject is the governing image of capitalism. Here, we are no longer enslaved by some external law or idea, such as the idea or image of justice. Capitalism no longer requires any sense of man or human nature to regulate and control its activity. Early capitalism – and we can see this in early novels – argued that exchange, labour and production were in our own human interests, creative of benevolent social relations. But late capitalism removes all notion of human nature, arguing for the value of exchange itself: no moral concept of man or the self ought to impede the free development of life. Capitalism is no longer impeded or limited by any external law. The subject is nothing other than the empty axiom that allows all life to flow across one single plane; he is nothing other than a potential for labour and exchange, devoid of any positive qualities. If we allow for nothing more than exchange, interaction and the flow of capital, then no single idea of the self or good will be elevated above any other. The subject is just that capacity to adopt any and every persona or value; the undetermined ironic subject who exists behind determined values is an effect of the dominance and immanence of the capitalist system, a system that precludes any outside. Capitalism is not the imposition of law or value; it is a system that produces any and every value as one more quantifiable item of exchange. Just as the ironic subject can adopt any discourse or persona, so capitalism can market any discourse or value. Feminism, environmentalism, Christianity, Buddhism, New-Ageism or Anarchism: all these can be sold as logos, images or concepts in the late capitalism that markets communication. Anything and anyone can be taken up in the imperative to exchange; we no longer need to recognise everyone else as part of a common humanity, for even cultural difference and exoticism can be marketed. Other cultures, religions and dissident discourses can all be allowed precisely because they enable the further flow of capital.

Irony represents both a tendency and a problem of capitalism. Irony has always posited some point above and beyond any particular context or value. In this sense it anticipates the tendency of capitalism to cross contexts and produce a universal point from which all values can be exchanged. When Deleuze criticises irony and representation he criticises this tendency to create a point of judgement that values and orders life, a point of view from which life is systematised and reduced to identity. Deleuze's humour or superior irony is therefore opposed to the politics of capitalism, communication and subjectivity *and* to the poetics of 'post-modern' irony.

The popular postmodern idea that everything is discourse, that there is no self, substance or perception outside signs, that individuals are constructions of social systems: this type of postmodernism is at one with a capitalism that reduces life to one undifferentiated plane of relative values. The postmodern refusal of all value is far from being revolutionary. There has always been a repressive or reactive tendency in human political life to reduce difference to systemic equivalence; if revolutions are undertaken in the name of 'man' or humanity, they are ultimately reactionary, subordinating action and difference to some general standard or point of value. Far from establishing some point outside difference from which life might be judged, humour allows the chaos of life and difference to disrupt any elevated value. According to Deleuze, a revolution can occur only in moving away from irony and the emptiness of subjectivity to humour. Here, instead of positing a form – the subject – that can remain above and beyond any identity, humour presents the singularities and differences from which general forms such as the subject or man emerge.

In Swift, for example, the direction of humour is clear: the focus on the body, the emergence of language from noise and nonsense, the narrative description of the particularities and desires that set themselves up as values and moralities, and even the finitude of 'man' who, when observed from above or below, appears as one more body, rather than a rational subject. Most importantly, instead of human nature being a moral ground or authority it is shown to bear a tendency towards cruelty, and a delight in the perception of cruelty. Humour allows us to say the unsayable, or say what we cannot mean. Whereas the ethics of irony posits ideas and concepts towards which we ought to strive, or what we *must mean* when we use words like 'justice', humour allows all the repressed and meaningless drives of the body to disrupt sense. Morality is possible when cruelty is given a *meaning*: the forceful and violent interactions of bodies are subjected to law. By establishing a human, moral or justifying point of view we are able to see cruelty, violence and force as exercises of law or punishment.

Humour, by contrast, displays the cruelty of violence: the unjustified or meaningless enjoyment of another's suffering. We are delighted by watching the other body fall; the body convulses with laughter when the moral subject or 'man' is once more presented as either subject to, or delighting in, cruel necessity. We laugh at misfortune, at the collapse of law, at misguided logic, at hypocrisy, or even, as in the case of Swift, at the violence we direct against our own bodies. Gulliver is risible because, like those he visits, he vainly subjects the human body to inhuman ideals of purity and constraint. It is this violence of humour, the force of life that assaults conscious intent and determinate meaning, that precludes the possibility of postmodern irony.

Postmodern cynicism, or the refusal of any force or value beyond the system of exchange, is at once a feature of capitalism and, in theories of postmodern irony, often presented as disruptive of capitalism. The possibility and desirability of this postmodern irony will be the subject of the next chapter.

8

POSTMODERNISM, PARODY AND IRONY

Rorty, Hutcheon, Austen, Joyce and Carter

Irony, as we have noticed in most of the sources from Socrates to the present, has been regarded as politically ambivalent. Irony is both questioning and elitist, both disruptive of norms and constructive of higher ideals. On the one hand, irony challenges any ready-made consensus or community, allowing the social whole and everyday language to be questioned. On the other hand, the position of this questioning and ironic viewpoint is necessarily hierarchical, claiming a point of view beyond the social whole and above ordinary speech and assumptions. Advocates of 'postmodern' irony have acknowledged these risks. Indeed, how we understand and value postmodernism depends very much on our definition and evaluation of irony. We might want to reject the very problem of a level of sense or meaning behind signs. We might want to embrace a postmodern society without meta-narratives, privileged viewpoints or ideals of legitimation. Alternatively, we might want to redefine irony. If there is nothing other than signification, with no subjects who signify or world to be signified, then we would be left with a world of 'saying', without any possibility of underlying truth or ultimate sense. Such a world would be radically ironic, for *no* speech act could be legitimated, justified or grounded. To describe postmodernity as a society of the simulacra, where copies and repetitions have no original, where systems have no centre and where images have no prior model of substance imaged, is to see the postmodern present as finally having liberated itself from the constraining myths of an ultimate real.

RICHARD RORTY: IRONY AND PRAGMATISM

Richard Rorty argues that irony is the only possible ethic of modern liberalism. We cannot believe in a foundation that would underlie or supersede the difference and specificity of cultures: 'we have no pre-linguistic consciousness to which language needs to be adequate, no deep sense of how things are which it is the duty of philosophers to spell out in language' (Rorty 1989, 21). We should recognise that 'we' are effects of the vocabulary we speak, and that we can only renovate or renew such vocabularies from within: 'The ironist spends her time worrying about the possibility that she has been initiated into the wrong tribe, taught to play the wrong language game . . . But she cannot give a criterion of wrongness' (Rorty 1989, 75). Those who 'go Socratic', Rorty argues, try to renovate their language by an appeal to reality, but Rorty's ironist sees 'no reason to think that Socratic inquiry into the essence of justice or science or rationality will take one much beyond the language games of one's time' (Rorty 1989, 74–5).

For the ironist, renovation of language comes about through *private* irony or continual self-creation, while at a public level we have to be nominalist, recognising that our concepts have no corresponding reality but only a stabilising function (Rorty 1989, 87). We recognise that our fixed political institutions and our moral vocabulary – terms such as justice, democracy and even liberalism – have no inherent meaning: 'I take pragmatists and deconstructionists to be united in thinking that anything can be anything if you put in [*sic*] the right context, and that "right" just means the context that best serves somebody's purposes at a certain time and place. Metaphysicians think that there is a Right Context' (Rorty 1996, 43). Publicly and pragmatically, we must adopt a common political vocabulary: in the case of modern Western democracies we think of justice, rights, humanity and freedom. We use such terms for what they can do, or for the open-ended conversations they may allow. We can neither find their intrinsic meaning, nor argue for their inherent superiority. Indeed, Rorty insists on a peculiarly private irony. We take part in the political language of democracy, all along aware that democracy is one possible language game among others. But we also have to acknowledge that a *culture* of irony would preclude the necessary agreement and stability that enable democracy to function, 'I cannot go on to claim that there could or ought to be a culture whose public rhetoric is *ironist*. I cannot imagine a culture which socialized its youth in such a way as to make them continuously dubious about their own process of socialization. Irony seems inherently a private matter' (Rorty 1989, 87).

Irony, for Rorty, is not elevation above everyday speech; it is not a high literary technique that situates the author or speaker 'beyond' characters and speaking conditions. On the contrary, irony is a private attitude, an awareness that one's language is just one language among others. Rorty sets his understanding of irony and modernity against those, like the contemporary Frankfurt school philosopher Jürgen Habermas (1929–), who insist that insofar as we speak we presuppose a demand that others will recognise what we say to be valid. For Habermas this assumed validity is necessary not because there simply *is* some ultimately true extra-linguistic world, a metaphysical 'real', but because speaking together generates a 'lifeworld': a common and ongoing frame of reference through which we negotiate what we say, what we do and how we define our world (Habermas 1993). For Rorty, however, such a necessarily presupposed goal of consensus and legitimation merely assumes that others will agree to our stories about justification and understanding. Rorty argues that adopting a tone of irony would allow for a plurality of stories and, further, that we would value a world in which competing accounts were possible. We would not be troubled by, nor would we violently react to, other narratives and language games. Irony allows us to inhabit our own context, acknowledge the existence of other contexts *and* enable our own context to be open, fluid and creative.

There is a contradiction in Rorty's advocacy of irony, and one he is quite happy to inhabit. On the one hand he argues for the value of irony: that it is the only way we can abandon grand claims about truth and foundations, claims that have allowed the West to think of itself as a privileged home of reason. On the other hand, he does not want to establish irony, or the perpetual questioning of one's public language by private individuals, as a universal truth or theory. To do so would mean establishing the ironic viewpoint that questions Western values, as one more central Western value. Rorty parcels out this paradox into a distinction between public and private. Publicly and politically, we have to speak and act as if we believed and stood behind the values of the West; we commit ourselves to the language of rights, humanism and democracy. Privately and philosophically, we know such values to be contingent and context dependent; we remain ironic at a private level. This might mean that philosophers who play with and recreate language games *might* invent new ways of speaking that could be adopted publicly and politically, but such inventions would be ironic: not seeking to find *the* truth, but speaking with a sense of creation, renovation and infidelity (Rorty 1996, 17). What Rorty is seeking to avoid is the notion of the philosopher as elevated metaphysician who can abstract himself from everyday life and ask the big questions about the big concepts: what *is* man, what *is* truth, what *is* justice? Irony, of Rorty's kind, takes philosophy away from the position of transcendental social judgement, and does so by insisting that in postmodernity we no longer believe in truth, ground and foundations. We believe in writing, self-creation and the uncontrolled proliferation of language and texts.

But is this really the best way to understand postmodern literature, culture and irony? For examples of ironic or postmodern writing Rorty turns to philosophers like Derrida, rather than to postmodern fiction (Rorty 1989, 125). Derrida, however, far from agreeing that his concept of writing leads to play and the abandonment of the questioning power of philosophy, has insisted that we *cannot* simply doubt our language and recognise ourselves as effects of the context within which we are located. On the contrary, the very thought of the writing or textuality that produces speaking positions *both* places us strangely outside any context *and* produces one more position of elevated doubt that reinforces the power of philosophy to think of itself as above and beyond life. Far from abandoning or escaping metaphysics, Derrida's concept of writing disturbs or solicits metaphysics. Whether there can be a genuine 'play' beyond metaphysics is a possibility that Derrida neither definitively asserts nor denies. But he makes one thing very clear. It is the belief that we can simply abandon all claims to truth and metaphysics by merely inhabiting a context provisionally or ironically that is the most metaphysical and violent of all. To speak from any context – even the context that insists that all language is context-dependent – is to be placed in a position of *decision* and determination. One should acknowledge the force and inherent assertion of speech and language, rather than claiming that irony allows us to never really be at one with what we say or who we are.

There are two objections that we can make to Rorty's celebration of irony and his broader claim that we can escape metaphysical striving by abandoning the desire to 'get beneath the propositional to the non-propositional' (Rorty 1996, 43). First, irony cannot avoid being metaphysical, for it posits another meaning – an ideal or immaterial sense. Could there be a proposition if there were no non-propositional referent? Second, irony is often a way of keeping a language in place rather than, as Rorty claims, a way of renovating language. To use a discourse ironically allows the continued articulation of that discourse and leaves that discourse in place. Postmodern literature has been dominated by texts that express a masculinist, imperialist, racist or elitist discourse in order to present the violence of that discourse. Twentieth-century novels and films, from J.G. Ballard's *Crash* (1973) and Bret Easton Ellis's *American Psycho* (1991) to Quentin Tarantino's *Reservoir Dogs* (1992), display the violence of a desire and sexuality that is self-enclosed in a system of signs, clichés, slogans and advertising images. But whereas Ballard frames his technological nightmare of postmodernity with an introduction (added in 1995) that signals his clear disapproval of the world he presents, later faithful depictions of a postmodern world of pure simulation and violence with no moral voice are less obviously ironic. Both *American Psycho* and *Reservoir Dogs* present the dismemberment of bodies alongside the enjoyed and popular signs of everyday life; the violence can be read, not as a local perversion or evil, but as symptomatic of a world where the immediacy and surface nature of desire and gratification precludes any moral voice or limit. One could read such works as ironic *critiques* of the world they present, but this would require an explicit reading. And even if one were to decide that such texts were, or ought to be, ironic, this would still allow the violent content to be displayed, enjoyed and popularised. Indeed, part of the sense of both *American Psycho* and *Reservoir Dogs* is the imbrication of violence, torture and dismemberment with sexual and everyday desire. Even if we were to decide that such works were ironic, how do we avoid the enjoyment, repetition and reinforcement of violence that these texts also make possible? If masculinity, or a Western 'phallogocentrism' that can acknowledge no limits to its own desire and self-projection, is being repeatedly ironised as self-consuming, irony may be one more way for this subject of domination to sustain itself (Braidotti 1991). Violence is presented, with the critique of this violence already anticipated and silenced. Any objection to these works as violent or masculinist could be rejected as being too literal, as having missed the subtlety of the irony. In criticising himself the white male subject of capitalism allows its images and fantasies to be given one more viewing.

LINDA HUTCHEON AND THE POLITICS OF POSTMODERN IRONY

The political nature of this problem of irony has been explored by the Candian theorist of postmodernism Linda Hutcheon. When the West decides to be ironic about itself it cannot avoid some relation to its others; it cannot avoid repeating the very colonialism it adopts only ironically. Hutcheon details one striking example of a Canadian museum exhibit that, instead of presenting its archives from other (dominated) cultures from the point of view of knowledge and authority, decided to adopt an ironic viewpoint (Hutcheon 1994, 178). For example, one image of a white woman educating the indigenous population in the art of hygiene was presented and labelled as such, with the viewer supposedly being able to recognise the patronising tone both of the image and its description. The colonialist images of the past were presented *as colonialist* and *as images*: as speaking and looking in a certain style of paternalism, authority, objectification and imperialist grandeur. The curators were aware of the very politics of speaking about others. If one cannot present other cultures themselves, and if one cannot be placed in a position of authoritative truth in relation to other contexts, then one should play up and emphasise that any exhibition of other cultures is just that: an exhibition. The image of the other is always *decided*, collected and determined from a governing and colonially complicit point of view. However, this decision to present the colonising gaze ironically, by repeating all its demeaning and objectifying images, failed to achieve its aim; many of the indigenous viewers of the exhibition saw the images as one more presentation of the white Western view of its others.

Hutcheon's analysis of the incident details the ways in which the irony of the exhibition was misread. Not only did many viewers not notice the quotation marks around descriptions of exhibits, the indigenous viewers themselves felt that even a marked irony repeated the occlusion of their stories, culture, voices and specificity. Hutcheon's reflections are interesting and salutary precisely because she acknowledges the problem and risk of irony but can come to no conclusion:

> it is far too easy to forget the dangers in the face of the valorization of irony's subversive potential by much feminist, gay and lesbian, post-colonial and poststructuralist theory and practice . . . the particular intersection – in the communicative space set up by meaning and affect – that makes irony happen is a highly unstable one, sometimes even a dangerous one. Whether it will become too dangerous, too risky is for the future to decide. Will there ever be another – safe – 'age of irony'? Did one ever really exist?
>
> (Hutcheon 1994, 204)

Unlike Rorty, Hutcheon recognises that such gestures of irony, far from avoiding the old myths of the West as the privileged viewpoint of reason, once again allow the West to speak in the absence of others. Even if the irony had been better managed, rendered more explicit or made less ambivalent, would irony, Hutcheon asks, have been an appropriate gesture? Not only are there some issues that might deserve more respect than others, such as the genocidal crimes of colonialism, there are also risks inherent in such post-colonial acts of irony and self-distancing.

For Hutcheon, irony is not and should not just be a disbelief or distance from what one says (as it is for Rorty). Irony has a political and ethical force. One speaks the language of colonialism and reason ironically in order to display its violence, force and delimited viewpoint. However, this critical repetition does not only risk being unnoticed or misunderstood. It still allows the voice of colonialism to speak, even in quotation marks. Hutcheon herself can reach no conclusion on this issue.

On the one hand she maintains the value of irony in creating a distance from Western discourses and narratives of reason. It is precisely because, from a position of postmodern postcolonialism, one cannot find or desire a better position of truth and authority, that one adopts irony to present any authority or history as one fiction among others. On the other hand, not only can such gestures of distancing and irony fail to be read, they also allow the West to keep speaking itself, even if one is speaking with a full sense of the violence and limits of one's context.

FREE-INDIRECT STYLE: AUSTEN AND JOYCE

Irony, as we have noted, produces and implies aesthetic *distance*: we imagine some authorial point of judgement that is other than the voice expressed. But the stylistic implications and complications of this distance also lead beyond irony. If it is the case that an author or speaker can be other than what they manifestly say, it is also the case that complex forms of irony can make the recognition and existence of this distanced authorial position impossible to determine. It may be the case that the text resists a clearly elevated or distanced position from the discourse it expresses. What is implied, not said or other than the narration, is not some clearly perceived ironic position that 'we' might recognise, for such a point of elevated recognition is precisely what the structure of the text seeks to destroy.

Modernist free-indirect style moves well beyond the clear location of irony and earlier uses of what is now identified as free-indirect discourse. We might say that Austen had already used free-indirect style in *Pride and Prejudice* (1813), describing characters in the elevated, manufactured and obsequious tones they would themselves use. But we would also have to say that while Austen herself never speaks in the novel, all the voices and the dialogues that characters maintain with each other allow a social whole to emerge, where some characters speak with a sense of the social whole, and others merely repeat received values. Austen presents two styles of dialogue: characters who do nothing more than voice received opinions (including characters, such as Mr Bennett who continues to look at his wife as an object of ridicule and satire). Other characters, by contrast, speak with an openness to others, not merely judging what they say, but allowing their actions and character to fill out a picture of personhood that lies beyond mere speech. It is the *narrative* of the novel, the structured description of actions, places and the changes of human relations that allows certain voices to be seen as sincere and open, and others to be seen as mere rhetoric and dissimulation. The plot allows some characters to emerge as those who have been capable of insight and development, while others remain within the style of repetition and received ideas through which they were originally described.

Austen's use of voices and dialogue is centred in some grounding value: the value of social dialogue and exchange itself, as opposed to merely received and repeated values. Her good characters alter their opinions and values when presented with contrary events; they speak with a view both to self-reflection and self-renewal, admitting that there is more to life than merely adhering to what one says. Good sense and character are social and stylistic. Characters with a sense of the social whole allow their moral discourse to alter, expose itself to definition and articulate questions of how one ought to speak (Oldmark 1981, 2). Both Elizabeth Bennett and Darcy develop an awareness of their place in the community and a recognition of the effects of their own speech. By contrast, Austen presents characters who are nothing more than rigid repetitions of style: Mr Bennett's satire, Mr Collins's pomposity and Lady de Burgh's ritual propriety. Such characters cling to their own personality and style of speech as if it were nothing more than a social role or a play; they have no sense of creating themselves in relation to others, or of acting in ways that go beyond mere social rule and expectation. Jane Austen's use of free-indirect style is ironic; she speaks in the language of characters and their received morality, but she also allows a higher point of view through characters who speak sincerely with a sense of moral discourse as dialogue and question, rather than fashion or truths 'universally acknowledged'.

Modernist free-indirect discourse, by contrast, is not grounded in character. Style itself speaks, with characters becoming effects rather than authors of language. The early stories of James Joyce's *Dubliners* (1914), for example, problematise the moral tradition of irony, which traditionally generates a position of judgement above the limits of context or discourse. Not only do the stories allow for a high modernist ironic reading, which would place the reader and author in an elite and impersonal point of judgement above the commodified and machine-like voices of everyday life, they also allow for a postmodern irony, where discourses are presented as forces in their own right, as though language circulated with its own energy and power of transformation. There is no position *from which* narration emerges, no impersonal or ineffable point of pure creativity that maintains itself only as a principle of style and creation. Rather, narrations are effects of the collision of text; speakers are points through which language or text passes. 'Text' expands from being language to include all the noises, accidents, forces and traces of life.

Consider Joyce's 'An Encounter', which is written from the first-person point of view of a young boy who plays truant with his friends in order to embark on an 'adventure'. Because the story is written in the first person it is not, strictly speaking, an example of free-indirect style, which usually adopts the idiom and style of a character in the third person. But Joyce's first-person, or the 'I' of narration, is already invaded by impersonal voices. Not only does the story speak as though a moralising adult were describing his experiences as a child – 'A spirit of unruliness diffused itself among us and, under its influence, differences of culture and constitution were waived' – this adult voice is itself derived from popular culture (Joyce [1914] 1992, 11). The story not only mentions that the boys read '*The Union Jack, Pluck* and *The Halfpenny Marvel*'; the describing voice also speaks in the tone of 'boys' own' adventures: the escapade is referred to as an 'adventure'; the boy refers to other boys flinging stones 'out of chivalry'; they arrange a 'siege'; they carry 'provisions'; and refer to Leo Dillon as a 'funk'. The narrating adult voice is already that of a circulated discourse, and already the stylised, rather than actual, repetition of the child's point of view. The narrator is not a transparent subject viewing a world so much as a series of received voices and notions. The recollection is never fully aware of what it is saying; the voice is traversed by boy's slang ('skit', 'miching', 'josser'), the moralising tone of boy's literature, and the upright bourgeois, but 'liberal' (ibid. 17) dismissal of popular culture: 'Though there was nothing wrong in these stories and though their intention was sometimes literary . . .' (ibid. 12).

At the heart of the story is an unstated event, a suggestion that the boys see the old man masturbating:

> – I say! Look what he's doing!
> As I neither answered nor raised my eyes Mahoney exclaimed again:
> – I say . . . He's a queer old josser!
>
> (Joyce [1914] 1992, 18)

In *not* viewing or describing the event, the voice of narration is itself exposed as partial, silent, suggestive of 'indecency', but deprived of the power to say what is being experienced or happening. The voice is limited precisely because of its propriety, its inability to see the invasion of the child's happy world by the sexualising adult. As the story progresses the adult's sexual intrusion *and* the sexual delight of the adult adopting the voice of the boy is made explicit. The 'old josser' talks to the boys of 'sweethearts', adopting a boy's viewpoint, taking a delight in the description of infant eroticism:

> He began to speak to us about girls, saying what nice soft hair they had and how soft their hands were and how all girls were not so good as they seemed to be if only one knew.
>
> (Joyce [1914] 1992, 18)

Both boys' literature and the 'strangely liberal' voice of the old man prohibit child sexuality, but the description of what is prohibited enables the voice to repeat, imagine and eroticise the child's point of view; there is a pornographic pleasure taken in the very discourse of punishment, and the imagination of transgression:

> He began to speak on the subject of chastising boys. His mind, as if magnetised again by his speech, seemed to circle slowly round and round its new centre. He said that when boys were that kind they ought to be whipped and well whipped. When a boy was rough and unruly there was nothing would do him any good but a good sound whipping . . . He said that if ever he found a boy talking to girls or having a girl for a sweetheart he would whip him and whip him; and that would teach him not to be talking to girls. And if a boy had a girl for a sweetheart and told lies about it then he would give him such a whipping as no boy ever got in this world. He said that there was nothing in this world he would like so well as that.
>
> (Joyce [1914] 1992, 19)

There is no longer a strict border between the moralising voice of boys' literature, which enjoys its judgement and proprietorial view of boys, and the sexually violent imagination of the old man. What is displayed, in

'An Encounter', is the prurient delight of the voice of elevation and punishment, the enjoyment and sadism of moralism. Further, the child is himself caught up in this world of received voices, blindly repeating the discourse that he finds disturbing but that he can neither free himself from nor understand. In seeking the old man's approval, in wanting to be acknowledged and admired by the moralising sadism, the boy pretends to have read books that are, for him, merely mentioned names (Joyce [1914] 1992, 17). The narration is not an ironic voice that elevates itself above corruption; the act of elevation or judgement itself is corrupt, stifling and intrusive: both the adult voice of the story describing the adventure and the old man's delight that 'Every boy . . . has a sweetheart' (ibid. 17). The discourses of morality are, in *Dubliners*, shown to be productive of a paralysing and blind moralism that is trapped within its enjoyment of a pleasure that can only be suggested through cliché, innuendo and slang. Any reader of this story who feels that the corruption is an object, and that the sexuality is there to be viewed, has missed the force of the narration. In order to read or perceive the sexual allusion one has to interpret or decode the sexual message; unlike the narrative voice, which remains blind, the reader can see the sexual sense; in so doing it is the reader who, like the old man, reads an erotic sense into the world of boys and sweethearts and 'nice warm whipping' (ibid. 19).

POSTMODERN IMMANENCE

One way to understand postmodernity is to see it as a radical rejection or redefinition of irony. If irony demands some idea or point of view above language, contexts or received voices, postmodernity acknowledges that all we have are competing contexts and that any implied 'other' position would itself be a context. Postmodernity would be a society of simulation and immanence with no privileged point from which competing voices could be judged. One would have to accept one's own position as one among others, and as thoroughly unoriginal. One could be ironic, not by breaking with contexts but in recognising any voice as an effect of context, and then allowing contexts to generate as much conflict, collision and contradiction as possible, thereby precluding any fixity or meta-position.

Alternatively, one could see postmodernity as the impossibility of overcoming irony. Any attempt to reduce the world to discourses, contexts, language-games or relative points of view would itself generate a point of view of recognition: the point of view of the postmodernist who continually affirms the end of meta-narratives, the point of view that is *other* than the beliefs of feminism, Marxism, nationalism or any other belief in identity.

Neither position is possible, and yet both seem inevitable. Postmodern irony in its radical form works with this contradiction. Insofar as one speaks one must adopt or generate a point of view, one must say something. Even speaking ironically, or being other than what is said, requires one to express a position. And the point of view above such a position, the disembodied, impersonal, implied and absent ironic narrator has – from Socrates to the present – created its own style, context, manner and morality. Far from speaking from 'nowhere' postmodern literature has problematised the impersonal point of view, the point of view that would be other than life. It has done so by presenting the dual *force* of all saying.

Traditional irony is intuited or suspected because one assumes a principle of non-contradiction. If the text is contradictory, absurd, clichéd or self-refuting, then we must assume that what is said is *not meant*. However, one cannot remain in a position of pure *not-saying*; for the not-saying is itself an act of speech. Postmodern texts have shown all the ways in which not-saying or ironic detachment generates a specific said. Saying is always *saying that*. The voice from nowhere has a style, position, commitment and force. One must be aware of the force and violence of a closed and unquestioning context; at the same time, one must also be aware that in speaking one nevertheless says something. But just as there can be no position of ironic not-saying, for the position above speech generates its own 'said', so there can never be a position of pure saying. All speech is haunted by irony. Not only can we question whether what is said is really meant; any act of speech can be repeated and quoted in another context, generating unintended forces. Further, and more importantly, insofar as speaking creates some event of decision, force and difference, or makes a claim about what is other than itself, it must refer to what is not itself. One can only make a statement about the world, or really say something, if one recognises the force of contradiction. To assert that something is the case is only a forceful speech act in a context where one could or would assert that it is not the case. As the contemporary Yale school critic J. Hillis Miller has observed, if something is universally and unquestionably true then it does not need to be said. Saying something unquestionably true can never be a speech act of one's own: universality can have no copyright (Miller 2001, 70). To recite a multiplication table is not to *say* anything at all; one only speaks, or speaks with force, if what one says can be contradicted, if what is asserted can also not be asserted.

On the one hand, to speak is to adopt a position and style, to say that something *is*. On the other hand, such a saying or position could only make sense, or be a position, if it is articulated against what it *is not*. Is one really *speaking* or saying anything if what is said is what *must* be true? An utterance has force or speaks only to the extent to which it is what is not already assumed. If one wants to speak and be heard, to be taken as saying something, then one must commit to *this* rather than that. One must rely upon the principle of non-contradiction, a commitment that in saying *this* one negates or rejects its contrary. At the same time, this very commitment also demands and requires contradiction, for to be saying something, to be asserting *this* with any force, is also to acknowledge the force and validity of what one is not saying. Addressing an other or communicating is not the circulation of the already known. An assertion has *force* or makes a difference only if it makes a claim about what lies beyond the speech act.

To make sense or interpret what someone says not only requires some meaning behind the signifiers or words used. There cannot just be the circulation of signs, with no logic, order, hierarchy or conflict. To *speak* is to be recognised as saying something, rather than emitting noise. In listening or interpreting one must direct oneself to what the speech act in itself is not. We interpret a speech act as sincere or ironic depending on whether we take what it says to be true or to be contradictory: contradicting either what the speaker has said or usually says, or contradicting what we take to be true. Irony relies on the force of contradiction; we assume irony if what is said cannot be meant or is not the case. But irony also inhabits contradiction: we *cannot say* 'a' and 'not-a', or we *cannot say* what we all assume or know to be false, so the speech act must be ironic. However, some of the most complex forms of irony intensify contradiction; they do not *clearly* contradict the true or the logical in order to present themselves as in opposition to what is said; they do not allow for a truth or sense behind the speech act. The speech act produces a conflict of sense, expressing both sides of an assertion with equal force.

This inhabitation of contradiction or sense of irony can mark texts that are not presented as ironic. Andrea Dworkin, the radical American feminist, has been a tireless critic of pornography, with a great deal of the force of her position relying upon what she takes to be the obvious violence of the pornographic text. Her *Pornography: Men Possessing Women* (1981) quotes a great deal of pornography, and presents this pornographic material as an act of representational violence against women. To read Dworkin literally and sincerely requires a clear distinction between the author and the material she quotes; it also requires a clear distinction between the *use* of pornographic material – those who read and view the violent material – and the *mention* of pornography – those feminists, like Dworkin, who can repeat the material in order to show, but not commit, its violence.

Now, on the one hand, Dworkin wants to *not say* or *not mean* what she is quoting, she positions herself and her readers as other than the discourse that is being repeated, judged and objectified. On the other hand, however, Dworkin's text nevertheless *does* say what she insists ought not to be said. Her text can only work critically, like any argument, by giving voice to its other. But when arguments concern the very force of speech and representation, it is the very mention of the object, such as the quotation of pornography, that gives further life and force to the object it aims to destroy. If irony is saying one thing and meaning another, we can see an irony in Dworkin's text: she says that she is other than, opposed to, innocent of, the violence of pornography, but in her critique and objectification of the discourse of pornography she cannot avoid speaking through, or mentioning, its voice.

This unintended contradiction – that one can only be other than pornographic by repeating the discourse of pornography – is manifestly exploited in much postmodern ironic literature. Whereas Dworkin's text presents itself as simply other than the violent voices it would innocently mention, a great deal of post-colonial and feminist literature has acknowledged the essential complicity of voice. To speak from a position outside Western reason, to present oneself as *other than* the objectifying, elevated and moral voice of conscience is, once again, to place oneself in a position of elevation. The tactic for dealing with this is to say and not-say, to be ironic.

It may be the case that there is no already given, innocent and pure voice outside reason. It may be the case that in order to think what is other than Western phallogocenrism we have to rely on the very concepts of essence and identity that have marked Western thought. Feminists have referred to this strategy as 'strategic essentialism'. To appeal to 'woman' as reason's 'Other' reinforces the traditional dichotomies of male/female, active/passive, rational/irrational, universal and contingent and so on. The strategy lies in repeating or saying this discourse in order to demonstrate its force. One cannot be *other than* the voice of reason, for to set oneself up as the truer voice would be to employ all the strategies of reason. But one can repeat the discourse of reason in order to show its force, what it does, and the figures through which it is sustained. When Angela Carter writes *The Bloody Chamber* (1979) or when Luce Irigaray writes *Speculum of the Other Woman* ([1974] 1985) they both articulate a female voice, a voice of imagery, fluidity, sensuality, emotive complexity and empathy, that is *other than* the universal, disembodied, rational and elevated judgement of reason. They take up the traditional images of the feminine in order both to affirm the value of those images – the joy of embodiment, sensuality, ambiguity and fluidity – and to demystify those images. The fecund, multiple, corporeal and poetic feminine is a repetition of *reason's myth* of the feminine. In expressing this female voice as *other than* masculine, they acknowledge that 'the feminine' is already masculine, produced through the negation of reason, as a critique of reason. The voice they articulate is both affirmed and denied. It is affirmed as female in order to counter the myth of the feminine upon which male reason has already formed itself. Only by imagining itself as other than the body, contradiction, the passions and chaos does male reason erect itself as universal. But the female voice is also ironised and negated; the feminine articulated by Carter and Irigaray is articulated *as* mythic. The feminine is presented as *reason's* other. Carter and Irigaray both write from a point of view of female autonomy, as other than the violence and judgement of reason, and recognise that the articulation of this female voice maintains the dichotomy between reason and its other.

This tactic of saying and not-saying characterises a broad variety of post-structuralist positions. On the one hand, we continue to speak the discourse of rights, humanism, universal reason and truth; on the other hand, we also recognise the violent and local figures through which these discourses are sustained. Post-structuralist ethics is aware of complicity: to attack the Western tradition of domination, rationalism, judgement and law is only possible through the invocation of a higher law or judgement. Derrida's response to this has been to affirm both the ethical possibility of law, or its elevation above any received tradition, and the impossibility of the law, for one always speaks from within a tradition. On the one hand, one *wants to say* that Western reason has been used to domesticate, subordinate and tyrannise its others, but such a judgement also employs the very sense of reason and properly universal justice it would deny. We can only continue to speak through the voice of the law with a full sense of its complicity, impossibility and contradictory force.

Against a postmodern irony, such as Rorty's that would simply allow us to speak and not really mean what we say and that would happily allow us to say and not-say at one and the same time, both Deleuze and Derrida, in quite different ways, take the necessity recognised by the tradition of irony to new possibilities. For Derrida, all speech is potentially ironic, both because a concept has a sense we neither author nor control *and* because there are *non*sensical forces at work in the articulation of concepts. From this point of view, reading literature today would maintain both the force and the problem of irony. We would need to acknowledge the problem of sense or meaning beyond manifest intent, as in classical irony, but we would also need to read for the inhuman, machinic or errant forces that preclude such a sense from governing the text.

ANGELA CARTER

Angela Carter's collection of stories, *The Bloody Chamber*, was published in 1979 and provides a dynamic response to one of the crucial problems of radical feminism. How does one think outside the masculine myths of 'woman' without presenting the feminine as some ineffable and timeless essence. To begin with, one can read Carter as an exemplary postmodernist. Her stories are written in the voice of fairy tales, with 'The Bloody Chamber' being a first person re-telling of 'Bluebeard's Castle' from the female protagonist's point of view. A received and traditional narrative is re-told from the point of view of its classically objectified and silent other, the sexually violated women. The text inhabits a narrative to show its force, foregrounding the values and positions it creates. However, there is also a utopian or deconstructive dimension to Carter's text. Carter's narrative does more than repeat the narratives of tradition *as* narrative; it is more than a playful postmodern inhabitation of a discourse that it also disavows. Not only does Carter add another voice to the text; she rewrites the very notion of voice. She does not just add a 'female' voice to a masculine narrative; she destroys the simple way of thinking about the opposition between male and female. She shows the feminine to be a masculine construction, an image, fantasy or projection of male desire. The female character in 'The Bloody Chamber' constantly views herself in mirrors, sees herself from the point of view of male desire, and adopts all the jewels, dress, fantasies and poses that place her in the position of created sexual object. In narrating the story she looks back to a time when she was both an unselfconscious and a passive object of desire and recalls the moment at which she adopts and internalises the male gaze that fixes her as female:

> That night at the opera comes back to me even now . . . the white dress; the frail child within it; and the flashing crimson jewels around her throat, bright as arterial blood.
>
> I saw him watching me in the gilded mirrors with the assessing eye of a connoisseur inspecting horseflesh, or even a housewife in the market inspecting cuts on the slab. I'd never seen, or else had never acknowledged, that regard of his before, the sheer carnal avarice of it; and it was strangely magnified by the monocle lodged in his left eye. When I saw him look at me with lust, I dropped my eyes but, in glancing away from him, I caught sight of myself in a mirror. And I saw myself, suddenly, as he saw me, my pale face, the way the muscles in my neck stuck out like thin wire. I saw how much that cruel necklace became me. And for the first time in my innocent and confined life, I sensed in myself a potentiality for corruption that took my breath away.
>
> (Carter 1979, 11).

In this sense, 'woman' does not exist; 'she' is only that feared lack or absence created by the masculine assertion of presence. In order for a text or image to represent anything at all it must presuppose an absent or lost presence which it aims to recall. Carter's stories show the mythic production of the lost origin. Her female characters are viewed through the lens of a male desire that can be active, representing and masterful only through its production of a passive, represented and slavish feminine. The opposition between male and female then structures all the oppositions between subject and object, for the masculine is just that which is *other than* the represented, *other than* that silent body which cannot speak or represent itself. Carter exposes the feminine *as* a mythic presence produced through the idea of subjectivity and representation; only with the idea of a world there to be represented, and a subject who actively represents can we have the sexual hierarchy. We can only think the opposition between subject and object, presence and absence, signifier and signified through sexual imagery. The feminine is just that imagined lack perceived from the point of masculine subjectivity.

However, while denying or exposing the feminine as a lie, or while saying that woman does not exist, Carter also speaks in the voice of the feminine. The feminine is a fiction and illusion *and* it is also the only reality outside the play of mirrors. Carter produces a female voice or subject that disrupts the fiction of sexual difference. Indeed, the only way to destroy the fantasy of sexual difference – of woman as man's necessary negation or other – is to repeat and intensify the fantasy, both by showing the production as a production *and* by producing differently. Carter parodies the female subject who would take on all the active, violent and masterful strategies of the masculine subject, exposing such projections of the self-authoring subject to be a fiction. Often her female characters take on heroic, active but also *absurdly* masculine roles; the masculine model of the subject is powerfully adopted at the same time as it is parodied: 'what other student at the Conservatoire could boast that her mother had outfaced a junkful of Chinese pirates, nursed a village through a visitation of plague, shot a man-eating tiger with her own hand and all before she was as old as I?' (Carter 1979, 7).

Her work is therefore ironic, negative and deconstructive. It is ironic because it inhabits the simple mythic world of sexual difference in order to expose its absurd simplicity. It is negative because it takes what is conceived to be outside language and subjectivity – woman – and shows that otherness to be an effect of representation. It is, most importantly, deconstructive because it does not just repeat and parody the opposition between male and female; it also takes the affirmative step of gesturing to all those forces of desire and difference that precede all myth, meaning and representation. Many of her stories enact a utopian promise of going beyond the human or beyond the subject for whom the world is merely so much passive material to be mastered and re-presented. The fairy stories of myth and tradition are presented as so many ways of inscribing a border between animal and human. Carter repeats tales of werewolves, for example, in order to show the ways in which the human self was, and is, haunted and doubled by what is not itself. The subject is neither self-authoring nor transparent. The human is a collection of features that we have perceived from inhuman life: 'her cunt a split fig below the great globes of buttocks on which the knotted tails of the cat were about to descend' (Carter 1979, 16); 'I could see the dark leonine shape of his head and my nostrils caught a whiff of the opulent male scent of leather and spices that always accompanied him' (ibid. 8); 'his white, heavy flesh that has too much in common with the armfuls of arum lilies that filled my bedroom in great glass jars' (ibid. 15). Carter's writing is composed of layers of scents, tastes, perceptions, recollections and quotations, with her characters' bodies never being self-contained objects so much as sites of competing affects. Against all these bodies and layers of sensibility, Carter sets the absent male gaze, the point from which all sensations are organised and rendered both sexually different and meaningful. To be a subject, or to speak, is to be complicit with this objectifying gaze. There can be no pure and innocent femininity outside this structure precisely because the female body is produced as female only through this desire:

> He stripped me, gourmand that he was, as if he were stripping the leaves off an artichoke – but do not imagine much finesse about it; this artichoke was no particular treat for the diner nor was he yet in any greedy haste. He approached his familiar treat with a weary appetite. And when nothing but my scarlet, palpitating core remained, I saw, in the mirror, the living image of an etching by Rops from the collection he had shown me when our engagement permitted us to be alone together . . . the child with her sticklike limbs, naked but for her button boots, her gloves, shielding her face with her hand as though her face were the last repository of her modesty; and the old monocled lecher who examined her, limb by limb. He in his London tailoring; she, bare as a lamb chop. Most pornographic of all confrontations. And so my purchaser

unwrapped his bargain. And, as at the opera, when I had first seen my flesh in his eyes, I was aghast to feel myself stirring.

(Carter 1979, 15)

In *The Bloody Chamber* masculinity is described as a mask, as achieving its power only in not being seen; it is only by viewing the body as masked, as clothed, that a male subject is posited as unseen, behind all the staging (ibid. 9). Similarly, it is only through the threat of law, prohibition and punishment, only through a violence directed against the female body, that the male subject is produced as authority.

Sexual difference is not, for Carter, a topic to be treated ironically. On the contrary, the very structure of irony is itself sexual. The point of view that observes, objectifies and is *other than* any determined body, or the point of view of narration, voice, desire and speech, has traditionally been defined as different from the feminine. Indeed, the feminine is just what is other than, or different from, the pure gaze of subjectivity. For this reason, Carter's narrating female voice is not a point of view outside traditional difference. Rather, insofar as she speaks, Carter's narrating female character is also other than her own desired body. 'The subject' is itself a fantasy of difference, created through narratives that differentiate desiring gaze and voice from desired and viewed body.

Masculine and feminine are images or figures of a difference that is inherent to all thinking and speaking. As de Man and Derrida have noted, to use a concept or speak is to intend or posit some being or sense that is there to be presented, and to create a subjective point of view of one who speaks. One cannot adopt a postmodern play that frees itself from metaphysical commitments, a commitment to presence. But one can look at texts to see the ways in which they constitute subject positions and points of view over and against a posited presence. Carter's narrative shows the ways in which this structure of subject and object, presence and absence, sign and sense has a sexual imaginary. To speak is to be other than the object, and the primary imagined object – that original desired body from which all speech must detach itself – is the female body. There is, therefore, a critical deconstructive dimension to Carter's postmodernism where she presents the point of view of speech and subjectivity as created through a narrative of difference, a fantasised sexual binary: the desiring, disembodied male gaze and the desired, silent female body. Following Derrida, we might say that insofar as one speaks one must adopt a discourse of presence, constituting oneself as a subject over and against a re-presented presence.

There is also, however, an affirmative dimension to Carter's irony. She does not just present the classic image of the speaking and viewing subject as masculine; she also intimates a new mode of difference. Here, the feminine would not just be that which is other than the voice of speech and representation, not just that towards which the active and objectifying gaze is directed. Carter's writing suggests that bodies themselves have a differential power. Bodies become human, become animal and, in 'The Company of Wolves', her rewriting of 'Red Riding Hood', animal and human bodies fall in love and live happily ever after. Difference is not just the imposed relation between male and female on otherwise equivalent bodies. The body is not a presence that is then taken up in representation; nor is it an imagined and lost presence forever desired by a self-enclosed and disembodied voice of representation.

Just as Derrida insists that speech intends or posits some sense beyond the sign, and cannot therefore be reduced to a closed system of difference, so he also argues that signs create forces beyond sense and presence. Carter, similarly, not only looks at the ways in which the traditional sexual binary posits some lost presence – the female body there to be viewed – she also looks at the way the inscription of this fantasy and the bodies it represents can have a force that exceeds sense. Her stories are ironic repetitions of the production of the feminine as a lost absence; but she adopts this voice and then shows that it is not a simple or negated outside. The body disrupts inside and outside, male and female subject and object.

Carter's characters constantly undress to reveal an underlying animality, or a becoming-animal to use Deleuze and Guattari's phrase. The human is not some basic essence that we all share; nor is it a common ground. On the contrary, the human in Carter's stories is achieved through performance and clothing.

This allows us to add a further dimension to Carter's irony. Not only do her texts inhabit and disrupt the traditional images of male and female that have been used to differentiate object and subject, she also creates new styles of voice. If traditional speech and point of view create an 'I' who speaks over and against a presence that is there to be re-presented, new styles of writing would destroy the singularity of point of view. This would be postmodern, not because it set itself 'behind' or above all the discourses that it surveyed but did not intend. Rather, the text would destroy the position of speech and point of view, producing not a subject/object or subject/predicate logic, but a humorous play of surfaces. Carter's stories often repeat phrases from other stories, without quotation marks or a defined speaker. In 'The Bloody Chamber' a phrase from Red Riding Hood – 'All the better to see you' – is printed as though it were the speech of the Count, but it is not in quotation marks and is typographically set off from the paragraphs that surround it. Carter uses the space of the page, the literal text, to display the voices of myth and tradition that traverse our narratives and perceptions. Carter presents these lines, not in sentences or quotations, but almost as objects dropped onto the page, without a clear attribution, voice or point of view: are these phrases *said*? In 'The Erl-King' two similes or hybrid perceptions are similarly set off from the text, to be followed by description and, again, a fragment from Red Riding Hood. Voices, in Carter's stories, invade, wander, quote, parody and perceive with neither a clear sentence structure nor an organising point of view:

> Eyes green as apples. Green as dead sea fruit.
> A wind rises; it makes a singular, wild, low rushing sound.
> What big eyes you have. Eyes of an incomparable luminosity, the numinous phosphorescence of the eyes of the lycanthropes.
>
> (Carter 1979, 90)

Both Derrida and Deleuze work within and beyond the tradition of irony. Derrida's deconstruction insists that the use of concepts cannot avoid positing or intending a sense that can be invoked across contexts and independent of any specific use. One may never disclose this sense, but the intention or direction towards this sense is necessary to concepts. A deconstructive reading extends traditional irony, not just by showing the ways in which the concepts we use have a force beyond what we want to say, but also looking at how this difference, between what is said and what is posited as present, is created in each text. The difference between signifier and signified, presence and absence, subject and sense is inscribed through concrete and material figures. One might therefore look critically to the ways texts create effects of presence, or all the ways in which narratives imagine and inscribe a body that is other than the point of view of speech. Carter uses the position of the feminine in a critical and utopian manner; if the feminine is produced as *other than* the male subject, then it can be repeated to gesture to what lies beyond sense and subjectivity.

CONCLUSION

Reading literature ironically requires that we think beyond the traditional philosophical commitment to propositional, translatable and non-contradictory thinking, recognising that truth is not simply there to be referred to by an innocent language. Truth requires thinking through the contradictory force of language, its essential difference from both what *is* and what remains beyond question. To read literature ironically also requires, however, the continued force of philosophy's truth and non-contradiction. We can only read texts ironically, seeing the tensions and relations between what is said and not-said, what is and is not the case, if we commit ourselves to a sense and truth towards which speech and language strive. There cannot, then, be a simple abandoning of the structures of truth and reason or the difference of irony in favour of a postmodern world of textuality, where signs coexist without conflict, hierarchy or tension.

Irony can, then, neither be achieved nor overcome. One cannot remain in a naively postmodern position above and beyond any discourse. The liberal ironist who has freed himself from metaphysical commitment, who speaks with an enlightened sense of his difference and distance from what he says, remains blind to the ways in which this discourse of detachment has its own attachments. Rorty's disengaged and sceptical pragmatist is, like Carter's presented male gaze, always defined against the determination, fixity, identity and opacity of desires and bodies. At the same time, one cannot be simply at one with, or immanent to, a pure field of material difference. One cannot *be* postcolonial or postmodern, liberated from any position of decision or judgement. To be embodied is not an event of pure surface or becoming; one becomes in a certain style or manner. There is always a certain irony, always a predicament of disjunction between what one is and what one means, both for oneself and for others.

GLOSSARY

Allegory: A narrative or series of images which stands in a relation of symbolising resemblance, but also difference, from an original referent. A classic example would be George Orwell's *Animal Farm* (1945), a barnyard tale where events and characters stand in a one-to-one relation to the Russian revolution. Paul de Man used the term allegory more broadly to signal any use of literary or poetic language that presented itself as standing in for some outside world.

Aphorisms: Witty phrases or observations that are self-sufficient or free-standing rather than being part of an argument or connected series of propositions.

Aporia: A gap or point of indeterminacy in a text.

Bildung: The modern German word for formation, which also refers to individual formation or education but which also has artistic resonance, deriving from the word *Bild* for picture.

Constative: A speech-act that, unlike the performative, does not produce or create a relation but names or designates something already existing.

Context: One way of determining the meaning of a text, phrase or sentence is by appeal to context, or the particular situation, conventions and expectations that surround language. Philosophers in the twentieth century, particularly those who followed the work of Ludwig Wittgenstein, argued that there were no such things as meanings or mental entities that lie behind words. Rather, meaning is just how a word works or is exchanged in a context. Philosophers who stressed the importance of context were associated with 'ordinary language philosophy', which examined the uses of words, rather than supposedly eternal meanings.

Cosmic or tragic irony: Where the expectations of a character or community are thwarted by life's events, events which often seem to pass judgement on life or that seem to be the outcome of fate.

Death of the Subject: A movement in twentieth century French thought, usually associated with Roland Barthes (1915–80) and Michel Foucault

(1926–84), which argues that language, texts and knowledge ought to be analysed without the assumption of a grounding author, intention or individual subject.

Deconstruction: The philosophy of Jacques Derrida (1930–) and his followers, including the twentieth-century literary critics of the Yale school. Deconstruction focuses on an opposition, such as the opposition between speech and writing, where one term (speech) is usually taken to be the origin of the other. Deconstruction then demonstrates that the accidental or supposedly secondary term is necessary for the first. One could not speak if there were not already an organised, repeatable and general system of marks that went beyond any individual speaker.

Dialectic/dialectical: A method that achieves truth by presenting the conflicts and contradictions of various positions and voices and then produces the true and reasoned position as the resulting resolution of such differences.

Différance: If a language or system is a set of differences then this is only because there is a process of *différance*. For Jacques Derrida, any term in a system has to be marked out from other terms and identified and repeated through time; we have to anticipate future uses of a term as the same. The differences of a system are therefore never fully present but always deferred through time, and marked by spatial traces.

Discourse: When one speaks one does not just use a system of signs or language, one also relies on discourse, which includes all the specific conventions, conditions, oppositions and relations of a particular political and historical moment. One can speak about a self in the discourse of literary criticism, or the discourse of biography, or the discourse of personal evaluation. Discourses have varying conditions and locales. It was once legitimate to use biography and personal response in literary criticism, and the discourse of literary criticism was also once, in the eighteenth century, located in popular magazines rather than universities. One could also argue that there was no discourse of literary criticism before the eighteenth century, and so discourse creates the objects and knowledges of which it speaks.

Dramatic irony: If the audience sees or knows more than a character, or if a character's speech is undermined by subsequent action, then we can say that there is a dramatic irony, an irony that plays on a disjunction between character and audience point of view.

Immanence: The opposite of transcendence, where transcendence refers to some point outside or above experience, such as God, truth, or being, that could provide an ultimate referent point for experience. Philosophies of immanence refuse to posit a position, value or ultimate voice outside life and experience.

Linguisticism: Usually used as a pejorative, linguisticism refers to positions that overplay the power of language or that fail to recognise a real world or truth outside language.

Logocentrism: Western thought has been defined as logocentric because it assumes some ultimate point of truth or presence, a founding word or logos, from which various positions and voices might be judged.

Meta-narrative/meta-position: According to the French theorist Jean-Francois Lyotard, postmodernity displays an incredulity towards meta-narrative. Any story, such as Marxism, humanism or theories of scientific progress, that provides an account and explanation for other stories and cultures is a meta-narrative. By setting themselves in a position above and before other stories, meta-narratives disavow their status as narratives.

Metaphysics: The tradition of Western philosophy that considers those truths, such as the truths of logic, meaning or reason, which cannot be explained physically or in terms of natural objects.

Mimesis/mimetic: Any sign, image or text which copies or reproduces its object. Associated with realism.

Parody: The use of a particular voice or style in order to display its peculiarities and blindness. Parody therefore tends to suggest a proper or rational way of speaking against which the parodied voice is set. The contemporary American Marxist Fredric Jameson argued that parody was opposed to pastiche, which was strictly postmodern.

Pastiche: A collection, series or juxtaposition of style and voices with no sense of an underlying normality from which they depart.

Phallogocentrism: If logocentrism is the commitment to some ultimate point of truth and presence, phallogocentrism is the sexual imaginary through which this logic is effected. One imagines some ultimate inchoate and undifferentiated origin, which requires the active, forming and inseminating power of reason to bring it to life and self-presence. The silent origin is imagined as a feminised body that requires the universal voice of man, who is man only through the phallus or the body part that is other than the lack of the origin.

Poiesis: The ancient Greek term from which the modern concept of poetry is derived. Poeisis referred to a form of creation that produced an external or detachable object.

Polis: The ancient Greek word from which the modern concept of the political is derived. The *polis* originally referred to a community of individuals that was larger than easily managed tribal collectives, but smaller than imperial states. The polis is often contrasted with modern society precisely because the *polis* includes the moral and philosophical reflection that is now considered to be apolitical.

Postmodern: A notoriously difficult and contested term that, for its opponents, signals the twentieth century's abandonment of truth and reason in favour of a world that is known only through images, signs or copies. For its defenders the postmodern is a liberating attitude that remains suspicious of any single foundation or ultimate position of truth.

Post-structuralism: Whereas structuralism argues that in order to understand any sign or event one needs to consider the system of terms or differences within which it is located, post-structuralists question how structures emerge (their genesis), and how the study of structures must always rely on one term (such as the terms structure, language or culture) which cannot be explained from within the structure itself.

Pragmatism: A tradition originating with the American philosophers William James and Charles Sanders Peirce who argued that the only criteria we have for judging a particular position or belief is whether it improves or enables life. Truth is defined as what produces success or agreement.

Praxis: Action or activity that is not necessarily subjected to a systematic set of rules (*Techne*); nor does praxis have to have a separate and detachable produced object (*Poiesis*) or criterion.

Rhetoric: The art of using speech or writing to persuade or influence.

Romantic irony: Usually associated with German Romanticism of the early nineteenth century, Romantic irony argues that life is a process of creation, flux and becoming and that any perception or representation we have of life must be partial and at odds with the absolutely fluid nature of life. Language is therefore at odds with or in conflict with life, and so one can only write with a sense of the inevitable disjunction between the word and the world.

Satire: According to Elliot (1960), satires have their origin in ancient fertility rituals and sacrifice, where those who were ungenerous become the object of invective. Satire can therefore be traced back to an attack upon those who are life denying or anti-social. In Roman times, and with the figures of Horace and Juvenal, satire takes on certain formal qualities. In general satire takes the form of an attack by way of ridicule, irony or parody.

Signifier/signification: A signifier has meaning only through its position in a lawful and arbitrary system of exchange. The signifiers 'blue' and 'grey' organise the colour spectrum; the signifiers 'empathy' and 'sympathy' structure the way we think about the emotions; the signifiers 'man' and 'woman' organise human bodies. On the model of signification, these words only have sense within some lawful system of divisions; they do not have a direct representational relation to things themselves.

Sophistry: The sophists were originally those who in Ancient Greece sold their skills and services as effective speakers. In general, sophistry is a belief that the most forceful or artfully presented argument is the superior argument, rather than an argument that is true.

Speech-act: The twentieth century philosopher J.L. Austin (1911–60) formulated speech-act theory in his landmark book, *How to do Things with Words* (1962). Here, language was considered not so much as a vehicle for information as an action. Promises, for example, create relations of obligation; naming ceremonies produce identities; and marriages use the words 'I now pronounce you man and wife' to create a marriage. For speech-act theorists, including J.L. Austin's principle philosophical heir, John Searle, if we want to understand language we should look at *how it works* in a context, and not try to find timeless conceptual meanings. In this sense, language is *performative*: it produces and acts, rather than represents.

Strategic essentialism: One adopts a voice as representative of one's essence or identity, such as the voice of woman, but does so only to work against or transform the logic that produces persons as essentially determined. The term is usually associated with the contemporary post-colonial feminist critic Gayatri Chakravorty Spivak.

Subject/subjectivity: Whereas individuals or humans are selves with a specific identity and are perceivable as part of the world, the subject is the condition or process of consciousness from which the world or self is constituted. Subjectivity is therefore different from the social, embodied and specific individual; the subject is the point from which society and self is viewed and effected, but not itself an effect.

Techne: The Ancient Greek word from which the modern concept of technology is derived. Techne referred to any skill or practice, such as medicine or musicianship, which had a regular and repeatable set of procedures.

Textuality: Textuality should not be confused with texts, books or the marks of language in a narrow sense. Textuality is the process of positive difference whereby what something *is* is achieved through a process of differencing and distancing. Textual differences have to repeat and re-mark themselves through time and space. The marks and sounds of a language have their identity only by bearing the possibility to be repeated, but one could see all difference this way. There is no essential human self, only an ongoing repetition and mutation of voices from which we discern 'the human'.

Transcendent: That which lies outside experience, whether that be some notion of an ultimately real world, or some eternal origin such as God or truth.

Transcendental: A movement in philosophy usually associated with Immanuel Kant who sought to provide ultimate conditions for all possible experience.

Trope: Any figure of speech, any use of language which departs from literal or direct usage to indirect or connotative usage; tropes include metaphors, similes, irony and other instances where a word has an implied other meaning.

Will to power: According to the German philologist Friedrich Nietzsche, we should reverse the standard relation between those in positions of power (masters and slaves) and the forces of power. Instead of arguing that some selves are stronger than others and therefore become masters, Nietzsche argued that life in general was a field of forces or power which then created positions and selves; the master is the effect of active forces, the slave of reactive forces. We need to see language, history and beliefs in terms of forces and powers rather than the individuals or subjects who are produced by power.

References

Albert, G. (1993) 'Understanding Irony: Three Essays on Friedrich Schlegel', *MLN*, 108.5: 825–48.

Alford, S.E.(1984) *Irony and the Logic of the Romantic Imagination*, New York: Peter Lang.

Apel, K.-O. (1998) *From a Transcendental-Semiotic Point of View*, M. Papastephanou (ed.), Manchester: Manchester University Press.

Aristotle (1934) *Nicomachean Ethics*, trans. H. Rackham, Cambridge, Mass.: Harvard University Press.

Auden, W.H. (1979) *Selected Poems*, E. Mendelson (ed.), London: Faber and Faber.

Austen, J. (1972) *Pride and Prejudice*, T. Tanner (ed.), Harmondsworth: Penguin.

Austin, J.L. (1962) *How to do Things with Words*, Oxford: Clarendon Press.

Ballard, J.G. (1995) *Crash*, London: Vintage.

Beckett, S. (1986) *The Complete Dramatic Works*, London: Faber and Faber.

Behler, E. (1993) *German Romantic Literary Theory*, Cambridge; New York: Cambridge University Press.

Blake, W. (1957) *Complete Writings*, G. Keynes (ed.), Oxford: Oxford University Press.

Blissett, W. (1959) 'The Secret'st Man of Blood: A Study of Dramatic Irony in Macbeth', *Shakespeare Quarterly*, 10.3: 397–408.

Booth, W. (1974) *A Rhetoric of Irony*, Chicago: University of Chicago Press.

Borges, J.L. (1965) *Fictions*, A. Kerrigan (ed.), London: Calder.

Bowie, A. (1997) *From Romanticism to Critical Theory: The Philosophy of German Literary Theory*, London: Routledge.

Boyle, F. (2000) *Swift as Nemesis: Modernity and its Satirist*, Stanford, Calif.: Stanford University Press.

Bradley, A.C. (1905) *Shakespearean Tragedy: Lectures on Hamlet, Othello, King Lear and Macbeth*, 2nd edition, London: Macmillan.

Braidotti, R. (1991) *Patterns of Dissonance*, Cambridge: Polity.

Brooks, C. (1947) *Modern Poetry and the Tradition*, London: PL (Poetry London).

Browning, R. (1988) *The Poetical Works of Robert Browning Volume 3*, I. Jack and R. Fowler (eds), Oxford: Clarendon.

Butler, J. (1993) *Bodies that Matter: On the Discursive Limits of 'Sex'*, New York: Routledge.

—— (1999) *Gender Trouble: Feminism and the Subversion of Identity*, New York: Routledge.

Byron, G.G. (1973) *Don Juan*, T.G. Steffan, E. Steffan and W.W. Pratt (eds), Harmondsworth: Penguin.

Camery-Hoggatt, J. (1992) *Irony in Mark's Gospel: Text and Subtext*, Cambridge: Cambridge University Press.

Carter, A. (1979) *The Bloody Chamber and Other Stories*, London: Gollancz.

Chaucer, G. (1966) *The Merchant's Prologue and Tale from The Canterbury Tales*, M. Hussey (ed.), Cambridge: University Press.

Cicero (1942) *De Oratore*, 2nd volume, trans. E.W. Sutton, London: Heinemann.

Coleridge, S.T. (1951) *Selected Poetry and Prose of Coleridge*, D.A. Stauffler (ed.), New York: Random House.

Deleuze, G. (1990) *The Logic of Sense*, trans. M. Lester, C.V. Boundas (ed.), New York: Columbia University Press.

—— (1994) *Difference and Repetition*, trans. Paul Patton, New York: Columbia University Press.

Deleuze, G. and Guattari, F. (1983) *Anti-Oedipus: Capitalism and Schizophrenia*, trans. R. Hurley, M. Seem and H.R. Lane, Minneapolis: University of Minnesota Press.

—— (1986) *Kafka: Toward a Minor Literature*, trans. D. Polan, Minneapolis: University of Minnesota Press.

—— (1987) *A Thousand Plateaus: Capitalism and Schizophrenia*, trans. Brian Massumi, Minneapolis: University of Minnesota Press.

De Man, P. (1979) *Allegories of Reading: Figural Language in Rousseau, Nietzsche, Rilke, and Proust*, New Haven: Yale University Press.

—— (1983) *Blindness and Insight: Essays in the Rhetoric of Contemporary Vriticism*, 2nd edition, rev., London: Methuen.

—— (1996) *Aesthetic Ideology*, A. Warminski (ed.), Minneapolis: University of Minnesota Press.

Derrida, J. (1973) *Speech and Phenomena and Other Essays on Husserl's Theory of Signs*, trans. D.B. Allison, Evanston: Northwestern University Press.

—— (1974) *Of Grammatology*, trans. Gayatri Chakravorty Spivak, Baltimore: Johns Hopkins University Press.

—— (1978) *Writing and Difference*, trans. A. Bass, London: Routledge and Kegan Paul.

—— (1982) *Margins of Philosophy*, trans. A. Bass, Sussex: Harvester.

—— (1988) *Limited Inc*, trans. S. Weber and J. Mehlman, Evanston: Northwestern University Press.

—— (1989a) *Edmund Husserl's Origin of Geometry: An Introduction by Jacques Derrida*, trans. J.P. Leavey, Lincoln: University of Nebraska Press.

—— (1989b) 'How to Avoid Speaking: Denials', trans. K. Frieden, in S. Budick and W. Iser (eds) *Languages of the Unsayable: The Play of Negativity in Literature and Literary Theory*, New York: Columbia University Press, 3–61.

—— (1995) *On the Name*, T. Dutoit (ed.), Stanford: Stanford University Press.

—— (1997) *The Politics of Friendship*, trans. G. Collins, London: Verso.

Dollimore, J. and Sinfield, A. (1985) *Political Shakespeare: New Essays in Cultural Materialism*, Manchester: Manchester University Press.

Donatus, A. (1864) *Ars Grammatica*, H. Keil (ed.), in *Grammatici Latini* vol. 4, Leipzig.

Dostoevsky, F. (1972) *Notes from Underground/The Double*, trans. J. Coulson, Harmondsworth: Penguin.

Drakakis, J. (ed.) (1995) *Alternative Shakespeares*, London: Methuen.

Duke, P.D. (1985) *Irony in the Fourth Gospel*, Atlanta: John Knox Press.

Dworkin, A. (1981) *Pornography: Men Possessing Women*, London: Women's Press.

Eagleton, T. (1990) *The Ideology of the Aesthetic*, Oxford: Blackwell.

Eco, U. (1992) 'Postmodernism, Irony, the Enjoyable', in P. Brooker (ed.), *Modernism/Postmodernism*, London: Longman, 225–8

Elliott, R.C. (1960) *The Power of Satire: Magic, Ritual, Art*, Princeton: Princeton University Press.

Ellis, B.E. (1991) *American Psycho*, London: Picador.

Foucault, M. (1970) *The Order of Things*, London: Tavistock.

—— (1972) *The Archaeology of Knowledge and the Discourse on Language*, trans. A.M. Sheridan Smith, New York: Pantheon.

Fowler, H.W. (1968) *A Dictionary of Modern English Usage*, 2nd edition, E. Gowers (rev.), Oxford: Clarendon.

Freud, S. (1984) 'Beyond the Pleasure Principle', in A. Richards (ed.), *On Metapsychology*, trans. J. Strachey, Harmondsworth: Penguin.

Garber, F. (1988) *Self, Text and Romantic Irony: The Example of Byron*, Princeton: Princeton University Press.

Gearhart, S. (1983) 'Philosophy Before Literature', *Diacritics*, 13.4: 63–81.

Good, E.M. (1965) *Irony in the Old Testament*, Philadelphia: Westminster Press.

Green, D.H. (1979) *Irony in the Medieval Romance*, Cambridge: Cambridge University Press.

Greenblatt, S. (1980) *Renaissance Self-Fashioning: From More to Shakespeare*, Chicago: University of Chicago Press.

—— (1988) *Shakespearean Negotiations: The Circulation of Social Energy in Renaissance England*, Oxford: Clarendon.

Habermas, J. (1993) *Justification and Application: Remarks on Discourse Ethics*, trans. Ciaran P. Cronin, Cambridge, Mass.: MIT Press.

Hadot, P. (1995) *Philosophy as a Way of Life*, A. Davidson (ed.), Oxford: Blackwell.

Hallward, P. (2001) *Absolutely Postcolonial: Writing between the Singular and the Specific*, Manchester: Manchester University Press.

Handwerk, G. (1985) *Irony and Ethics in Narrative: From Schlegel to Lacan*, New Haven: Yale University Press.

Hartman, G. (1970) *Beyond Formalism: Literary Essays 1958–1970*, New Haven: Yale University Press.

Hassan, I. (1987) *The Postmodern Turn: Essays in Postmodern Theory and Culture*, Columbus: Ohio State University Press.

Hazard, P. (1954) *European Thought in the Eighteenth Century: From Montesquieu to Lessing*, London: Hollis & Carter.

Heidegger, M. (1967) *What is a Thing?* trans. W.B. Barton, Jr. and V. Deutsch, Lanham: University Press of America.

Husserl, E. (1970) *Logical Investigations, Volume One: Prolegomena to Pure Logic . . .* trans. J.N. Findlay, New York: Humanities Press.

Hutcheon, L. (1994) *Irony's Edge: The Theory and Politics of Irony*, London: Routledge.

Irigaray, L. (1985) *Speculum of the Other Woman,* trans. G. C. Gill, Ithaca: Cornell University Press.

Joyce, J. (1992) *Dubliners,* T. Brown (ed.), Harmondsworth: Penguin.

Kant, I. (1959) *Foundations of the Metaphysics of Morals and What is Enlightenment?* trans. L. W. Beck, Indianapolis: Bobbs-Merrill, The Library of Liberal Arts.

—— (2000) *Critique of the Power of Judgment,* trans. P. Guyer, Cambridge: Cambridge University Press.

Kennedy, G.A. (1980) *Classical Rhetoric and its Christian and Secular Tradition from Ancient to Modern Times,* London: Croom Helm.

Kierkegaard, S. (1989) *The Concept of Irony, with Continual Reference to Socrates: Together with Notes of Schelling's Berlin Lectures,* trans. H.V. Hong and E.H. Hong, Princeton: Princeton University Press.

Knox, D. (1989) *Ironia: Medieval and Renaissance Ideas on Irony,* Leiden: E.J. Brill.

Kofman, S. (1993) *Nietzsche and Metaphor,* trans. D. Large, London: Athlone.

—— (1998) *Fictions of a Philosopher,* trans. Catherine Porter, London: Athlone.

Lacoue-Labarthe, P. (1993) *The Subject of Philosophy,* T. Trezise (ed.), Minneapolis: University of Minnesota Press.

Lacoue-Labarthe, P. and Nancy, J.-L. (1988) *The Literary Absolute: The Theory of Literature In German Romanticism,* trans. P. Barnard and C. Lester, Albany: State University of New York Press.

Lang, C. (1988) *Irony/Humor: Critical Paradigms,* Baltimore: Johns Hopkins University Press.

Lefebvre, H. (1995) *Introduction to Modernity,* trans. J. Moore, London: Verso.

Levin, H. (1931) *The Broken Column: A Study in Romantic Hellenism,* Cambridge, Mass.: Harvard University Press.

Lovejoy, Arthur O. (1936) *The Great Chain of Being: A Study of the History of an Idea,* Cambridge, Mass: Harvard University Press.

Lycos, K. (1987) *Plato on Justice and Power: Reading Book 1 of Plato's Republic,* Basingstoke: Macmillan.

McGann, J. (1968) *Fiery Dust: Byron's Poetic Development,* Chicago: University of Chicago Press.

—— (1976) *Don Juan in Context,* Chicago: University of Chicago Press.

—— (1983) *The Romantic Ideology: A Critical Investigation,* Chicago: University of Chicago Press.

Mann, T. (1971) *Death in Venice,* trans. H.T. Lowe-Porter, Harmondsworth: Penguin.

Mellor, A.K. (1980) *English Romantic Irony,* Cambridge, Mass.: Harvard University Press.

Mileur, J.-P. (1998) 'Revisionism, Irony, and the Mask of Sentiment', *New Literary History* 29.2: 197–233.

Miller, J.H. (1998) 'Indirect Discourses and Irony', *Reading Narrative,* Norman: University of Oklahoma Press, 158–77.

—— (2001) *Speech Acts in Literature,* Stanford: Stanford University Press.

Moretti, F. (1988) *Signs Taken for Wonders: Essays in the Sociology of Literary Forms,* trans. S. Fischer, D. Forgacs and D. Miller, London: Verso.

Muecke, D.C. (1980) *The Compass of Irony*, 2nd edition, London: Methuen.

Muecke, D.C. (1983) *Irony and the Ironic*, 2nd edition, London: Methuen.

Nehamas, A. (1998) *The Art of Living: Socratic Reflections from Plato to Foucault*, Berkeley: University of California Press.

——(1999) *Virtues of Authenticity: Essays on Plato and Socrates*, Princeton: Princeton University Press.

Nietzsche, F. (1968) *Twilight of the Idols/The AntiChrist*, trans. R.J. Hollingdale, Harmondsworth: Penguin.

—— (1969a) *On the Genealogy of Morals/Ecce Homo*, trans. W. Kauffmann and R.J. Hollingdale, New York: Vintage.

—— (1969b) *Thus Spoke Zarathustra: A Book for Everyone and No One*, trans. R.J. Hollingdale, Harmondswoth: Penguin.

—— (1979) 'On Truth and Lies in a Non-Moral Sense', in *Philosophy and Truth: Selections from Nietzsche's Notebooks of the Early 1870s*, D. Breazeale (ed.), Atlantic Highlands, New Jersey: Humanities Press, 79–97.

—— (1993) *The Birth of Tragedy Out of the Spirit of Music*, trans. S. Whiteside, Harmondsworth: Penguin.

Novalis (1997) *Philosophical Writings*, trans. M. Mahony Stoljar, Albany: State University of New York Press.

Oldmark, J. (1981) *An Understanding of Jane Austen's Novels: Character, Value and Ironic Perspective*, Oxford: Basil Blackwell.

Plank, K.A. (1987) *Paul and the Irony of Affliction*, Atlanta: Scholars Press.

Plato (1963) *The Collected Dialogues of Plato*, E. Hamilton and H. Cairns (eds), Princeton: Princeton University Press.

Quintilian, M.F. (1995–98) *The Institutio Oratoria of Quintilian*, trans. H.E. Butler, Cambridge, Mass.; London: Harvard University Press.

Rawson, C. (1994) *Satire and Sentiment 1660–1830: Stress Points in the English Augustan Tradition*, New Haven: Yale University Press.

Rorty, R. (1989) *Contingency, Irony and Solidarity*, Cambridge: Cambridge University Press.

—— (1996) 'Remarks on Deconstruction and Pragmatism', and 'Response to Simon Critchley', in C. Mouffe (ed.), *Deconstruction and Pragmatism*, London: Routledge, 10–18, 41–6.

Schlegel, F. (1991) *Philosophical Fragments*, trans. P. Firchow, Minneapolis: University of Minnesota Press.

Searle, J. (1969) *Speech Acts: An Essay in the Philosophy of Language*, Cambridge: Cambridge University Press.

—— (1994) 'Literary Theory and its Discontents', *New Literary History*, 25.3: 637–67.

Sedgwick, G.G. (1935) *Of Irony, Especially in Drama*, Toronto: University of Toronto Press.

Shelley, M. (1992) *Frankenstein Or, The Modern Prometheus*, M. Hindle (ed.), Harmondsworth: Penguin.

Shelley, P.B. (1971) *Shelley: Poetical Works*, T. Hutchinson (ed.), Oxford: Oxford University Press.

Sim, S. (2002) *Irony and Crisis: A Critical History of Postmodern Culture*, London: Icon.

Simpson, D.(1979) *Irony and Authority in Romantic Poetry*, London: Macmillan.

Sophocles (1942) *Oedipus the King*, trans. D.Grene, in *Greek Tragedies: Volume One*, D. Grene and R. Lattimore (eds), Chicago: University of Chicago Press.

Spencer, T. (1954) *Fair Greece! Sad Relic: Literary Philhellenism from Shakespeare to Byron*, London: Weidenfeld and Nicolson.

St. Claire, W. (1972) *That Greece Might Still be Free: The Philhellenes in the War of Independence*, London: Oxford University Press.

Swift, J. (1967) *Gulliver's Travels*, P. Dixon and J. Chalker (eds), Harmondsworth: Penguin.

—— (1984) 'A Modest Proposal for Preventing the Children of Poor People from Being a Burthen to their Parents or the Country, and for Making them Benficial to the Public', in A. Ross and D. Woolley (eds), *Jonathan Swift: A Critical Edition of the Major Works*, Oxford: Oxford University Press.

Thirlwall, C. (1833) 'On the Irony of Sophocles', *Philological Museum*, 2.

Vlastos, G. (1991) *Socrates: Ironist and Moral Philosopher*, Cambridge: Cambridge University Press.

White, H. (1973) *Metahistory: The Historical Imagination in Nineteenth-Century Europe*, Baltimore. Johns Hopkins University Press.

Wilde, A. (1980) 'Irony in the Postmodern Age: Toward a Map of Suspensiveness', *Boundary 2: A Journal of Postmodern Literature and Culture*, 9.1: 5–46.

Wittreich, J. A. (ed.) (1970) *The Romantics on Milton. Formal Essays and Critical Asides*, Michigan: Ann Arbor.

INDEX